NIMBUS

BOOKS BY THE SAME AUTHOR

The Survivors
The Queen of Spades
Afghanistan
Modern Iceland
Three Tomorrows
The Science of Winning Squash
Afghanistan: Key to a Continent
Flashpoint Afghanistan
The Third Man

NIMBUS

TECHNOLOGY SERVING THE ARTS

John Griffiths

NIMBUS

IN ASSOCIATION WITH

ANDRE DEUTSCH

First published in Great Britain in 1995 by
André Deutsch Limited
106 Great Russell Street
London WC1B 3LJ

ISBN 0 233 98888 2

Typeset by Falcon Graphic Art Ltd
Design by Jeffrey Sains

Cataloguing-in-Publication data available for this title
from the British Library

Printed in Great Britain by
BPC Hazell Books Ltd
A member of
The British Printing Company Ltd

for Numa Labinsky
In memoriam amicitiae

ACKNOWLEDGEMENTS

I am greatly indebted to all the very many Nimbus directors, employees and performing artists, and the music critics and editors who gave me so much of their time so frankly and willingly. Many are referred to in the text, but not all, and all alike are due my thanks.

The Nimbus inner family – Michael and Gerald Reynolds, Adrian Farmer and Jonathan Halliday – not only endorsed Numa's courageous decision to commission an honest history of the company, but were incredibly open and helpful at all times, and extended a hand of friendship to boot.

My biggest debt is to Count Numa Labinsky, who died so tragically just four days after this manuscript was completed and handed over for editing. He thus never saw the story of which he is the central and dominant character, but in almost the last of our many long discussions, as if prescient of his own death, he threatened to haunt me if I did not do an honest and imaginative job. I trust he will rest content with an effort that began as a literary task and ended, thanks to his friendship, as a labour of love.

SOURCES AND REFERENCES

Quotations from texts are either identified within the narrative or by a number referring to the endnotes. As printed communication comes today in so many forms the nature of the text – memo, fax etc. – is usually identified. If it is not the text is from a letter. Quotations not so identified are all taken, usually verbatim, from interviews with the author between May and December 1993.

Nimbus divided into two independent companies with different shareholders on 1 October 1992. After that date they are referred to as Nimbus Manufacturing on the one hand and Nimbus Records, or Nimbus Technology (and Engineering) on the other. Before that date I write just of Nimbus distinguishing between its various operations only when necessary.

CONTENTS

INTRODUCTION	XV
CHAPTER ONE	1
CHAPTER TWO	23
CHAPTER THREE	33
CHAPTER FOUR	48
CHAPTER FIVE	78
CHAPTER SIX	101
CHAPTER SEVEN	122
CHAPTER EIGHT	138
CHAPTER NINE	154
CHAPTER TEN	171
CHAPTER ELEVEN	202
CHAPTER TWELVE	217
CHAPTER THIRTEEN	234
EPILOGUE	256
APPENDIX A	260
APPENDIX B	261
APPENDIX C	263
ENDNOTES	273
INDEX	277

LIST OF ILLUSTRATIONS
BLACK AND WHITE PLATES

13 Numa with writer Colin Wilson.

15 Numa with actress Mary Wimbush who recorded his poetry.

25 Numa with Gerald.

29 Numa recording Vaughan Williams' *Songs of Travel*, accompanied by Adrian Farmer.

37 Bernard Roberts, whose complete Beethoven Piano Sonatas direct to disc brought Nimbus their first international acclaim.

38 Gennady Rozhdestvensky, the Russian conductor.

40 Numa and his protégé, composer George Benjamin, 1993.

41 George Benjamin, composer, with Mark Elder.

49 The houses at 46–48 Handsworth Wood Road, Birmingham, bought for flat conversion.

50 Typical interiors of the Hermes flats and Handsworth Wood Road properties.

52 The bungalow bought to live in but eventually extended for studio use.

53 Stensham Court, a rejected candidate for Nimbus's new home, subsequently destroyed for redevelopment.

55 View of Wyastone Leys taken by Gerald Reynolds in 1969.

56 Notice for sale which first attracted the Founders' attention to their future home.

56 The overgrown approach to Wyastone Leys.

60 The Swiss tenor, Hugues Cuenod.

61 Michael Reynolds, accompanist Geoffrey Parsons, Numa and German baritone Gerhard Hüsch.

62 Geoffrey Parsons 'accompanying' Gerald Reynolds assessing sound balance for Gerhard Hüsch.

63 The multi-memo recording technique subsequently abandoned for surround sound.

64 Vlado Perlemuter, aged fourteen.

65 Sir William Glock, former Head of BBC Music.

66   Vlado Perlemuter recording the Ravel piano cycle.

69   Vlado Perlemuter inspecting his golden disc with Adrian Farmer at his eightieth birthday concert at the Bath Festival.

70   Vlado Perlemuter supervising Michael opening a bottle of 1949 Clos de Vougeot to celebrate a triumphant concert.

72   Martin Jones, British pianist, at the time of his recording of the complete Mendelssohn cycle.

75   William Blair playing Puck in a complete recording (Shakespeare and Mendelssohn) of *A Midsummer Night's Dream.*

76   Nina Walker and Montserrat Caballé at La Scala, Milan, 1975.

78   Gerald, Numa and Michael, after the completion of the rebuilding of the house and the establishment from scratch of the recording studio and the LP plant.

80   Early press report in the *Ross Advertiser* of 13 February 1980, showing the Founders at work.

82   Michael Reynolds adjusting the controls at the mixing desk.

82   Gerald Reynolds at the LP cutting lathe.

84   Graham Eddy at a semi-automatic LP press.

85   Nimbus staff in the LP press shop.

90   Mike Lee, the first commercial director.

94   Youra Guller, Romanian pianist, in her eightieth year doing her last recording, the last to be made in the Birmingham studio.

98   John Wallace, trumpet player.

103   Signing the CD Manufacturing Licence with Philips at Eindhove, Holland.

106   Dr Jonathan Halliday at Nimbus's first CD laser mastering machine, 1984.

107   Numa and accompanist and fellow director, Nina Walker, dressed in clean room gear.

109   Batch metalising of CDs.

114   The new factory in the shadow of the house.

115   Celebrating the purchase of the first CD moulding pres, 17 July 1984.

116   The delivery of the CD press, 1 August 1984.

117   The CD press fully operational and making its first discs (the first CDs to be pressed in Britain), 22 August 1984.

118   Dr Jonathan Halliday holding the first disc.

119   Gerald, Numa and Michael, holding another first disc.

121 Numa after the deal with British Telecom to put all British telephone directories onto a single CD-ROM.

123 Jim Drennan of Midland Bank Industrial Finance, subsequently Chairman, with Numa in the newly constructed factory.

126 The factory coming up to full production of 15,000 discs per day.

127 A 1985 press release.

128 Gerald and HRH the Duke of Kent on a private visit on 3 July 1985.

129 The staff at the changeover period from LP to CD production.

130 Cwmbran, the new factory.

131 CD injection moulding machines at the Cwmbran factory.

132 The American factory in the shadow of the Blue Ridge Mountains in Virginia.

133 Numa exploring new technology in Virginia.

139 Oscar Shumsky, Russian-American violinist.

141 Oscar Shumsky recording a Mozart violin concerto.

147 Shura Cherkassky, the Russian pianist.

152 Marta Deyanova, Bulgarian pianist and now Mrs Gerald Reynolds.

152 Tim Souster operating the electronics for *Equalisation,* his 1982 composition for brass quintet and electronic interference.

152 Adrian signing up Sir Michael Tippett to record some of his works.

152 Soulima Stravinsky, son of Igor, who recorded his and his father's piano music.

153 Amaryllis Fleming with her five string Amati 'cello, specially used for the Bach 'Cello Suite No. 6 written for that instrument.

153 Cyril Smith and Phyllis Sellick, piano duettists.

153 Cis Amaral, editor of *Performance* (A magazine published by Nimbus) with pianist, Claudio Arran.

153 William Mathias, composer, with Numa.

153 Alfredo Kraus and Raúl Giménez, his sometime pupil, at the Nimbus piano.

157 Peter Laister.

174 Martin Best with his lute, leader of the Martin Best Medieval Ensemble.

180 Monica Huggett, leading for Mary Verney in the First Beethoven Piano Concerto with the Hanover Band in their first recording which, on 20 January 1982, was Nimbus's first orchestral and first digital recording.

181 Geoff Barton and Jonathan Halliday in the control room for the first

Hanover Band recording using digital equipment.

188   The Hanover Band conducted by Roy Goodman in a dinner concert at the Banqueting Hall in Whitehall.

191   William Boughton conducting the English Symphony Orchestra in Symphony Hall, Birmingham, in the first recording made there, prior to its official opening.

192   The control room of the Great Hall, Birmingham University.

194   Gerhard Hetzel, concert-meister of the Vienna Philharmonic, with Adam Fischer.

195   British actress Ann Todd who recorded poetry and prose readings for Nimbus.

196   Sir John Gielgud who recorded Oscar Wilde's *The Happy Prince*, with Adrian Farmer.

197   Christ Church Cathedral Choir, Oxford, surround director Stephen Darlington.

198   Principal Conductor of the BBC National Orchestra of Wales, Tadaki Otaka.

199   British pianist John Lill.

203   Numa, Adrian and Norman White with the 78s that started the *Prima Voce* series.

213   Paco Peña and Eduardo Falú discussing Flamenco from the old world and the new.

213   Indian musicians, Subhen Chatterjee, Sudha Datta, Girija Devi and Ramesh Misra.

214   Wu Man, a virtuoso of the Chinese Pipa.

214   Indian musician Ram Narayan and his daughter Aruna Narayan playing sarangis.

215   The Trebunie family of musicians from Zakopane in the Tatra mountains, Poland.

215   The Familia Valera Miranda from Cuba.

216   Indian musicians, Shruti Sadolikar with Anand Kunte and M Kothare.

216   Fong Naam, Thai classical musicians.

231   Numa with Peter Elliott, Vice President of the Nimbus label in the United States.

232   Numa with Thompson Dean of DLJ, Merchanting Banking New York, celebrating another successful step towards the sale of CD plants, Autumn 1992.

233 The board of the new Nimbus company relaxing after their escape from Captain Maxwell's jaws.

237 Numa singing in the small recital room at Carnegie Hall, New York.

238 Numa and Adrian rehearsing for the recording of Arie Antiche
–9 in the music room of Numa's house.

240 Immediately post-Maxwell, Numa starts expanding again.

241 HRH The Prince of Wales with the Directors, having just opened the Performing Arts Centre on 5 May 1993.

244 The signing of Nimbus's first sale of mastering equipment to China.

253 Anthony Smith, currently Sales and Marketing Manager, with his predecessor Roger Bateson at the start of Nimbus's UK distribution.

255 Numa with the three horns used in recording the *Prima Voce* discs.

LIST OF ILLUSTRATIONS
COLOUR PLATES

Numa Libin, *c.* 1960

Michael Reynolds, *c.* 1960

Nina Walker

The exterior of the studio extension in Birmingham

The interior of the Birmingham studio.

The ruined ballroom at Wyastone before conversion into the chamber music studio.

The chamber music studio in all its glory.

The four seasons at Wyastone Leys.

Aerial view of Wyastone Leys.

The Maxwell deal in a very brief lull in between storms that had already begun.

William Boughton conducting the English Symphony Orchestra in the Symphony Hall, Birmingham.

The Haydnsaal at the Esterhazy Palace, Eisenstadt, Austria with Adam Fischer conducting the Austro-Hungarian Haydn Orchestra.

Roger Jones, Gerald and Jonathan outside Buckingham Palace after receiving the Queen's Award for Technological Achievement, 1987.

Gerald Reynolds.

The farmhouse near Charlottesville, Virginia bought as Nimbus's American headquarters.

Planning for the American factory in the boardroom at Wyastone Leys.

Dr Jonathan Halliday.

Numa, relaxed and in charge.

Numa with Welsh composer Alun Hoddinott.

The building of the Nimbus Foundation's Performing Arts Centre.

Count Labinsky in his fulfilled dream of a concert hall.

HRH The Prince of Wales in the house at Wyastone Leys to open the Performing Arts Centre.

The completed Wyastone Leys estate in 1993, showing factory, house and Performing Arts Centre.

The combined old and new team.
Gary Helfrecht, Vice President of Nimbus Technology and
    Engineering America.
Jonathan with Roger Nute, NTE's General Manager.
New mastering equipment being constructed.
Final assembly of a laser beam recorder.
Installed master preparation line.
The new automated master preparation line launched in October 1994.
Glass master disc before baking.
The auto spin developer.
The Nimbus Halliday laser beam recorder in action.
Numa contemplating his paintings.
Numa's last painting.

INTRODUCTION

The young singer staggered aboard the grubby Bakerloo line train in unusually buoyant mood, for he knew that somehow his cumbersome parcel would be a passport to a world he was destined to enter: the world of recorded sound. As with all the crucial points in his life, this was something he had sensed rather than deduced. He should not even have been in London that morning for he had taken the wrong day off from his minor part in one of Shakespeare's 'Falstaff Plays' in Stratford to attend his singing lesson with Roy Henderson. Henderson, a kindly man, unable to give him time, had sent him off with the old-fashioned disc record cutting machine which had fascinated the young man as it stood in the corner of the room during his lessons. So, for once, his tortured, love-hungry soul was relatively at peace, open to the influences of the outside world, to any benign gesture from the fate that he firmly believed predestined the general direction of his journey through life.

At that moment there stepped into the carriage and into his life the man with whom he was to share his next forty years. He was accompanied by a young friend carrying a large model aeroplane which they had been flying at Wembley as part of the Festival of Britain. The singer experienced a disturbing surge of feeling, a certain recognition that there was a man with whom he would happily spend the rest of his days. As he glanced down the clanking, half-full carriage, from time to time common sense told him not to be absurd; he would never even see him again. Indeed in the mêlée of the crowd at Paddington Station he soon lost sight of the pair.

Having stowed his recording machine safely in the guard's van he decided to pursue the euphoric mood of the day and blow his last 7s/6d on dinner in the restaurant car. Sitting abstractedly in the plush of the post-war, slightly faded splendour of a GWR brown, cream and gold dining Pullman that had not yet succumbed to the drabness of British Rail, he barely raised his eyes when the attendant politely asked if he would mind joining a gentleman at an adjacent two-seater table as there was a shortage of places.

'Typically English,' thought the young singer, as he encountered the draughty blast of the open upper window at the other table. He turned to his companion to ask him politely if he would mind shutting it only to stare into the gentle gaze of his icon of the Underground. 'There is no such thing as luck,' he averred to the end, 'there is some form of immutability, some destiny we are too blind and too dumb to understand.' After a few desultory pleasantries the two young men (the aeroplane flyer had elected to stay in his compartment) found themselves talking earnestly about their lives and ambitions. The singer was so easy to talk to, 'a great communicator with a friendly manner.' Exchanging telephone numbers they found that they both lived near each other on the wrong side of the tracks in Birmingham. The singer's new companion turned out to be an electrical engineer with an interest in electronics, so it seemed only natural to invite him to come and help unravel the mysteries of the newly acquired recording machine.

In the event it was many days before the invitation was taken up, yet in that double chance encounter was born not only a life-long personal relationship but a record company destined to have a significant impact on the cultural life of Britain and considerable influence beyond its shores. The young singer, who later performed under the pseudonym of Shura Gehrman, was Count Numa Labinsky – then just plain Mr Libin – the future president and dynamic heart of Nimbus Records. His companion was Michael Reynolds, who was to become his partner and co-founder of the company. The journey they embarked on that afternoon in 1951 was to prove a long and fruitful, if often arduous, one.

CHAPTER ONE

In January 1985 a short memo was circulated to all members of the staff at Nimbus Records and its associated companies:

> Please note that as from 1 January 1985 I adopted my father's true name and title and shall in future be known as Count Labinsky, Christian names: Alexander Numa. Please amend your records accordingly. A sample of my new signature:
>
> Yours faithfully, A N Libin

The significance of the moment was probably lost on most of the recipients, but for the first time Numa Labinsky* had decided to take his destiny entirely into his own hands and determine for himself who he would be. Just how difficult a decision that was can be seen by looking back over the tortuous path of his earlier life, a necessary process to fully understand the work of art that is Nimbus. Without at least some understanding of the man who was its creator, and for twenty-five years remained its driving force until his untimely death on 28 January 1994, there can be no full appreciation of the unique and remarkable nature of this company. Yet to attempt to understand a character so complex, versatile and creative is not easy.

Alexander	**Shura**	**Numa**	**George**	**Bill**
Libin	Gehrman	Labinsky	England	Zobinoff
Designer	Singer	Poet	Artist	Novelist
Actor	Philosopher	Entrepreneur	Mechanic	Coal Miner
Collector	Fantasist	Philosopher	Linguist	Prankster
French	Russian	Jewish	English	Catholic

---

* For the purpose of our narrative we shall refer to him as Numa or the Count throughout in all contexts unless, as with singing, they obviously demand the use of one of his other names. The chapter is almost entirely based on interviews with the Count and those closest to him. Before his death he completed a short autobiography (published by André Deutsch in February 1995) which gives a much fuller picture of these earlier years than wouldbe appropriate here.

Simply to set down the matrix of his personae and his fields of endeavour indicates how elusive the quarry may be. When every conversation with him had been, on his part, a consummate performance (and it must be confessed a highly enjoyable supporting role on mine) running the gamut of the emotions, employing every trick of gesture and voice, and skipping from subject to subject with a grasshopper inconsequence which nevertheless usually brought him back to the original topic, it required a great effort of will not to play the rabbit before his hypnotic snake. The paradoxes abound. He was feared by many and yet inspired widespread affection, even among those whom he had wronged; he could be, and often was, astonishingly generous and loving, yet he was capable of malice and revenge; he boasted extravagantly yet could be almost paralysed by self-doubt and modesty; he alternated the seriousness of the philosopher with the mischief of a schoolboy prankster.

Numa was born at 61 Murdoch Road, Handsworth, Birmingham, on 19 June 1925 to a Russian émigré father and a French mother. The register of births records his names as Alexander Numa Libin. His father's name was also Alexander Libin and his mother's maiden name was Blanche Crohin – Numa was always proud of his Jewish blood and was puzzled by his father's anxiety to conceal it. His preferred name, Numa, is from the Arabic Naoum. It is also a family tradition that it is linked with Numa Pompilius, the second elected Roman king who was related to Romulus and in a peaceful reign of forty-three years established many cultural festivals and temples, including the first to Janus, god of doorways and bridges.

The Russian diminutive form of his first name, Alexander – Shura – played an overshadowing role in his psyche throughout his life and he used it whenever he wished to say something 'other' about himself, to redefine his role. He would constantly refer to Shura 1 and Shura 2 when trying to account for ambivalence in his actions and attitudes. He was haunted by the image of a twin, Shura 2, an alter ego with whom a perfect silent communion existed and which he vainly sought to recapture for sixty years or more. This alter ego was loved more dearly than any other being in childhood and represented the kind of wordless, perfect communication of minds he tried to achieve in his music, and in his last years in his drawing and painting. All his life it was only through his singing that Numa felt able to communicate again with this other Shura, this other self, and through that personalised channel to convey his haunting sense of loss, of yearning for the unattainable perfection of oneness with others. During one early interview in the summer of 1993 he was most insistent that I record his belief that 'to live an entirely private life means above all to be deprived of things essential to a truly human existence. The true deprivation of total privacy lies in the absence of others, the lack of caring for any other. Whatever remains is without significance and a man consequently diminishes himself and becomes invisible to other human beings if he withdraws his being in this way.' The need for spiritual communication was also at the root of his lifelong compulsion, obsession rather, both to sing and to convey through ever-improving techniques of recording and reproducing music the spiritual exultation that comes from a great musical performance experienced at a live concert.

Numa was born in Britain because one of his father's numerous wild business ventures had taken him to Birmingham to try to set up a chain of bakeries to feed the bread-hungry Midlands. From his father he inherited entrepreneurial recklessness, albeit with far greater success, and an extravagant and dramatic sense of style.

As soon as he was born Numa's incurably French mother hurried him back to their house on the Franco-Belgian border at Leers, near Roubaix (famous for its tapestries and its slaughter houses) and to the matriarchal bosom of a family providently well-endowed with musical genes. His maternal grandfather and several of his female great-aunts were more than competent amateur singers.

His suspicion of women in general stems from these early days. Although several women influenced the development of his early singing career relatively few, his great-aunt and his first regular accompanist among the rare exceptions, got in any degree close to him. He recollects crawling beneath the tablecloth at his mother's elaborate hen tea parties and running his hand up the thighs of the ladies to see if they screamed. A great many of them didn't. It was then, too, that he first identified Baudelaire's 'odeurs mysterieuses' for which he retained a lifelong revulsion. More specifically he disliked his mother – though, tragically, it took him many years to realise that he loved her too. He felt she had betrayed him by trying to trade gifts for love. He often found himself at odds with his sister Jeanne as well, four years his senior and, he felt, his intellectual superior. Of the female members of

3

the household he cared only for his great-aunt, whose quiet devotion to the needs of the family, both in France and later in Birmingham, he came to see as almost saintly.

By contrast, the adult men loomed large, if sometimes indistinct, in Numa's childhood – the mad gardener, the blond athletic giant Vassily (his father's Russian friend and secret lover) and above all, his father himself. Often absent, but always affectionate to his son, one minute driving a Bentley and indulging in every extravagance, and the next bemoaning imminent bankruptcy and selling off another family heirloom to meet the debts; inventing, dreaming, talking, scheming, until his sudden death when Numa was only fourteen. Numa was haunted ever after, not so much by the shock of the event as by the guilt of being unwilling to comfort his hysterical mother. That failure brought home to him that he had no hope of spiritual survival in his now female-dominated household.

Numa had strongly asserted his independence and his individuality from earliest childhood. When sent as an infant to the Dame School in Roubaix, he repudiated what he saw as the teacher's stupidity by walking the six kilometres home and refusing to return even when put on a regime of bread and water for several days. There followed a succession of Jesuit priests as private tutors and with them, too, he exercised his intellectual independence, for example, challenging as inappropriate the concept of virgin birth – 'if God wanted to be a man he should have done what man has to do and been conceived in the usual way.' The attitude provoked many a beating, but the beatings did not deter him from being drawn in early adolescence to the idea of becoming a priest himself.

From childhood Numa had been a collector of inanimate objects in which, nevertheless, he detected an animus. 'You get a life force from certain objects, from stones, from amethyst for example.' His toys as a child were stones and the fossils he collected with fascination, as if he understood the encapsulation, the defeat of time, which in the shape of the records produced by Nimbus – and the *Prima Voce* series in particular – was later to be his greatest achievement. The vast numbers of washing machines, lawn mowers and sewing machines with which his home was encumbered was not just evidence of a squirrel instinct but of a struggle, not unlike that of the modern sculptor, to find new images in these ostensibly inanimate objects.

4

With his father dead and Vassily banished, Numa fled from an uncongenial home to an England already looking anxiously across the Channel at the mounting threat of war. He spoke almost no English but knew that his father had owned two quite substantial houses in Birmingham, so he returned to the city of his birth. There, despite his youth, he persuaded his father's agent to let him live in one house and to have the rent from the other – a princely £4 a week – to live on. This he occasionally supplemented by singing.

Numa had already recognised his homosexuality before leaving for England, but had not defined it as such, beyond the knowledge that he could, indeed needed to, love men. While he could, and sometimes did, love women in the Platonic sense, he chose, for companionship on a daily basis to live with men. This had presented no problem for him during his upbringing in France nor had he considered it anything but natural and acceptable until he arrived in England, where he was shocked and amused to discover that any overt expression of affection between men provoked an uneasy hostility.

Shortly after arriving in Birmingham he had befriended, and been befriended by, a young working-class Glaswegian, Tom, with whom he set up home at 4 Handsworth Wood Road. He scoured and painted the house and searched the second-hand markets for bits of furniture, while green-fingered Tom turned the garden jungle into a miniature Eden. Numa was to spend much of the next thirty years decorating and renovating old houses. Next he learned to be an English gentleman and acquired fluency in the native tongue of which he became a considerable master, its foreignness hardly ever betrayed by a misaccentuation or turn of phrase. Tom tended him and Numa tended his voice, became absorbed in the process of becoming a professional singer, searching for a teacher committed to traditional methods that had almost died out and discarding those who failed to meet his need to sing in a specific and highly personal way. His first concert with an orchestra was at Wolverhampton Civic Hall, and he chose to sing the 'Nuits d'Eté' of Berlioz, a work which he loved to sing at that time. He sang as a male alto, and the performance which he gave, according to him, 'was very good.'

Fundamentally Numa remained a male alto all his life although, for reasons we shall see later, he became a bass baritone in his early twenties. He was hurt when on first taking Tom to hear him at a concert his friend remarked, 'You were all right – but why do you have to sing like a woman?' This was an attitude he was to encounter evermore often the older he grew. After one of his wartime concerts, 'in tents and ghastly tin huts to fifty or sixty men all bored out of their tiny minds', the Officer in Charge scathingly informed him that his 'was the kind of voice he expected to hear from a cathedral choir stall not from a grown man.' He knew then that if he were ever to be accepted either as a person or an artist in England he would have to change his voice, which, at the age of twenty, was still comfortably alto with no sign of a break. He decided to turn his voice around and added about five-and-a-half notes of what he called a deep bustle, accepting that his high voice was a freak of nature and that to the best of his knowledge he was the only member of his generation to have this dual gift. Thus he became a bass baritone, for sing he must at whatever price. And there was a price, even so early, for in changing both his vocal and his personal style he became what his companion called 'a posh, fucking bastard' and, to Numa's great sorrow, Tom left him. Fortunately Numa did not make the voice transition until Ninon Vallin, protégée of Debussy and distinguished interpreter of Fauré, had been moved to tears by Numa's alto singing of a Fauré song. He had been to one of her wartime concerts in Birmingham and praised her performance with such insight and acumen that Vallin asked him if he sang himself. When he acknowledged that he did, she asked him to sing for her. This encounter was to have a significant effect on his career immediately after the war.

Nimbus exists because of Numa's obsession with singing, more particularly with singing in a special way that ensured, in worldly terms at least, that he would not win great fame as a singer. If he had enjoyed the success as a performer and the understanding as an apostle of bel canto, that he felt his talent deserved, Nimbus would not have come into being because its founder would have been appearing on the concert platforms of the world instead. For Numa, the twentieth-century convention of singing in the naso-pharynx was anathema. He saw it as not only destructive to the voice but to the performer's ability to convey the true emotional depths of the music. For Numa the production of vocal tone originated in the larynx and nowhere else. It did not come from the mouth or nose, or behind the eyes. Head and chest resonance have to be used, but only when the launch from the larynx has been mastered. 'Whether all singers and their teachers would agree, is another matter.

But then, why should they? What works for Gehrman [Numa's nom de voix] need not work for others.' The larynx then is the true source of good vocal music, but also necessary for success is command of the disciplined, time-consuming method necessary to exploit its power – precisely the long apprenticeship that most of his contemporary singers, and those of subsequent generations, were unwilling to serve.

The length of his own apprenticeship is truly impressive though it was punctuated by his many wartime concert performances as an alto and interrupted by the necessity to make a living for the demanding female family – mother, sister and great-aunt, that had by now descended on him in Birmingham.

His mother's unexpected arrival on his doorstep confronted him with the need to make what today would be called 'serious money', for her expectations were not only high but presented with such overwhelming confidence in their fulfilment as to make it almost impossible not to comply with her demands. The first of these was that he should resuscitate another of his father's moribund ventures, this time in what was traditionally known in Birmingham as the 'toy' trade, making cufflinks and other dress jewellery. A substantial residue of stock and a small team of dedicated workmen coupled with Numa's ingenious realisation that in wartime there would be a good market for such items engraved with regimental insignia and suitable sentiments, meant that he was soon able to give his mother the considerable income of £400 a month. Upon this she built a small social empire as queen of the exiled French community in the West Midlands, a guileless and successful black marketeer whose 'deadly charm' and determined spirit made all who met her do as she bid them – even the redoubtable Général de Gaulle for whom Numa grudgingly gave up his bed. Numa himself, for all his suspicion of his mother's charm, inherited no little part of this formidable capacity to get others to help him fulfil his dreams. The 'toy' business was soon extended no less successfully into the more patriotically appropriate field of making hyperdermic needles.

By this time, Numa felt free to join Sir Barry Jackson* as an apprentice actor at the Birmingham Repertory Theatre. He was accepted on the strength of his singing from *Boris Godunov* of Boris's 'I have achieved the highest power' in Russian and, rather aptly, of 'Lend me your aid' from

* Sir Barry Jackson 1879–1961. Founder of Birmingham Rep, Director at Stratford after World War II and pioneer promoter of the work of George Bernard Shaw.

Gounod's *Queen of Sheba*. He was thrown out a year later for refusing to sing the banal tunes in *1066 and All That*. In the interim he had helped to pull in audiences eager to see what his next blunder on stage would be – as, for example, when in the role of Hercule Poirot he entered, not through the French windows as the script required, but through the fireplace. He happily accepts Barry Jackson's verdict that he was the worst actor he had ever seen, but it is the compulsive actor in him that distinguished his lieder singing from that of almost any other performer.

He was scarcely less inept off-stage, succeeding in crashing Jackson's beloved Austin – virtually irreplaceable in wartime – because he would not admit that he could not drive. This enthusiasm for driving and crashing novel bits of hardware he never lost. Two incidents may serve to illustrate his passion for machinery, if not its obedience to his desires. When they were first manufacturing LPs at Wyastone Leys, Colin Dix, one of Nimbus's first employees, arrived to work on a Honda 90cc motorcycle and came out of the office one day to find Numa sitting astride it. 'How do you start the engine?' asked Numa. Colin showed him. 'How do you make it go?' came the next inevitable question. Colin indicated that you turned the throttle on the handle but before he could explain that there was no clutch on this model, Numa had revved up and gone flying over a steep bank to land in the rose bushes below in a tangle of kicking legs and spinning wheels reminiscent of Mr Toad. A couple of years later he took another ride, pillion, on Colin's 850cc motorcycle, up the steep winding drive, of Wyastone Leys, flat out and much faster than he anticipated, 'singing at the top of his voice as if he were rehearsing an opera.' Numa's passion for machinery was clearly a chronic condition for just before Christmas 1993, at the age of sixty-eight, he was to be seen in the cab of a large JCB working on an extension to the garden cottage, experimenting joyfully with all its seven levers to the plaintive admonitions of the driver, 'not to get carried away, Sir.'

In 1943, at the age of eighteen, he was confronted with a more serious challenge. He was now old enough for conscription but as a lifelong conscientious objector refused to be enrolled. The tribunal which determined whether or not exemptions from military service could be granted did not much care for Numa's logic-chopping retort to the standard: 'what if a German was raping your sister?' question, wrote 'coward' on his papers, and sent him down Baggeridge colliery near Wolverhampton to be a conscripted coal miner. Once he had survived the rather gruesome initiation process of having a dead mouse put in his sandwich and his water bottle pissed in, the miners, realising that his total ineptitude at things mechanical (despite his love and understanding of them) was likely to imperil their lives as well as his own, took 'Bill', as they called him, under their wing and let him hide at the far end of a long abandoned working with a lamp and a book. There, among other things, he read the complete works of Francis Thompson.

One other event in the closing stages of the war made its mark on Numa; he met and fell in love with René Ramond, a French Air Force gunner some six years his senior, who came to visit his mother's quasi salon for the French exiles in wartime Britain. To the surprise and slight chagrin of Numa's mother, René showed keen interest not only in Numa but in his singing, a subject that mother and sister had found embarrassing, since for them to perform in public in the way Numa insisted on doing was little better than prostitution. René did not understand or appreciate the music itself, but he did understand and accept its central importance in Numa's life. When, just before the end of the war, René was killed on his very last mission, Numa was devastated and all his earlier sense of loss rekindled. When the war ended, it was partly this sense of loss and partly the continuing search for his musical destiny that sent him back to Paris at the first opportunity. There he telephoned Ninon Vallin and tentatively asked if he might see her. The next day he called clutching a small bunch of violets. She thanked him and asked him to sing her the Fauré song again. No sooner had he begun in his new bass voice than she screamed, very musically, and told him to stop. What, she demanded, had become of the voice she had heard which had moved her so? What was this baritone voice doing, or trying to do, replacing the extraordinary alto voice she had found so beautiful? She did not accept the validity of his claim that he had abandoned the old high voice because of its unbearably painful associations, but nevertheless agreed to help him and sent him to her friend, the famous conductor, composer and singer Reynaldo Hahn.* Hahn was already an old man but still believed in teaching by example, by singing as much as he could to demonstrate what the larynx does. The teacher/pupil relationship became a close and affectionate one so

9

that when Hahn died in 1947 Numa felt once more that he was fated to lose all the people who mattered to him in life.

He had been earning a precarious living singing at the soirées and salons of the upper-classes whose patronage he found distasteful. Now he rejected it and, having gained the friendship of the jazz clarinetist Sidney Bechet, sang instead in the nightclubs and brothels of Paris. It was at this period that he made his one and only 'experiment in promiscuity' in the course of which he had two men and two women in two days. He was so physically and emotionally disgusted with himself, and frightened by the possibility of disease, that he bathed his genitals in a solution of dilute carbolic acid to their considerable, but fortunately temporary, detriment, pain and shame, and came to the irrevocable conclusion that sex without love was worthless.

In 1947 he resolved to return to England where he took singing lessons with Joy MacArden* ('she taught me to imagine the sound before I made it'), and Roy Henderson*, whose gift of the disc recording machine ('the hair on the back of my neck tingled when I first saw it') was, in part at least, the conception of Nimbus Records. Henderson recognised in Numa a potentially world-class singer – a recognition which at the time caused the young pupil to roll about on the carpet with laughter. Henderson's 'mad Frenchman' managed to secure some singing engagements through his old wartime Council for the Encouragement of Music and the Arts (now the Arts Council) contacts. Leslie Heward helped him to get several in Birmingham and while, at first, they were not very exciting it was essential for him to develop the habit of performing for the small music groups which were dotted all around the Midlands in those days.

In 1950 he became unofficial singer in residence at the Barber Institute in the University of Birmingham (Sir Jack Westrup, Professor of Music at the University, invited him to give regular weekly recitals), probably the first post of its kind in Britain. He also secured some work with the BBC, mostly on Children's Hour at £3 a time, though he failed to pass the full BBC audition. As Numa Libin he enjoyed a

---

* Numa was fortunate in his teachers. As well as Vallin, there was Reynaldo Hahn (1875–1947), the Venezuelan-born French musician and companion of Proust; Roy Henderson (b 1899) the Scottish baritone who became a professor at the Royal Academy of Music in 1940; the Dutch soprano Joy MacArden (1893–1952), a much respected teacher in Melbourne and Birmingham and pupil of Emma Calvi, Blanche Marchesi and Roberto Tamanti to the last of whom she sent Numa for lessons.

certain amount of success, getting engagements with the Birmingham Symphony Orchestra, the Bournemouth Symphony Orchestra and the Liverpool Philharmonic and even working again for the BBC. The reaction to his performance was often deeply divided and usually controversial and remained so throughout his subsequent recording career. As Shura Gehrman, a pseudonym coined by Sacha Zarcos who told him his German sounded much more like Platdeutsch, northern German, and that if he didn't want to sound like a South Kensington German he had better put an h in German! The Shura, of course, was another recognition of that alter ego with whom he was always trying to come to terms and appropriate for the 'other' voice of this man of many voices.

Just how good a singer was he then? The answer to that question is invariably a highly personal one, for critics have taken diametrically opposite views of his recordings, as the following samples of their reviews demonstrate. To take two recent opinions of his two voices first:

> Shura Gehrman is, in my uninhibited opinion, the greatest bass singer alive, and he may very well be the greatest bass of this century.[1]

> In conveying what each song means to him, Shura Gehrman often achieves an intensity of feeling that is deeply moving, and this is even more so when he sings not as a baritone but as a male alto. There the sound can be beautiful and astonishing, and the articulation of the words crystal clear, as in everything he sings.[2]

Not all critics were as kind and comments on his singing have been widely divergent and not infrequently a little bemused:

> His singing is far more expressive than is the current style in art song singing but, in fact, it is so expressive in a Schubert album titled *The Man Who Steals the Flame* that it is embarrassingly grotesque.[3]

> Gehrman's pronunciation is rarely faulty, though, I feel other aspects of his interpretation to be more questionable. His is a wide ranging voice; he builds from pianissimo to fortissimo with ease, yet at each extreme it is not always easy to understand the words. Moreover, the wide dynamic is too much even for the higher linear speed of the grooves of this 45 rpm disc: at high volume the groove sounds to be on the edge of distortion and breakdown. This exaggeration of tone is not wholly suitable for this music, though Gehrman, with his firmly focused voice, is always stimulating.[4]

There is a melancholy in the voice of Shura Gehrman which connects immediately with this dark and moody cycle. (Die Winterreise) Lost love, over and over again invades the collection, and Gehrman reaches his lowest and highest point in The Grey Head, in which a young man laments on how far he must travel through life before he can welcome death.[5]

... I confess that, after listening to Gehrman's disc of Schumann (*Dichterliebe*), Brahms (*Four Serious Songs*, etc.) and assorted Schubert, I find myself on the shadowed side of that debate. I hear an emotionally overwrought singer of let's say, unbridled technique, holding forth in a cavernous sounding studio.

Shura Gehrman delivers the songs with passion, earthiness and vehemence especially on 'John Barleycorn'. Gehrman's is a voice of unusual resonance and range of tone. A singer in the lieder tradition – a singer who is in effect an actor singer – of a type who have all but disappeared.[6]

If Geraint Evans is a great artist, Shura Gehrman is – why, co-owner of Nimbus Records. Doubtless the voice of this singer-entrepreneur resounds in the self-righteous preface to the Nimbus catalog, wherein one reads: 'Today's recording industry plunders its musical treasury indiscriminately; its musical judgment flounders (sic) at a level of mediocrity compounded by the sheer quantity of its output.'
Could this fulmination be the squish of sour grapes?[7]

Shura Gehrman is unique ... the singing voice is always in command. But what he does with it is extraordinary ... instead of meticulously (intellectually) working out his phrasing, dynamics etc., he tries to recreate what he had found in the music. ...
You may at first be surprised or even stunned, but you ... will have to come to terms with this phenomenon. Fundamentally, his is a typically Russian soft-grained, velvety bass voice, with a very secure foundation and a beautifully open and direct quality ... some three hours later I realised that I had experienced something which can only be described as a revelation ... he succeeds in blowing the cobwebs off what has become known as the lieder tradition.[8]

At full tilt Mr Gehrman's voice is a fearsome, clarion-like instrument, bearing down on a phrase with doom-laden menace ... scowled out with a venom so fierce as to amount to parody.[9]

The Times described *Winterreise* at the time of its issue as a 'hideous performance' and its reviewer felt he should not have issued his discs through his own company since his 'voice was, to say the least, eccentric.'

Colin Wilson, contemplating the fierce hostility of Numa's critics, felt he 'could grasp the essence of the problem. The notion of a certain cool detachment has entered deeply into the modern concept of musical performance, as if the performer would feel it infra dig to offer the audience anything but fine technique.'[10]

Numa with writer Colin Wilson.

Perhaps we should leave the last outside word on the impact of Shura Gehrman's singing to a 33-year-old Dutch professional singer, Jan Kist, to whom I spoke in November 1993. Earlier that month he went into a record shop to get a copy of Schubert's *Die Schöne Müllerin* which he wished to hear in German. They only had an English version, *Fair Maid of the Mill* sung by one Shura Gehrman. Reluctantly he let them put it on for him and, in his own words, was totally astonished. 'It was an apocalypse. I realised that for ten years I had been singing the wrong

13

method; that if I went on pushing my voice this way it would never be free.'

He immediately wrote to Shura Gehrman to ask if he could come and learn how to sing in that 'free' way. He duly came over in mid-November and worked with Gehrman. 'Everything changed completely. It was a perfect, smooth way. I was singing with the whole body. It simply works. I have wings now and I'm not tired. I could go on forever.' Kist was so converted by the experience that he gave up girlfriend and job – 'singing in choruses where, Numa says, you can't hear yourself properly' – and planned to come to Wyastone Leys to study with Numa in 1994.

Numa's own view was succinct. 'They think I'm awful and I think they are doubly worse.' He went on to explain: 'If you listen to my singing there is a dying and swelling of each note, which is considered wrong, but it is right, and part of bel canto. This is not as noticeable on the thin [alto] voice but it is how you keep the voice fresh.' And whatever his critics said he had 'no intention of stopping singing until I am recognised to be a very unusual singer and that I am not a quack . . . that is my due because there are no better singers.'

Simply to consider such a remark conceited is to fail to understand Numa's consuming passion about a particular method and quality of singing. Moreover, the conceit and the exhibitionism are no more than a fragile carapace around a deep sense of insecurity common to many dedicated artists.

Numa could be as frank with other singers as he was with himself but, like most determined proselytisers, he failed to see that his candour might cause pain and offence and was genuinely surprised at the quarrels and upsets that ensued, for example, from his criticism of Dietrich Fischer-Dieskau's lieder singing, telling Vanessa Leigh she sang like a whistling kettle, disparaging the performances of the likes of Elisabeth Schwarzkopf, and advising Geraint Evans to go and study with Tamati as he was the only one who could teach him the open platform. One of the very few singers of whom Numa did approve was another 'natural' and fellow pupil of Henderson, Kathleen Ferrier, about whom he wrote a moving poem when she died.

His impatience with fellow artists was not the product of contempt but of despair at the apparent inability of performers and critics alike, in his view, to distinguish between what he regarded as flawed technique and genuine good singing. As he wrote to his friend Sir William Glock: 'Remember you have listened to Mr and Mrs Pig too long [singing]. If you go and see bad movies long enough you think they're good.' He would not encourage bad singers simply to avoid hurting their feelings. As he said: 'If you want to be a bear or a howling banshee that's fine but it's not singing. I have vast areas of ignorance but I am aware of the technical aspects of singing. It's an obsession and anything out of my life that is good comes from that. If music is cut out then I have very little to contribute. Paradoxically I've had to suffer from being able to do very little.'

But Count Numa Labinsky was far more than a fanatical and dedicated singer and musician, far more than a highly successful entrepreneur. For many years he designed (and had made) costly jewellery, some of it of exquisite delicacy and some much more crude, radiating a kind of vulgar energy. His poetry*, which he composed in his head in French and then translated into English, tumbles headlong, the words almost tripping over themselves in their haste to express the complex and

Numa with actress Mary Wimbush who recorded his poetry.

* André Deutsch has published a volume of Numa's poems and drawings.

15

emotionally charged ideas he wished to capture. For several years he endowed research at Liverpool University into artificial intelligence on a non-computer basis, until the project was brought to a sadly premature end by the death of one of the key researchers. In the summer of 1993 he suddenly became obsessed with the need to draw and paint, something he had never done before. The paintings are fierce and commanding, the drawings have a metaphysical originality evocatively executed in manner far from the technical naivety one might expect from an absolute beginner. It is as if he were able to tap into some primal source beyond himself and channel its energy to fulfil his own needs and ambitions. Of the drawings and paintings he says:

> I don't know what prompted me to do it. I remembered René Ramond, I remembered my mother's face, I remembered Shura, I remembered my great-aunt's face and drew a whole lot of it from within. I never even knew that I could draw. Of course, it's primitive. Don't expect a Watteau or a Fragonard. The only lesson I ever had was from that fat man, Matisse, living in some strange part of France, when I saw him once painting with a stick. He hated religion and he turned to me and said: 'Are you a believer?' I said, 'no.' 'Are you afraid of dying?' I said, 'I don't know.' He asked, 'Do you like food?' I said 'yes' and again he asked, 'Do you like wine' and I said 'yes' and he said 'All right, you come with me', so I went. I confess I am in love with the line drawing, it isn't a talent but something more horrifying than that, it's a need. I thought that music was my great need but I can stand quite far away from music, because I have done it all my life, in a way that I cannot from this compulsion to draw.*

So it seems, contradictorily, that he was at the same time very much in charge of events and at their mercy. It is no coincidence that so many of those who worked with him, from the relatively junior to the most senior, from the longest serving to the newer recruits, use the similes of childhood to describe him, a child at once innocent and full of devilment, mischievous and anxious to please, assertive and vulnerable. One of Nimbus's very first employees describes how he started out by insulting her, being cruel or telling other people she was no good but then eventually decided that she was OK. Thereafter she became his 'darling'. She took to him and loved him like a naughty child – 'you do whatever is necessary because they need protecting. They couldn't be allowed to know what people said about them because they would find that hurtful.'

Another senior colleague says that while Numa could be unforgiving about some things, he did some unforgivable things himself to vulnerable people – a sin Numa was the first to confess. 'He was also a man of enormous character, charm and occasional kindness, whom I treated consistently as if he were a spoilt child.'

Those who encountered Numa only occasionally and in formal situations were frequently taken in by these 'childish' manifestations, which were, in fact, quite calculated and no part of his private, as opposed to his public, behaviour. Such ploys were used to disarm or divert attention and even sometimes to defuse tension. A classic example occurred at the last, rather uncomfortable, meeting with Peter Laister. Numa was in considerable pain and at a critical stage in the proceedings retired to the adjacent room, to which his doctor had been called, for a morphine injection. When he returned a few minutes later he was leaning heavily and groggily on the doctor's arm, apparently in dire need of support. The distraction and the sympathetic reaction took the heat out of the situation and put everyone in a more conciliatory mood. Only later, after the meeting, did it emerge that he had been perfectly capable of returning under his own steam and had actually asked the doctor to walk him in quite deliberately. The untutored observer, who did not know him well, might have been taken in by the apparently childish behaviour, particularly as Numa did sometimes have a genuine air of childish innocence.

The corollary of these child-like qualities was that he retained throughout his life a child's capacity to give and receive love with uninhibited generosity so that even former employees with whom he had fallen out retained great affection for him. Many, from highest to lowest, remained loyal friends throughout his life as was evident from the flood of letters sent to Michael and Gerald Reynolds when he died. Perhaps the impact of his affectionate disposition was best summed up in a letter of condolence from Gloria, a shop-floor worker in the American plant, who wrote, 'he always seemed attentive to what was being said to him and this made one feel important in the scheme of things.'

After an operation in 1966 to remove his gall bladder, cream and chocolate were forbidden foods but his companions still had to conduct 'chocolate hunts' to find where he might have hidden a cache bought in town, or that he had persuaded some unsuspecting newcomer to smuggle into him.

Cigarettes were another forbidden fruit. In the late seventies when Michael and Gerald were trying to get Numa, who had been quite a heavy smoker, to give up the habit, he used to sneak around the factory trying to scrounge a cigarette off the workers. One day he was standing with Colin Dix on the steps of Wyastone Leys with an obviously proprietorial air when a delivery van called. Colin signed for the goods and as the driver was about to go, Numa sidled up to him and begged for a cigarette. 'Not effing likely!' came the reply. 'If you can afford to live in a house like that, mate, you can afford to buy your own fags.' The incident is indicative of Numa's love of naughtiness and a certain innocent naivety about the ways of the world.

Numa loved to shock and astonish, sometimes for the sheer hell of it – in his Paris days he blew up one *pissoir* and poured red wine down another adjacent to a cafe frequented by many ladies, simply *'pour épater les bourgeois.'* In Birmingham he once made friends with an impoverished working-class old lady called Kitty whose son had become a doctor, married and gone off to live in suburbia. Numa was so incensed by the son's snobbish rejection of his mother that he persuaded Lady Shrewsbury* to dress Kitty and herself 'up to the nines' and accompany him on an unannounced visit to the doctor's house. The show he and Nadine Shrewsbury put on of being the old lady's bosom friends shamed her son into acknowledging her properly. Throughout his business life he continued to use his shock tactics for a purpose – though he obviously got a considerable kick out of them too.

While this smacks superficially of the schoolboy, it had a deeper underlying motive: to shock and disconcert by eccentric comment and behaviour. Knowing that a group of German businessmen would arrive in crumpled suits to negotiate a deal over dinner, Numa had all his team turn out in the most elegant dinner jackets. Then, having put the visitors at a disadvantage, he drove a hard bargain.

When a 'pricey' PR company came to pitch for Nimbus business Numa marched into the meeting in white silk pyjamas and dressing gown, eyed the head of the firm up and down and announced, 'you're too fat! Now I'm going for a pee pee!' (The firm was in fact hired.) By

*He met Lady Shrewsbury when they shared an accompanist and became friends while organising her festival, Opera at Ingestre, with John Pritchard and the Liverpool Philharmonic.

wrong-footing his interlocutors Numa aimed to seize the high ground, assess their responses under pressure, and make his own dispositions. In my case he asked me at our first interview when I began to masturbate.

But he also had a very real sense of his own worth and dignity. A former company secretary, Stuart Garman, related the occasion in the summer of 1989 when Numa and three other Nimbus directors were on a visit to JVC in Japan.

> At the first meeting we were told to go to one of JVC's factories and we had to go by train, a very public ordinary hard-benched train. Numa didn't really appreciate that, he wanted to be taken by car. Reluctantly he accepted that it would be quicker by train. We were met by two rather junior young men from JVC and had to stand in the taxi queue while it drizzled with rain. Numa paced up and down that taxi queue getting more and more vocal and angry. 'How could the President of Nimbus Records be kept waiting in the rain and be expected to use an ordinary taxi?!' He was steaming and really got very upset. When we got to their plant we were met by the Assistant Manager and taken round this audio factory where we were shown a variety of historical moments in JVC's life, including dummy head recording which Numa hated. Then, to cap it all, His Master's Voice logo with Nipper listening to the gramophone, which is a JVC trademark in Japan. JVC had invented stereo and television and all those things that are part of a typical Japanese tour showing off their wares. Numa took great exception to what he felt was chipping away at the empire. Next we were asked to listen to some recordings of something like Mantovani with strings screeching. Numa simply hated it and made it quite clear that he would tolerate neither false claims nor what he regarded as discourteous behaviour.

As Stuart knew from personal observation, this was in total contrast to the treatment of guests at Wyastone Leys. There it was not just that Numa insisted on every practical detail being right to welcome a guest, from tidy flowerbeds to clean toilets, quality soap to beautiful flowers, but that he insisted in seeing that it was so by personal inspection and, if necessary, personal action. Moreover he ensured that every business guest felt that his visit had been fruitful by demanding and getting a carefully prepared and well-packed agenda tailored to the individual. It was not surprising that Numa was offended by JVC's behaviour. Nevertheless, as Stuart explained, 'the Japanese couldn't understand what the problem was and took us back to the station, where we had to run for the train. In the train Numa lambasted each one of us in turn, demanding that we agree that we had been badly treated. All this in a crowded train, Japanese looking over the tops of their seats at what was going on. In the end he convinced himself this was the beginning of the Third World War. And he was not going to speak to them ever again unless he got a full apology, despite the fact that meetings had been arranged and reporters were going to see us the following day. A more senior JVC representative came to meet Count Labinsky in the hotel the following morning but was hit between the eyes with a tirade for an hour-and-a-half. How dare he treat visitors to his country like this? Numa was offended by the very sight of JVC. Numa simply forbade anyone to go to any of the meetings that had been set up and that was the beginning of a short but beautiful holiday.'

Numa, as Gerald explained, had been offended not for his own sake but for the slight to the company and its directors, which was in marked contrast to the courtesies extended by Sony. He also recognised the importance of not allowing oneself to be put down, to lose face, in negotiations with the Japanese.

There was a wonderful counterpoint in Numa's life between fierce assertion of his own worth and a contrite recognition of his own faults, of which his Jesuit tutors would have thoroughly approved. I juxtapose at random from my interview notes: 'Basically, I know I am a weak man and therefore can be strong . . . It's absolutely essential to tell you that I'm very rarely wrong on fundamental concepts. I'm only wrong when I am swayed and listen to others . . . I think I'm a prig but also very mischievous . . . My response to the press is human – when they say nice things I like them, when they say horrid things I don't, I'm simply normal enough to be hurt – I am hurt . . . A famous singer has to believe in himself or herself and have a certain amount of "I am the best" . . . But I wasn't sensitive enough, I was far too conceited, too obsessed with myself.' And so on.

While Numa's volatile temperament was in part the product of his own passionate and artistic nature, the volatility had been greatly exacerbated by serious physical illness as Michael recalls with tender concern.

Some time in 1964 Numa had a very heavy cold and I was bed-bound with a bad back I think, at the time, so I couldn't do any of the work.

Numa insisted on putting up the curtains in a flat and kept eating these dreadful Veganin tablets to keep the fever down. He took so many they caused him tremendous hepatic colic which seemed to start off a succession of painful illnesses for him in that part of his body. After that he had these abdominal pains and a lot of sickness as well. In 1966 he had an operation to remove his gall bladder. The specialist told him he could now eat anything. It was near Christmas so he tucked into the good food and he had a mince pie that set him back where he was before with a terrible pain. Yet despite being sick after nearly every meal he made some amazing recordings between 1969 and 1975. When we got to Wyastone Leys he started with Palpheum which tended to change his character. He seemed to be very much on a knife edge and used to lose his temper more quickly. He went on to Pethidine later, which proved to be better at the time but the quantities crept up until they were forty or fifty a day some days.

Numa castigated himself a little unfairly for this dependency. 'Doom descended on me when I was forty-seven and I was in so much pain, but I think I have behaved as a great coward over the past three years and because I withdrew a lot, I took to the tablets.'

Pethidine is heroin based, and therefore both highly addictive and a depressant. Numa's extraordinary resilience and strength of character was demonstrated to me as I watched him break this pethidine habit in less than three months while I was first interviewing him. With the help of a sympathetic and psychologically skilful young local doctor, he escaped from what had become a serious addiction by the same self-discipline that he had applied to his singing. In the months immediately prior to his death he took virtually no pethidine at all. It is no coincidence that ridding himself of chemical props and replacing them by willpower resulted in another of those creative outbursts – nearly a hundred paintings and a resumption of making recordings, this time, once again, with the male alto voice – with which his career had been punctuated.

The pattern of the apparent contradictions that can be seen in so many of the public aspects of Numa's character and experience accounts in part for the unique features of Nimbus as an organisation. His conduct of the business, and particularly the man management reflected these characteristics. At one moment abrupt, tough and angry, at the next considerate, generous and understanding; the losing of cases for wrongful dismissal at industrial tribunals counterbalanced by acts of generosity very rarely to be found in commerce and industry. On one occasion, for example, when he learned that a manual employee would have to wait more than a year for badly needed heart surgery, he paid for immediate treatment at a private hospital. In another case, noticing an employee struggling to work out whether she could afford the deposit for a house, he established how much was needed and paid it.

But his generosity to his employees was the tip of a more private iceberg in which he remembered dozens of individual anniversaries, or succoured a multitude of distresses without recourse to computer, diary or secretarial reminder but from his own memory because he wished to express his genuine concern. My own experience confirms this. Within a couple of months of beginning to work with him on this book I had to go into hospital for an operation. I mentioned this by way of explanation for an impending absence of a few days. Numa took a keen interest in how, where and by whom I was to be treated and I left gratified at his concern but thinking that was the end of it. The day after the operation my hospital bedside was transformed by a massive bouquet, a kindly note and two jars of Wyastone honey to speed my recovery.

This was typical of the private moral code by which Numa lived. He never hesitated to speak his mind, often with considerable passion, but when he had, usually with good cause, knocked someone down verbally he would always make a point of picking them up again before the day was out. He encouraged ambition in those who worked with him (he never permitted the phrase 'worked for') but would not tolerate that overweening ambition which tried to prosper at the expense of others or of Nimbus. Whilst he expected high standards he wanted them to be the product of self-motivation, not imposed. The closer to the centre of the family network an individual was, the more demanding was Numa's insistence that these standards be maintained.

All the above points describe an obsessive personality and, as Peter Laister, the chairman of Nimbus for six years until November 1993, pointed out: 'What Numa wanted, he wanted with total obsessiveness, but it did produce a great dynamism.' Nimbus's dynamic came from that obsession.

CHAPTER TWO

If Numa Labinsky was the plutonium core at the heart of the reactor, then Michael Reynolds is the shield that controlled and directed its enormous energy safely to positive ends. Michael is the calm at the centre of the whirlwind of creativity and technical innovation at Nimbus. When Numa challenged and threatened to explode, Michael merely smiled and gave a non-committal 'hum' rather than provoke an outburst with the wrong word.

Born on 12 March 1929, Michael Reynolds was educated at Stowe before joining the General Electric Company as apprentice electrical engineer, gaining his HNC in 1952. His main interest had always been in electronics, but his father, who saw no future in that field, steered him in the more general direction. Michael stayed with GEC until 1957 by which time he was a contracts manager – business experience he was to find invaluable at Nimbus, where he has tended to concentrate on the detail rather than the overall picture. This is something for which Numa sometimes criticised him but, as he points out in reply, someone had to translate the concept, the visionary idea, into concrete achievement. His brother, Gerald, describes Michael as, 'the stable, conscientious one who not only makes sure the details don't get missed, but retains a degree of detachment about business decisions when the rest of us are reacting emotionally.'

The relationship between Michael and Numa grew more slowly on Michael's part. As Numa realised, Michael was 'totally oblivious to the emotional chaos that he was causing.' But he did attend nearly all Numa's concerts with interest and enjoyment, if not awareness that Numa was singing for him. The two of them walked and talked until the small hours as they wandered the streets of Birmingham. Some nine months after they met they set up house together at 4 Handsworth Wood Road in Birmingham. Michael's father, chairman of Tube Investments Aluminium and son of the founder of Reynolds Tubes, was the kind of gregarious communicative person who quickly accepted Numa's foreignness and the situation into which his son had entered. He recognised also the value to Michael, who suffered from petit mal at a time when it was not so easily controlled by drugs, of such a secure relationship. Michael's mother, whom Numa described as 'rather county and sidesaddle,' took a little longer to win over, though in the widowed, closing years of her life she was closer to Numa than to her sons. Once his mind was made up, Michael did not, in any case, worry what his family might think. He was seeking a permanent relationship and in Numa discovered one which arose, initially, from a deep sense of companionship, though, as with most relationships, unsuspected crises still lay ahead.

Although Numa and Michael did not realise it at the time, the stool still only had two legs. In fact they tried hard at first to evade the determination of the third leg to stick itself on. Gerald Reynolds was thirteen years younger than his brother and very different in character and abilities. He described himself 'as a nasty, spotty little boy that used to take Michael's model electric trains to pieces and not put them back together again.' From his grandfather – maker of the once famous Armstrong Siddeley motorcar – and his father, Gerald had inherited a passion for all things mechanical, and for motor cars in particular. When he left Stowe (where he had spent most of his time in the school workshop making things), he joined the Rover car company in Birmingham and studied at Technical College in the evenings. He describes how, at the age of twenty (he was born on 19 May 1942), he used to beleaguer Numa and Michael in their house in Handsworth Wood because he hungered for the mental stimulus that only they seemed able to provide. The two older men would hear him coming – he had a distinctly heavy tread – and slip out of the back door to the cinema, leaving Gerald patiently camped on the front doorstep until they returned. His siege was successful in the end. With what Gerald describes as great generosity, Numa and Michael admitted him first to the circle of their friends and then later into the more intimate relationship which they shared. Contrary to the accepted wisdom on such matters, though Numa and Michael were extremely wary of extending their relationship to a *ménage à trois* at first, the love between the members of this symbiotic triumvirate not only survived but grew for more than thirty years.

It was Numa who showed Gerald that his work at Rover was leading him into a dead-end and not only brought the younger man into the property business that he and Michael launched in 1957, but encouraged him to attend the Birmingham School of Architecture. Not for the last time, Gerald showed his remarkable capacity for learning quickly under pressure, by acquiring in a matter of eight months the two A levels in Physics and Maths which he needed to enter the architecture school. For two years he spent his spare time giving Numa and Michael practical help in converting the large old houses they had been buying up into the luxury bachelor flats that were their speciality. His flair for design further improved the already high quality of the conversions. After two years Gerald realised that to complete the six year course would be a waste of time as far as what he could contribute to the business was concerned. Until you become a top level architect, choosing your commissions, you are likely to be doing pretty mundane work and he realised that there was as much labour in designing a semi-detached house and supervising its construction as there was in a grand scheme. He decided simply to join Numa and Michael and get on with it. This he did in November 1963.

Numa and Gerald taking the sun.

But Gerald had already performed in 1961 a far more significant service by resolving a crisis between Numa and Michael which could have brought their relationship – and thus the embryonic Nimbus – to a premature end. Numa, who confessed that he found Gerald's love for him very humbling, believed that Gerald understood him better than anyone. Perhaps this understanding arose from the fact that during that early time when Numa was still a concert singer Gerald would sit, day after day, listening to Numa rehearse, usually for five or six hours at a time (Numa was no laryngitic singer in the twentieth-century fashion, who needed a rest every twenty minutes), and attended his recitals as well. Since, in many senses, Numa *was* his music, to understand one was to understand the other and musical performance certainly featured large in the crisis that now arose.

Numa was scheduled to give, on Thursday, 18 May 1961, as part of the Bromsgrove Festival, the concert that was to be his breakthrough. Certainly the programme was a formidable one, that few, if any, modern singers would be prepared to tackle.

Thursday, May 18th at 7.30 pm (1961)

NUMA LIBIN (bass)

DEREK YOUNG (pianoforte)

LIEDERKREIS, opus 39	*Schumann*
DAS BUCH DER BILDER (Four settings of Rilke) – First Performance	*Derek Young*
LE BESTIAIRE	*Poulenc*
LE PAON	*Ravel*
FOUR CHANTS POPULAIRES	*arr. Ravel*
MONOLOGUE OF BORIS TIMOFEEVITCH from LADY MACBETH OF MTSENSK	*Shostakovich*
SONGS AND DANCES OF DEATH	*Mussorgsky*

On the eve of the concert – a timing Numa felt very bitter about – Michael announced (not for the first time, for he had been engaged when he first met Numa), that he was to be married to a Miss Sylvia Wood. Numa was too devastated to do or say anything and Gerald saw that he alone would have to persuade Michael to search his heart to see if marriage was what he really wanted to replace his relationship with Numa. Michael broke off his engagement.

26

This says much for the younger brother's perception and for his powers of persuasion, both of which become forcibly apparent once you get to know him. Gerald is tall, quiet and highly articulate. He moves with a panther-like lightness of step now, in contrast to his youthful plod, which hints at the predatory sharpness of his intellect. He is, as we shall see, a mechanical inventor of great brilliance and a shrewd businessman. It is hard to escape the conclusion that had it not been for his utter devotion to and respect for Numa and Michael he might have been before now a singularly successful captain of the Nimbus ship.

The Bromsgrove concert made, as usual, a considerable impact. The *Birmingham Post* praised Numa's performance, not knowing it was to be his swan song, and at the end of the concert a huge bald Russian approached Numa, with tears in his eyes, and invited him to return to Russia to sing. Numa claims that he refused the invitation because of his hatred of communism (he even refused to speak Russian) and fear of never coming back, but the fact is that he had that night taken a momentous decision, subconsciously at least, to give up public concert singing. If Michael could give up marriage, then Numa could sacrifice for Michael what he loved most and the pursuit of which had most often separated them.

The three men were never parted again, emotionally or geographically, and until Numa's death they were seldom out of sight and sound of each other. For the next seventeen years they evolved together not only a property empire but the basis of Nimbus Records.

Before we can look at those early years of the company however we must jump ahead almost two decades to the extension of this 'family' of like-minded men and to the recruiting of the two who complete the quincumvirate which is at the heart of Nimbus – Adrian Farmer and Jonathan Halliday.

Adrian Farmer, Nimbus's Director of Music and Deputy Chairman, came to the company almost by accident in 1979 when he was touring South Wales with Jack Brymer, the clarinetist, and David Lloyd, who was not only Brymer's accompanist but Adrian's tutor at the Royal Northern College of Music. Adrian, after winning the Kent Actor of the Year Award when still a boy, had his sights fixed on a stage career until he discovered the piano. At first, aged nine, he tinkled away at his neighbour's upright, but by the time he was twelve and at his secondary school, where he had to resist the bias towards science and engineering, he knew he was going to be a musician. Although no one in his family had ever been to university, Adrian's music master persuaded him to go to Birmingham to take a music degree which, at that time, was based on music theory and history – a background which now stands him in good stead in his present job. While at Birmingham he spent much of his time playing the piano and, to the chagrin of his professors, directing such offbeat operas as *Tantivy Towers* by Thomas Dunhill. Wishing to develop his piano technique after graduating from Birmingham he applied for and got a place at the Royal Northern College of Music where he specialised in accompaniment, and it was as a humble page-turner that he found himself in the Nimbus studio on that fateful day.

At that time the rehearsal room was in the derelict part of the house in South Wales which had become the company's new headquarters and was little more than bare boards, with piles of boxes all over the place. Lloyd had come to try his hand as accompanist to Numa and was showing off in front of his pupil, to whom he was deeply attached, by playing too loudly and frenetically. Numa, who never allowed himself to be outdone by anybody, responded by singing more and more loudly himself while Michael and Gerald sat po-faced in the corner. It was a disaster. As soon as Lloyd left the room, Numa turned to Adrian and asked, 'And what do you do?' When Adrian replied that he played the piano, Numa placed 'Trockne Blumen' from *Die Schöne Müllerin* down in front of him and told him to play it. Adrian played and Numa sang and when they had done Numa simply said, 'You can go back with *him* or you can stay here with me. It's up to you to make up your mind.' Adrian stayed and is still there almost fifteen years later. Lloyd left in a huff.

Numa and Adrian worked together for many weeks and although Adrian was fascinated by Numa as a man as well as a musician the mentor took no advantage of the pupil's vulnerability. Which, as Adrian recalls, was just as well, for musically he was to be brought down to earth with a bump.

> I thought everything was going fine, I suppose it was going to my head and one day Numa just knocked me down. I shall never forget it. He said, 'Do you really expect me to sing to an introduction like that, do you think that's of any use or consequence to me at all? Until

you learn to play much better than that I'm not going to work with you again.' The problem with working with Numa was that he demanded a constant change of colour of what you're working on from moment to moment. It's not about the right notes it's about knowing that if he made a colour you can match it immediately. It took years to work that out and not to feel that every time you sat on a piano stool you were on a tightrope and you can't perform very much under those circumstances because you are constantly terrified.

Numa recording Vaughan Williams' Songs of Travel, accompanied by Adrian Farmer, now Deputy Chairman.

Adrian went to Bernard Roberts, and to Nina Walker, Numa's first accompanist, for lessons, whose effect, by making him play with his whole body as well as his hands and his mind, was to produce a very fine accompanist indeed. The recordings which Numa and Adrian issued on CD in recent years were all worked on way back in 1979 and quietly gestated in the intervening years. Their last recording, Duparc songs and Fauré's *L'Horizon Chimerique*, are excellent examples of the synergy they found. Its importance to Adrian became apparent when he chose it as one of the half dozen most musically successful recordings from his time at Nimbus. 'One of the records would be a CD that hasn't been issued yet which was a personal turning-point. Last year Numa and I went to the studio together and recorded *L'Horizon Chimerique* and the six Duparc songs. It was repertoire we had worked on right from the beginning but had never really got quite the way we wanted it. We hadn't tried it for two years or so but it all came together, it was amazing, we just went on and did the next song and the next song; it was a *performance*!'

When he joined Nimbus, Adrian came to live in the headquarters house (as he still does), on a salary of £3,000 all found, and was very happy. Gradually he assumed wider responsibilities, first for producing recordings and then, gradually, for playing a larger role in deciding repertoire and choosing artists, and later looking after front covers and sleeve notes. Now he is deeply involved in the business and marketing side of Nimbus, from which he derives little personal satisfaction, being, by his own admission, a tardy and reluctant correspondent and disliking the telephone. A natural 'performer', like his role model, he has more than a touch of the Numaesque about him, unable to resist the bon mot and the witty retort however much trouble it may land him in. In recent years, as the three founders have become more reclusive, Adrian has more and more become the public and peripatetic face of Nimbus, though it is a role he does not particularly relish.

If Adrian is today the most public of Nimbus directors, the man who completed its inner core by joining in July 1981, Dr Jonathan Halliday, is its most reclusive. Tall, gaunt, dark and taciturn, Jonathan usually confines his conversation to muttered, barely audible monosyllables or loud and furious outbursts of anger. When he does choose to talk, the acutely critical and logical mind with its encyclopedic memory is impressively evident. Jonathan Halliday is not only an electronics genius but an accomplished musician and a trenchant critic in business matters.

In nature classes at his primary school instead of the task set, he used to draw the electrical circuits which his father, an electrical engineer, had introduced him to. His traditionalist teacher, Miss Puddock, was unimpressed by his assertion that 'circuits were nature, weren't they?'

When he went to a good grammar school in Maidenhead (where he obtained 13 O Levels and 5 A levels with distinctions in music, pure maths and physics), he rejected what he saw as its arbitrary authority although he later realised that its teachers had a great deal more commitment than the dons he encountered at St Catherine's College, Oxford, where he gained a first in physics, and at Clare College, Cambridge which he attended for his PhD in radio astronomy. Standards were, in his eyes, no higher at his first job at the IBA in 1975, working firstly on an adaptive aerial project and then for three years on the 'surround sound' system, a concept he was to help Nimbus develop much further.

He discovered a talent for music at an early age and was taught the piano by a man strong on technique and weak on musicality, which, he says, at least gave him strong fingers. He wrote music but was not excited by the modern idiom so ran foul at school and Oxford of the 'ruling clique that said the only music that counts is either very modern or pre-1600.' At Cambridge things were different; not only was romantic and classical music highly thought of but, because Clare College admitted women in his second year, he became a member of a first-rate choir.

While he was at the IBA – where he 'didn't feel he was doing anything useful' – living until his last year in grim bedsitters, he was pointed in the direction of Nimbus by Roy Howat, a musical friend with whom he had made contact through music summer schools while still at Cambridge.

At his interview with the Nimbus directors, to the comment 'so you're an electronics person' (which they were looking for) he riposted, 'I hate electronics but I'm good at it.' A rapport sprung up because 'they talked to me as a person' and because he found for the first and only time in his life a group of people whose invitation to live with them as well as work with them showed the degree of dedication which he sought. After a week's agonising he decided to accept the post of Head of Research and he, too, has been there ever since.

With the recruitment of Jonathan the circle was closed and Nimbus embarked on the next stage of its growth which was to completely change the scale and impact of its activities. While the three founders and the two other members of the Nimbus quincumvirate frequently pay tribute to many others who have contributed to the company's success, there is no escaping the fact that these five have been at the heart of its achievements for the last fifteen years. There are two reasons for this: firstly the complementary nature of their gifts and personalities and secondly their unremitting dedication to the Nimbus goals, manifest in their not only working together but living together. For them Nimbus is a twenty-four hours a day, 365 days a year preoccupation. Principles that can inspire such devotion and mutual loyalty must be potent ones.

CHAPTER THREE

Early in my research I came across, in the chaotic and labyrinthine files of Nimbus Records, a pencilled note in Numa's hand. It was not clear if it was a draft for a brochure, a press statement or simply an aide memoire. It was dated 21 September 1957 and read simply:

> We aim to record anything of a specialist nature not dealt with by big companies to any great degree.
>
> These recordings to be made available at lower costs than those produced by big companies.
>
> The quality will of necessity have to be excellent.
>
> At the moment we are engaged in recording stories for children and book readings beside chamber music and music for small orchestras.
>
> The music is mainly new, old or little known.

The catalogue for 1990 covering some 400 titles is very different in appearance. It is well designed and beautifully produced in colour, but the text has a familiar ring.

> In founding Nimbus nearly twenty years ago, I sought to promote talented artists at the outset of their careers and to re-introduce great artists who had withdrawn themselves from the public eye . . . these artists have been encouraged to protect a fundamental belief: that music is communication at the deepest level when expressed through the act of committed performance.
>
> . . . the company's resources are dedicated to the service of musical performance on record.

There are three principal technical elements in this pursuit of perfection in performance: the acoustics chosen for the performance; the use of a special kind of single microphone and the approach to the playing and editing of the music itself. Later in this account we shall come across various examples and follow the evolution of three elements, but here, as we begin to read the score, it is important to understand the principles involved.

The acoustics, whether in the studio or on the locations so much favoured by Nimbus, should be naturally reverberant and at all costs avoid the harsh, dry quality which typified so many early CD recordings by other companies. In the words of a Nimbus paper to a Japanese audio conference in 1991: 'It is very important when making a record for the performer to receive acoustic feedback from his environment. A musical performance is something that not only happens in a specific time but also a specific place, and the listener must hear that place to understand the performance. Recording in a reverberant acoustic has various effects. The performer feels the acoustic supporting the sound he makes and it gives him something to react to and work with.'

When the great pre-twentieth-century composers conceived a work, they had in their mind's ear a perfect balance between the various sound elements. Though this was primarily conditioned by the scope of their genius, it was also subject to the limitations of the instruments of the day (and, of course, but to a much lesser degree, of their players) and the acoustic of the places in which they were performed. Some of Nimbus's most successful recordings have been those played in the places, such as the Haydnsaal in the Esterhazy Palace, where the works were originally performed. The majority of the performance venues until the early twentieth century were either ecclesiastical, palatial, or in theatres designed for opera, all of which had highly reverberant acoustics. It was up to the musicians to recreate the balance envisaged in the score by their playing without any artificial aid, using their ears and musical sensitivity to provide the feedback and modification necessary to come as close as possible to reproducing the composer's intention.

The audience consisted of a conglomeration of individuals each hearing the music from a unique personal position, although in a good acoustic variations in the sound reaching one pair of ears compared with another would be very small. If a performance is to be captured in all its glory then that listening experience has to be recreated. To that end the members of the Nimbus team have spent the past thirty-five years developing the single microphone technique, culminating in the Ambisonic, or surround sound microphone, partly of their own design. This consists, in effect, of a multitude of individual microphones packed together in a space not much larger than the human ear and, like the human ear, capturing the sounds impinging on it from all directions. Where stereo can recreate lateral shifts in sound, Ambisonic seeks to capture those reaching the ear from in front, behind and all the angles in between as well. Thus once the microphone has been positioned the responsibility for balance lies totally in the hands of the musicians, just as it would have done in the original performances. If the flute or oboe cannot be heard it must play more loudly or the rest of the orchestra more quietly. To 'mike up' individual instruments separately and rebalance the sound through the mixing desk is, in the Nimbus view, a travesty which distorts the composer's intentions. As they put it in the paper referred to above, the ensuing sound is 'at best an engineer's opinion of the true sound and, at worst, a hopeless distortion of it.'

Such an approach is very demanding of musicians. As one orchestral player I spoke to put it: 'It can be a little annoying to have played a whole movement, only for someone to approach the microphone as if they were praying, shift it a millimetre, and ask you to play the movement all over again.' However, in contrast with conventional recording practice, once the microphone position had been accurately determined, there was no further need for adjustment throughout the recording.

Again and again, from correspondence in the Nimbus files and conversations with many Nimbus artists, it is clear that the vast majority of performers, from soloists to orchestral players, are only too glad to have their musical responsibility restored to them in this way.

The same paper also admirably encapsulates Nimbus's attitude to editing:

> When Caruso stood in front of an acoustic recording horn in 1904, he knew that he had to perform – that is he had to sing that four-minute aria from start to finish, and if he made a mistake he would have to start again . . . The same is true of performances today although sadly not of recording, which has become a different art altogether.
>
> It is only since the invention of tape that there has been a difference between the attitudes towards performing and recording . . . A performance is an emotional and intellectual experience, complete from start to finish. Any disruption of that by editing parts from elsewhere, can only lessen its emotional impact. . . .
>
> When we make a recording, it is treated as far as possible as a live performance. The microphone is the audience, and we record artists who are prepared to take the risk of letting occasional mistakes stand in order to preserve the integrity of the performance.

If there is to be little or no editing, then a performance has to be recorded as a whole, or at least in coherent parts such as a complete movement. The Nimbus thesis is that no two performances are identical even when the same musicians are playing the same piece on the same day. Thus, while to patch a series of takes together may ensure that there are no wrong notes, it will juxtapose incongruities in the indefinable element of musical *re*creation unique to each performance. This, in turn, will subtly undermine the wholeness of the work. That is not to say that Nimbus never edits, that would be absurd, but as musical director Adrian Farmer put one of the family mottos: 'I will use an edit to save a performance but never to create one.' Nimbus, therefore, looks for artists who are willing to accept that in order to make a good recording they must give a complete performance, no less than those early performers, cutting direct to a wax disc, had to do. Indeed, the modern performer's task is perhaps even more arduous, for where Caruso's recorded performance was limited by the technology of his day to three or four minutes the use of magnetic tape now allows the structure of the music to be the only determinant of the length of a take. After initial hang-ups and difficulties the great majority of Nimbus artists happily embrace this approach, finding that it enhances the quality of their performance, and consequently of their recordings. Those few that cannot adapt go elsewhere.

Probably the largest undertaking completed by Nimbus to date, (though this will be overtaken by the complete Haydn symphonies when they are completed in the year 2000) has been its two recordings, one on LP and a later one on CD, of the complete Beethoven piano sonatas played by Bernard Roberts. Roberts's reaction is interesting.

> I enjoyed the experience of recording them in both settings. Even the CDs are integral performances apart from the odd stitch for a major break down. An artist hates hearing, of course, a mistake in a recording played over and over again but they were dead right that recordings were becoming too clinical and they were right to record in this way.
>
> When we went to CD I thought it would be a good idea to do the Beethovens again because I'd not only developed but the constraints were a little less as you can stop if you make the most terrible mistake and you don't have to play the whole twenty-five minutes again to cope with one error near the end. I hope the second set are a bit more urgent and expressive as I think the direct-to-disc were rather careful because of my awareness of the consequences of making a mistake. It took about two years to get through the CDs which we finished in 1985, and this time we organised it so that each disc would be a mini programme in itself.

Bernard Roberts whose complete Beethoven piano sonatas direct to disc brought Nimbus their first international acclaim.

Sometimes the single take philosophy does not work out quite as expected. When Nimbus was recording Stravinsky's *Firebird* and *Rite of Spring*, with the London Symphony Orchestra under Gennadi Rozhdestvensky, Alan Wiltshire, the Nimbus producer, having explained the required approach to the conductor, spent the morning rehearsing various passages and getting the balance right before concluding with a recorded run through. He had intended to repeat the performance after the lunch-break. When the run through was done, Wiltshire turned to Rozhdestvensky and said, 'Yes, that was very nice, but there are one or two things I would like to do again.' With a smile, Rozhdestvensky replied, 'You said you were a one take company. You have had one take. There is a taxi at the door, and I'm off.' The speechless producer was left with no alternative but to patch up the tape they had with pieces recorded earlier in rehearsal. Nevertheless, the resulting CD is highly enjoyable. Of course with this approach things sometimes go irretrievably wrong and Nimbus has no shame in admitting that something like thirty per cent of what it records never sees the light of day because it does not meet the company's exacting standards. Nor are the performers the losers by this, for not only does Nimbus pay generous advances which are not recalled when no disc is issued, but the artist's reputation is protected by not disseminating any less than excellent performance. Until very recently Nimbus Records was the only British company, apart from Thorn EMI, able to control all aspects of the origination and manufacture of its records in this way.

Gennady Rozhdestvensky, Russian conductor who recorded the Stravinsky ballets with the London Symphony Orchestra for Nimbus.

The artist is very much central to the Nimbus approach. Much of its recording programme is determined by the performers themselves, or by seizing musical opportunities as they arise, rather than by a marketing dominated selection. Adrian Farmer places great emphasis on this approach. 'The opportunism is very important even though at the back of your mind you know you may be running a terrible risk and it may be an appalling mistake. Most of the good things that have come through which you're able to go back to and listen to over and over again have been choices largely driven by the artists themselves rather than having someone you quite like working with and telling them the repertoire you want them to do. That doesn't often produce something really extraordinary. I tend to take the enthusiasm of an artist doing work in his own area as a very significant factor in deciding whether to do something or not.'

This makes for an interesting collection of artists as the *San Francisco Chronicle* observed when Nimbus began to manufacture CDs in the United States in 1987. 'All the major superstars naturally have contracts elsewhere. Yet by tradition, record companies have tended to overlook many superb musicians, especially if they lack glamour. Nimbus has sought out such artists: pianists like Shura Cherkassky, Ronald Smith and Vlado Perlemuter; violinists Oscar Shumsky and Jaime Laredo (also featured as conductor); tenor Hugues Cuenod; the marvellous young conductor William Boughton and the experienced Gennadi Rozhdestvensky; Nimbus's idea is to seek out such artists and record them in their specialities.'[1]

The *Los Angeles Herald Examiner* also drew attention to Nimbus's unique approach: '. . . Nothing about Nimbus, in fact, appears to be routine – the dowdy colour graphics of its packaging, the sonics, the repertoire and the performances are nearly always representative of the company's individuality. On top of that, Nimbus CDs are generously packed with music – most contain more than sixty minutes' worth.'[2]

Such an approach is bliss for most musicians from the purely musical point of view and has undoubtedly led to many great recordings of which the performers can be rightly proud. Commercially it can be a great deal less useful. As a former music executive put it, 'they have had so many wonderful projects for recording so they record them, they package them, they almost do nothing else. They did put some ads in the *Gramophone* and things like that but that was about all.'

Most of the artists I spoke to grumbled about the lack of marketing and even the inability to get discs delivered to them for concert tours. However, despite the loss of royalties this might have entailed – and it has to be remembered that no artist is ever really satisfied with the marketing of his works – most of them also accepted with good-natured resignation that this was the corollary of the constructive attitude adopted towards them personally and towards their music-making.

Two examples must suffice to illustrate the way in which the somewhat eccentric approach of the Nimbus management could act to the performer's advantage. George Benjamin, a talented young composer who was being strongly and exclusively patronised by Nimbus, was preparing his work *Antara* for a Nimbus recording in France with which he was very unhappy. At the last minute he rang them to say that there was to be a potentially far better opportunity to record the work the following year and to ask if he might cancel the current recording and start again from scratch. He was delighted and surprised that they willingly agreed to do this, though his introduction to Nimbus had largely immunised him against surprise. He had just finished studying with Messiaen when, on New Year's Eve 1979, he received a telephone call out of the blue from Numa who, without any preliminaries, announced: 'I love Mars Bars, I hate Wagner and I want to make a record of your music.' Although Benjamin has made little by way of direct royalties from his CDs – as he observes, they were not made to make money – they have been frequently broadcast, with over twenty transmissions in France alone, because of their availability in that format.

On another occasion John Wallace, the celebrated trumpeter, wanted Nimbus to let him make a recording of Scarlatti pieces with the soprano,

Numa and his protégé, composer George Benjamin, 1993.

40

George Benjamin (*right*), composer, whose career was launched by Numa when Benjamin was eighteen, with Mark Elder recording his first orchestral piece Ringed by the Flat Horizon.

Helen Field. He drove to Leeds with Nimbus producer Alan Wiltshire to see her between performances to try to persuade her to take part. They played bits of the repertoire, Helen Field sang some of it and the deal was agreed. As the two men were returning south in high spirits, Wiltshire's car phone rang.

It was Numa saying scrap the trumpet and soprano thing, we want you to do Sousa. It was like a bombshell, nobody had ever mentioned Sousa before, it was the first mention of Sousa I'd ever heard. We seemed to be going from the sublime Bach, Handel and Scarlatti to Sousa, to the ridiculous, and I was mortified, thinking bloody hell that's typical Nimbus. I went back, did a bit of listening to Sousa and thought, well maybe we could do something with this, there's a lot here a lot of people have been missing. I'd like to get my hands on some of the things that are not marches and even it out a bit. It was a good idea from Nimbus. I got really hooked on it. Then I was on tour in the States with the orchestra a little later, in New York, and I had about a day off so I got on the next plane to Chicago, got myself to Champagne in Illinois, to the big Sousa museum, sweet-talked a lady

41

into photostatting a lot of the other music, spent the day with her, got on the plane, came back and got back just in time for a rehearsal for the Carnegie Hall concert. That's the way we put the Sousa together and then the Helen Field project came to fruition in the end anyway. Partly because the Sousa was a big success they let me have my way on the other one.

If the Nimbus approach to music and technology is principled, organised and systematic, its approach to the other essential ingredient of its success – people – is anarchic, spontaneous and highly subjective.

Nimbus is a homophile organisation. I deliberately do not use the word homosexual for, although the passions and jealousies in any nexus of relationships are evident from time to time at Nimbus, any carnal element is irrelevant to the dynamic which make this a uniquely successful organisation. The love of men; of maleness; of Man is not irrelevant – indeed it is one of the two essential ingredients in Nimbus's rare mix. The other is an obsession with the highest musical standards.

The majority of employees, of course, lead ordinary heterosexual lives, but the inner heart of Nimbus is a living brotherhood of men. Only one woman, the distinguished pianist and voice coach Nina Walker, has ever held a senior post – she was a director of Nimbus for many years – or had any significant influence on company policy or ethos. The company itself is run on lines of unquestionable masculinity. As Adrian pungently observed, 'In an arts business the effeminate man is extremely destructive and that is something we are all agreed about; there's no place for campery.'

Dr Jonathan Halliday has been heard to complain that Nimbus is like a monastery – and one whose walls he has, on occasion, been tempted to 'go over'. The monastic comparison is one that many others have made, too. On entering the company for the first time it certainly did give something of the air of a venerable abbey in which the devoted monks and their charismatic abbot were seeking the Holy Grail of musical perfection under the most rigorous and highly arcane set of rules. Undeniably the object of their quest is as elusive and, indeed, as ineffable as the deity of any more conventional order. Certainly there was an air of industrious, if slightly nervous, peace and contentment about the place, but in a way that was deceptive for perhaps a more apt analogy is that of the Mafia family, or a Scottish feudal clan. There is intense loyalty in both directions; a great deal of mutual support among members of the family right or wrong. The *capo di tutti capi* demanded total loyalty and there was a code of *omerta* – to speak or act disloyally was emotional, and usually occupational, death as Chandos Ellis, Nimbus's Company Secretary, described it to me. 'The advantage of the Nimbus group is that there is a great deal of trust and mutual support. If you make a mistake everyone muscles round to get out of it, and that's that: but breaking trust is quite a different matter. Woe betide you if you do not get on with your job in the manner expected of you.'

A dramatic illustration of this arose shortly after Robert Maxwell took over the company in 1987 (which we will examine later) when Mike Lee, one of Nimbus's outstanding servants, who sadly died of a cerebral thrombosis in 1988, publicised the results of a Nimbus test which cast serious doubt on the durability of CDs made by competitors. It was widely reported in the Press, which gave the partial impression that all CDs were blighted in this way and by implication, therefore, Nimbus CDs as well, and Mike was invited to appear on television – the Founders were in the United States – to elaborate. Robert Maxwell not only forbade him to make any contact with the media – essential as this was to dispel the misunderstanding – but wanted him fired at once, and Maxwell's son Kevin put in a brutal call to Mike to tell him he was a 'f***ing idiot and a dead man' as far as his job was concerned. When the Founders got wind of this they telephoned Adrian to pass on the message to Mike that 'he was one of the family, and will always be one of the family', and told Maxwell that they point blank refused to fire him. Maxwell backed off.

In his book, *The Quest for Quality* Ian Webb, writing in November 1987, observed that 'the common community of interest and long working hours leads some observers to describe their working practices as bizarre.'[3] The idiosyncratic approach to people is certainly evident in their methods of recruitment in which contacts are often made through personal networks rather than formal channels such as advertising and where the decision to employ or not to employ is based on assessment of the personal dynamics involved rather than on paper qualifications. Jobs are to a large extent fitted to people rather than people to jobs. Moreover, when the Nimbus family wants someone it does not readily take no for an answer.

Emil Dudek recalls his first job interview with Nimbus with a smile. 'My first interview was the weirdest I've had in my life. It seemed largely to consist of Numa taking a cigarette from me and saying, "I like his eyes, let's have him." The environment there was very exciting; it reeked of a family firm atmosphere.'

Emil joined as assistant to Dr Halliday, but they got off on the wrong foot and within a week, with characteristic explosiveness the company had fired him. What followed was typical Nimbus. 'I left on the Friday and on the Sunday, while my mother was up to her elbows cooking Sunday lunch, Numa and Michael and Gerald came round in a chauffeur-driven Bentley and said, "come back." I got nagged and nagged and nagged by Numa to come back and two years later I eventually said yes, knowing what Nimbus would drain out of me, but then I was ready for that. I joined as Gerald's assistant and within a week I was made mastering manager. I ended up being a manager with not very much to manage. So I concentrated on technical things.'

The 'technical thing' Emil concentrated on was the development of CD-ROM (Read Only Memory), a field in which Nimbus, as a result of his work, rapidly dominated the UK market. This is a classic example of how the Nimbus Founders' instincts about a person proved absolutely right and greatly to the benefit of the company. One or two other key figures on the technical side found themselves badgered into joining over a lengthy period and, once having joined, are still there. Inevitably, in such a rapidly expanding company, not every hiring was a success and as one long-serving employee put it, 'in the early days at Wyastone Leys we lost some really good people and we kept some idiots.'

Colin Dix, another long-serving employee who joined in 1977 (with a break from 1980–85) had a similar experience. Recruited as a maintenance engineer he found himself two weeks later in charge of the plant. Later on still, under the benign but still very remote management of Jonathan Halliday, he was the first person other than Jonathan to operate the laser beam recorder, and was largely left to develop the CD resist coating line on his own initiative. 'They created a job for you rather than the other way round and then left you to get on with it, unless they didn't like what you were doing,' Colin commented approvingly, observing with less enthusiasm, 'it's all standardised now and not quite so much fun as in the early days of CDs.'

The running of the company is no less individualistic and personal – some might even say capricious and arbitrary – but it centres on two beliefs that have proved of great value in generating staff loyalty and the flexibility to deal with both crises and opportunities as they crop up; absolute trust and the notion that responsibility must be taken rather than granted. Emil Dudek describes the way he used to have to insist on reporting progress to the directors for they never demanded reports, simply gave him a sum of money and trusted him to do what had to be done. If he, or any other executive, wanted to fly somewhere, he simply picked up the telephone and booked the flight, charging it to the company. There were no checks and it was simply assumed that the freedom would not be abused, with the result that it never was. As Ian Webb put it in his book *The Quest for Quality*: 'The structure is low and flat, there being essentially no middle managers.' A system described more intimately by an insider as being 'held together by the Founders ... such respect, such love was more than just an employer/employee relationship – it was family.'

As Howard Nash, who joined the company as finance director in 1987 says of it: 'There's always been a tremendous amount of communication so none of us have grown up with the habit of just doing something, but always on the basis of consulting with others. This was very informal, over lunch or over coffee, but it was always a very close understanding rather than recorded formally in minute books. We all became adept at floating ideas.' But this, he found, could lead to some disconcertingly fluid situations. 'It was very difficult to find a particular conclusion reached which you thought was advantageous for the business and then to find it upset over supper after you'd gone home, so that you had to start again the following morning.'

Emil Dudek's experience was similar. 'Literally if there was a fuse blown everyone would run up into the directors' boardroom to get someone to fix it. They ran everything hands-on, as it were. They were together twenty-four hours a day so things could always be discussed and decisions made quickly. It was an effective way of running a company but you could arrive in the morning and suddenly the philosophy and direction was completely different and nobody had told you about it.'

While this intimate approach clearly had numerous benefits there were some who found it intrusive and oppressive and the hands-on familiarity was not always appreciated. One former executive describes how he had a girl in his department with long blonde hair which she used to backcomb which provoked Numa because he didn't approve of such things. 'One day he came in and grabbed hold of it and said, "What's this?" And of course the girl ended up in tears. I'm surprised she didn't resign on the spot but the fact is that she didn't.'

Another former senior executive comments that they tended to dig deep into people's emotions and described how one temporary member of the family had to 'leave in the middle of the night. He couldn't cope with it. He simply couldn't get away. During the day he'd have been dragged back!' A number of other former employees commented that 'they used to interfere quite a lot in private lives.' But, interestingly enough, in retrospect none of them appeared to be resentful of this. Numa in particular liked to keep in touch with every minute detail of the company's operations, from leaving a waspish note about unwashed cups in the sink in the staff kitchen to monitoring the way telephones are answered, but as he said, 'If they're not answered properly then Nimbus will suffer, and I won't have that. On the other hand if somebody says to me I think you are wrong I will sit down and ask them to explain. Otherwise you don't fulfil your purpose. You should not be in charge of a colony of ants.'

Nothing at Nimbus is stronger than the bonds between the inner five, and particularly between the three Founders. Numa, explaining his reluctance to mix with the outside world, and more particularly with members of his blood family (he had been known to go off on holiday and dash back home the next day), put it very simply: 'I have no contact, or wish to have any contact, because I am now married, if you like, to Michael and Gerald. They are my family.' Numa preferred to reach out by telephone from his ivory tower to a vast network of friends, acquaintances and even strangers with whom he wished to make contact, in unforgettable conversations – often of an hour or more.

Adrian explained why the quincumvirate of the three Founders, himself and Jonathan, the inner family, has never expanded, though there were 'cousins and nephews', like Nina and Mike Lee, and a few others who were dearly loved and very close. 'The quincumvirate hasn't grown though there have been possibilities of other members joining the family. That's because five is enough, the collective energy is enough to direct things. We are all obsessed by what we do. If you are there on site you are part of it and if you are not there and not on site then you are not part of it. You cannot be a part-time member of the family.'

This obsession with what they did, with the making of the highest quality classical music recordings at whatever cost, accounts for another unusual feature at Nimbus among financially private companies – the *relative* poverty of the principal shareholders. Though it is highly unlikely that Numa's repeated lament that they will all finish up in the workhouse will ever come to pass, the surviving Founders, who with Jonathan and Adrian between them own virtually all the company now, have drawn astonishingly little money out of the business for themselves. Many of the years in which the company traded they drew no directors' fees at all, in others less than their lowest paid clerks. Even in the company's most successful year, 1986, the directors took out only £22,300 on average and when the highest fees, paid to the outside non-executive directors are excluded, the family average is well below £20,000 a year. In the four years in which they temporarily lost control of the company to Maxwell, and when they might have been expected to extract from it as much as they could, the average directors' fee was still only just over £30,000. It is true that in recent years they have lived well out of the company, spent money on good cars – there's a Bentley for company use – and elegant furnishings, but this is a matter of style, of aesthetics, not one of opulent ostentation or status seeking. Every year they have ploughed the greater part of their profits (and in years when there have been no profits, their borrowings) back into making music, whether by way of records and then CDs or, since 1991, into the Nimbus Foundation as well, a charitable trust which has already built the most acoustically superb concert hall in the whole of Wales. Indeed, they deliberately obscured the losses they were making on their own recordings and the subsidy that element of the business received each year. As former company secretary, Stewart Garman put it: 'They didn't want to identify that certain recordings were unprofitable. They wanted to keep the costs hidden because it would have highlighted the losses. We all knew that the label was unprofitable, but the reasons they continued with unprofitable recordings were very good reasons.'

Those 'good reasons' have been inherent in the conduct of the business since its earliest days.

CHAPTER FOUR

1957:
Item: 29 June, 6'9" Bechstein Grand from Daisy Brown   £100.0s.0d
Item: 1 July, Ferrograph Recorder   £90.6s.0d
Item: 12 July, Tape Splicer   18s.6d
Item: 19 August, Cardioid Microphone   £49.10s.0d
Item: 27 August, EMI TR90 Recording Machine   £575.0s.0d
Item: 10 September, 2 Lustraphone Ribbon Microphones   £19.19s.0d

Thus in 1957, bit by bit, Numa and Michael began to assemble their first recording studio, groping their way from a basis of virtual ignorance of recording technique and technology towards considerable knowledge and experience. They were driven by their dissatisfaction with the recording and replication standards of others, particularly the BBC, whose recordings of Numa eventually drove him to make no more with them from 1959–60 onwards. Financial pressure dogged those first tentative steps and by October 1957 they were being badgered for payment by a substantial number of creditors. However, they had already set in hand the development of a property mini-empire which was eventually to enable them to fulfil their musical ambitions. On 3 August 1960 they had registered Handsworth Wood Properties Limited, and on 10 August the Hermes Development Company Limited, a property management company (they had also registered Hermes Recordings Limited as the first vehicle for their recording activities on 24 April 1958).

On 20 August 1957 a rather nervous Numa, regretting Michael's absence at his sister's wedding and accompanied by the estate agent who had led them to expect a price of £1,500 to £2,000, found himself bidding for 48 Handsworth Wood Road, which was eventually sold to the new company for £3,800. Three days later they each borrowed £1,500 from the bank and applied for permission to 'convert No. 48 Handsworth Wood Road, Birmingham into seven "bachelor" flats', to be let at 5½ guineas a week, (increased in 1959 to 7½ guineas). In 1959 they borrowed £2,000 from Numa's mother, who also invested £1,000 at a rather generous 18.5%, and £5,000 interest free from Michael's father, in order to expand their property business. On 30 October they bought numbers 4 and 4a Handsworth Wood Road together for £2,000 and on 14 December, No. 46 for £6,500 – all but £650 on a mortgage to Lloyds Bank where their borrowing totalled £6,640 against a first charge. But, despite this very high gearing, their timing was right and the property business became a substantial success. By 1961 they were making a reasonable living through Hermes Development – £1,400 in directors' fees per annum – which rose steadily. By 1966 fees and/or profit were of the order of £4,000 a year and capital appreciation had been very rapid. As Numa admitted, 'houses were going for £4,000–£5,000 and in about six years they had escalated to £50,000 or £60,000. That enabled us to build a studio and found Nimbus Records. It was a complicated eighteen year diversion.'

The houses at 46-48 Handsworth Wood Road, Birmingham, bought for flat conversion.

In the early part of that diversion, as Michael observed, 'The property business then began to take on a lot more priority as making flats and letting them was profitable once you'd found the money to convert the flats, which we decided to do as best we could and not to skimp. Four and 4a were the first, 48 was the next and then we went to 6 and 8 Handsworth Road and we got a block from Nos. 4 to 10. We then got 48's neighbour, 46, joined the gardens together and so on and then No. 38, which had a garden which went a long way down. We bought the house behind that garden, 6 Butler's Road, quite a bit later.

Typical interiors of the Hermes flats and Handsworth Wood Road properties.

Although by the mid-sixties they were doing well enough to put in a manager – typical of the Nimbus family loyalty pattern, the son of their foreman who was unable to do physical work because of a kidney disease – in the earlier days, as with so much of their later business, they rolled up their own sleeves and got stuck into the building and decorating themselves: Numa, in his unstoppable way, knocking a load-bearing wall down on himself and Gerald, who became involved from 1961 onwards, coming to the brink of a nervous breakdown from the exhaustion and isolation of the work he was doing. Numa's enormous physical strength soon had him bouncing back from his accident, though he was to be much debilitated by a mystery illness developing in the next few years. Gerald administered his own therapy of hard work and reading Jane Austen and was soon embroiled again, not only in designing and building but in trying to get to grips with the somewhat disorderly book-keeping practices of Handsworth and Hermes. (By 1962 they had still not filed their first set of accounts going back to 1959, though when badgered by the Board of Trade they seemed to have successfully pleaded that they had not traded except to buy equipment and pay artists.) He remembers: 'We had a wonderful book-keeping lady called Mrs Drury and we came into the office one day and found her hunched in her chair with her head in her hands, lamenting "Oh my God, we're going to go bust, we're going to go bust." We weren't, but we just didn't know what was going on there. I must say, you do have to learn these disciplines.'

In fact, far from 'going bust' they were doing very well; well enough to devote more time to the music recording they had begun on 18 August 1957 with a trip to Brussels to record Musica Viva. As Numa lamented to me: 'By 1960 we had spent all our money, about £12,500, on Hermes Records, our first record company, but all the Musica Viva and Opera de Camera tapes were destroyed because we left them in front of a strong magnetic field.'

On 11 February 1961, Christiane van Acke and Mischa Podolski were paid £40 to make Hermes' first studio recording. Like so many subsequent early attempts, it failed to get over the very high quality threshold set by these zealous musicians, not on artistic but on technical grounds. The fact was that, because of the physical limitations imposed by lack of space, the first studio at 48 Handsworth Wood Road had a very dead acoustic. Luckily for the three recording pioneers they had, by 1965, added to their property empire 6 Butler's Road, a house backing onto their property at No. 38 Handsworth Wood Road which Gerald describes as having 'a back which looked like a charabanc. It was built in the fifties but it had these terrible kind of 1930s curved, metal-framed windows and it had the most depressing atmosphere, really very nasty. It took us a long time to exorcise it. I've never come across a place with such a strong, evil, negative atmosphere. And we seemed to be surrounded by weird neighbours who were either melancholic or just plain dotty. Not a pleasant place, but we transformed it.'

The bungalow bought to live in but eventually extended for studio use.

Whatever the drawbacks of the bungalow itself, it had one thing essential to their plans – large grounds. The three men had looked both in and beyond Birmingham at schools, barns, farms and a host of other large buildings that might be suitable for a studio. Eventually, baulking at the idea of travelling to work when they had for so long enjoyed living and working in the same place, they decided to build a studio from scratch in the grounds of their 'ghastly bungalow'. Shrewdly they had chosen

52

as their architect a bright young man who had worked for the local authority planning department. When a planning officer protested at the building of a studio as 'big as a pair of semi-detached houses – how dare they?', the architect retorted that 'if his client wanted a music room as big as a pair of semi-detached houses there was no reason he should not have one, it was his money.' He won the day.

Michael and Gerald started with a clean sheet of paper and designed the new studio from scratch. They also had to raise the money to build it and after much difficulty persuaded the trustees of their grandfather's Trust to release some of their capital in it. Michael and Gerald's mother also lent them money; the Reynolds parents were pleased to see at last two of their children running their own business. Indeed, at one stage in 1977, five members of the Reynolds family, including Gerald and Michael, were lending Handsworth Wood £131,173 unsecured, in some cases interest free and subordinate to a further secured loan of £35,000, thus putting themselves at no small risk. All of this borrowed money was later re-lent to the recording and record pressing companies.

Stensham Court, a rejected candidate for Nimbus's new home, subsequently destroyed for redevelopment.

The decision to press their own records was the logical consequence of the recording development and of the failure of the commercial record companies to retain in their pressings the quality which the three knew they were beginning to get in their recordings. Numa was all for burying an LP plant under the garden at No. 6 until Gerald dissuaded him by pointing out that the rising clouds of steam might attract the unwelcome attention of a planning authority they had already offended more than once. The rapid deterioration of the centre of cities like Birmingham and a fear that a Labour government might introduce severe property taxes which would cripple their source of funds, started them on the long search for a place where they could live and carry out all their work.

In 1964, when they bought their first decent motor car, a Triumph 2000 (they had made do until then with the clapped-out old van in which they carried their building materials), they began to explore the country now being opened up by the new motorway networks.

One day they were driving along the Wye Valley near Monmouth when Gerald stopped to take a photograph of a beautiful house in the distance. Volume IV of a book series entitled *Country Seats* describes it thus:

> The house, which is of stone, was built in the year 1818 and more or less rebuilt in its present form in 1861. It stands on the side of the Doward Hill, on the bank of the River Wye, in the midst of grand old woods and the most beautiful country of that so deservedly far-famed river. The grounds, in the midst of which the house stands, are the very perfection of beauty.
>
> There is a deer park, within which the aforesaid Doward Hill stands ... The remains of an ancient British Camp stand in the park on the table-land of the Little Doward Hill ... The Camp was afterwards made a Roman one by the conquerors ... The name of Wyastone is derived from the association of a prehistoric stone lying in the park there – 'The Wye Stone' as it was then known.

It is indeed one of the most striking situations in South Wales and not surprisingly, as they looked across a bend in the Wye at its substantial façade, the three men heaved a collective sigh of regret that they could 'never afford such a place.' Eleven years later they moved in, through a sequence of coincidences that would seem to confirm Numa's belief that the hand of fate has been behind the success of Nimbus.

View of Wyastone Leys taken by Gerald Reynolds in 1969. A prophetic photograph taken six years before the acquisition of the site.

Gerald vividly describes their advent:

In June 1975 we were again down this way looking at a number of properties which weren't suitable. The estate agent in Monmouth told us that Wyastone Leys could be the place for us. We'd had particulars of it but without a photograph. So, although it did look interesting on paper, we didn't realise it was the same house we had admired all those years before. We were on our way home and on one of our many stops at the Little Chef down the road for waffles with maple syrup, we said to each other, it's only just up the road we might as well have a look while we're here. As soon as we came down the drive, scraping our car through the overgrown undergrowth, it did feel like coming home, and we recognised it as the house we had looked at all those years ago. On this occasion we weren't accompanied by an estate agent and were only able to look at the outside but it always did have a very good atmosphere. So many large country houses are places to retire to or to run an estate from, but not for any real working activity.

Then we made arrangements to have a proper look at it. It was being sold through two agents, one in Hereford and one in Monmouth. The very laid-back young man from the Hereford agency came to show us round and opened the shutters in each room about an inch or so and showed us round by torchlight. Seeing it under those circumstances was a pretty daunting experience. We were more or less put off but we

55

HEREFORDSHIRE/
MONMOUTHSHIRE BORDER

Ross-on-Wye 8 miles, Monmouth 2 miles, M5/M4 Motorway systems within easy reach.

A SUPERB RESIDENTIAL PROPERTY IDEAL FOR PRIVATE OR INSTITUTIONAL OCCUPATION SITUATED IN A DELIGHTFUL POSITION OVERLOOKING THE RIVER WYE IN AN AREA OF OUTSTANDING NATURAL BEAUTY.

5 🏠 7 🛋 4 🛏 Oil 🔥 3 🏡 🌿 🌳

Additional features:
Billiards Room, 2 Staff Flats, Lift, Coach House, ideal for further conversion or development. Water Meadows running to the River Wye

FOR SALE FREEHOLD WITH ABOUT 43 ACRES.
Apply Hereford Office, 14 Broad Street, Hereford HR4 9AL.
(Tel. 0432 3087).   (01120/KGM)F

Notice for sale which first attracted the Founders' attention to their future home.

The overgrown approach to Wyastone Leys.

56

then wrote to the local estate agent, who showed us round properly, opened it all up and we knew it was the place we had been searching for. It was fortunate for us that somebody else had just lost their deposit on it so that they were in the mood to negotiate. My approach was 'I've got a cheque in my pocket, we're prepared to pay this amount, do you want it or not?' So we put down a deposit straightaway and then brought our bank manager from Birmingham to see it. His reaction was, 'which bit are you buying?' We said, 'all of it, including all these cottages.' So we signed the contract in July and actually moved in October.

The top floor of the house was just about habitable with modern wiring. The ancient central heating was good even with the boiler out of the ark, the plumbing was primitive with lead pipes, and much of the rest of the house was dilapidated with wet and dry rot and so on.

One passage still had a ghostly imprint on the wall below some hooks where people had obviously left oil-skins in the past and they had stuck to the wall. That shadow is still almost visible through the paint we put on since. The weather was very kind in that autumn of 1975 for there was no frost until February of 1976. It was as if the place was welcoming us. My sister got divorced at the time and so she, too, moved in with a houseful of furniture, two horses, two dogs and two cats.

The banks wouldn't lend us enough money to do what was necessary although we were in the process of selling off the property interest in Birmingham but this naturally took time. We only got £25,000 for the bungalow in Birmingham which wasn't a bad price for that part of Birmingham but in relation to what it had cost us to do it meant we made a loss on that. We'd already been with Lloyds for many years but they treated us with great caution. The banks insisted that we sold off some of the property on the estate, so we sold the top lodge and the cottage that we now live in to my sister, which I was against, for £12,000 or so. She sold it when she left for £55,000. We couldn't afford to buy it then but we had an option clause on it and it eventually cost us £200,000 – sixteen times what we had got for it a dozen years earlier. We'll buy the top lodge back one day.

So we started with a tiny overdraft, a house to be renovated and converted and we'd also offered my mother an apartment in the house not expecting that she would want to move in quite so quickly. We had to divert our builder and our efforts from the LP plant to getting an apartment ready for her. Originally our own building team came down and used to stay in the house, but being city folk, they simply couldn't come to terms with the fact that out here in the country at night it's actually dark. Barry Jones, the son, used to say when we were going to put the cat out for the night, 'you can't go out there in the dark, what if something jumps on you?' I suppose we were the ideally suited people because we had been used to dealing with old properties and from our childhood background all of us were used to the country and preferred it. There was a famous night when the Joneses came back a little drunk from the local pub, Harold Jones, the father, woke up in the middle of the night and saw a grey figure at the foot of his bed – I think there probably was a fairly benign kind of ghost around. He was so terrified he jumped into his son's bed and, I think, wet himself and that was it, they got in their car next morning and left, never to come back again. So we had to find a local builder, which was a good thing in fact.

Wyastone Leys and the Nimbus Headquarters today bear resemblance to that dilapidated dream the founders recognised as 'home' only in so far as it is still a place of great beauty and still centred on the main house – though little operational business is conducted in that building now.

But we have let our story run ahead of itself and must return to Birmingham, to Numa's decision to resume a singing career in 1968 and the consequent building of the second studio in 1969, for it was to have momentous consequences not only for Nimbus and its founders but for the recording of serious music in Britain.

It took the emotional impact of his mother's death to return Numa, and his alter ego Shura Gehrman, from the role of property developer to the serious business of professional singing again. Numa was unequivocal about the Damascene nature of this event. 'It took my mother's death in 1968 to unleash an enormous amount of remorse because I was not a good son and then she came to me and said, I'm dying I should like to die with you, would you please help me. I didn't cry in front of her but I said yes, of course.'

Remorse led to action, for Numa was so moved by his mother's unfounded deathbed lament that she had done nothing with her life to recognise that by not singing he was wasting his talents. He did not, after all, have to get involved in the world-trekking weariness and loneliness of the international concert performer for he could confine himself to records – providing there was a record company that met his high standards. Since he did not believe that there was, he was obliged once again to embark on his quest to create one fit for the great performers of the day.

Once the new studio was built at No. 6 it had to be equipped. By that time the record industry was less monopolistic and secretive than it had been, so gurus such as Arthur Haddey at Decca and Angus McKenzie gave their advice freely. McKenzie played the three of them a surround sound recording he had made at St John's Smith Square using a discrete four channel system. Although the musicians sounded a little disembodied the audience noise was impressive and created such a sense of atmosphere that the newcomers decided that this was the way they wanted to record. To see what results they could get, they bought a Sony 4 channel domestic open reel machine and recorded Numa singing *An die ferne Geliebte*. This not only involved the listener through its added sense of dimension but produced a tonal quality far more faithful to that which the performer was delivering. The embryo quadraphonic approach was clearly what they were seeking; a performer's medium in contrast to stereo which seemed to be an engineer's medium, as they had discovered by their own work with the best professional stereo equipment. On Decca's advice they bought Studer four track machines from Bausch, because 'they were built like a battleship'. Numa was the guinea pig, together with pianist Martin Jones, because the lower frequencies from the bass voice were much harder to record and, as Gerald put it, 'Numa's voice was enough to tax and test any recording system and the subsequent parts of the chain.'

Numa wanted to have as Nimbus's first recording artist the Swiss tenor Hugues Cuenod of whom he had long been an admirer and generously remained so until his death despite believing that Cuenod did not return the compliment. In this belief he was wrong as Cuenod – still an astonishingly active 92-year-old giving master classes at Aldeburgh – made clear when I spoke to him at his home in Vevey near Geneva in the spring of 1994. Cuenod's view was a more balanced one: 'I think he is much better than he sounds – and he has a marvellous voice. His intelligence is superior to his very personal technique and I like it very much. There are some things only he does, can do or would dare to do in his very personal interpretations – he can be remarkably good and remarkably bad. Hearing him for the first time is like ringing a stranger's door-bell and having him open the door with no clothes on – one can be taken aback by the sincerity of it all.'

When Nimbus first contacted Cuenod's agent, Howard Hartog,

he quoted 'a ridiculous sum' so Numa telephoned the singer himself who gave them the recording for nothing. Thus Cuenod and his accompanist Martin Isepp (whom Nimbus had recruited for him from Glyndebourne) had already been booked for a serious commercial recording in circumstances where a postponement would have been embarrassing when the decision to switch from stereo to some form of quadrophonic was made. The stereo control room was far too small for the new approach so they hastily threw out all the culinary equipment from their kitchen to make way for speakers, recorders and other electronic apparatus. Such cooking as there was time for was hastily done in another corner of the house and the paint was barely dry on studio and control room when Cuenod and Isepp arrived to record Debussy's settings of poems by Baudelaire and Mallarmé. Tentatively Gerald placed the microphone more or less where he thought it should go and to Cuenod's astonishment they were ready to record within ten minutes

– an unheard of speed for recording sessions of the day. So good was the later recording of Erik Satie's *Socrate* – a piece Cuenod had always wanted to record – that the Swiss tenor exclaimed, 'My God, the way I sound here you'll have me singing Wagner next.'

Cuenod did not sing Wagner for them but he did make many other recordings for Nimbus, although most of them were not actually released. There were eighteen relatively unknown Schubert songs and others by Haydn and Mozart in keeping with the Nimbus practice, admired by Cuenod, of filling in gaps in the recorded repertoire or works neglected by others. Cuenod also recorded songs by Duparc and

The Swiss tenor, Hugues Cuenod.

Fauré of which Numa 'loved the Fauré, but not *Mirage* – do it again!' When that possibility arose a few years later Cuenod no longer wished to do it and when he later heard a Nimbus recording of *Mirage* sung by a, to him, new and unknown bass-baritone, Shura Gehrman, he suggested they ask the artist to record *L'Horizon chimerique* also. He had no idea that Gehrman was his friend and record producer Numa Labinsky who did, indeed, also later record and release *L'Horizon*.

When Cuenod's first accompanist, Isepp, left for America he was replaced by Geoffrey Parsons with whom, through Nimbus, he struck up a most fruitful artistic relationship. As a result Parsons also made several other recordings for Nimbus. Cuenod's own relationship with the Founders remained a happy one for the next twenty years. As he said: 'I got more pleasure recording with Nimbus than with anyone else because they let me perform the way I wanted to, without interference. The atmosphere, first in Birmingham and then in Monmouth, was so good, so kind, that I always felt I was going to meet my friends rather than just record producers.' Cuenod, in turn, has been honoured by Nimbus as the only living artist to have a recording resurrected for the *Prima Voce* series.

Left to right: Michael Reynolds, accompanist Geoffrey Parsons, Numa and German baritone Gerhard Hüsch.

Geoffrey Parsons 'accompanying' Gerald Reynolds assessing sound balance for Gerhard Hüsch.

The recording team as well as the artists found the new approach very different from their experience with the stereo recordings they had been making. As Gerald observed, 'With stereo you set things up and then you spend the whole of the rest of the session being dissatisfied, thinking, oh my God what could we do to improve this? It doesn't sound that good. It doesn't sound anything like the artist sounded in the studio. With surround sound it does. You get positive feedback. The artist gets positive feedback and the producers and engineers get positive feedback, so it's a very different experience. Although microphone position is critical within a matter of inches we soon learned how to get that right.'

However, other technical obstacles confronted them still. They had started on half inch tape with four tracks laid down but quickly went to one inch tape with four tracks which, using Dolby, gets a very big dynamic range, so they never had to apply any compression or limiting at the time of making the recording. Yet they simply couldn't find people who could translate the quality they were obtaining to an LP as the dynamic range was very difficult to cope with. The recordings were encoded to stereo and various people attempted to cut LPs from them

The multi-mono recording technique subsequently abandoned for surround sound.

but could not get a good enough quality. Therefore they briefly flirted with cassette tape because by playing four-channel heads designed for bi-directional replay in one direction it was possible to achieve surround sound from a discrete four-channel replay. The trouble was that the level of hiss coming off a good cassette machine was bad enough on two loudspeakers but was quite intolerable on four. Gerald had made very good studio replay amplifiers and was amazed at what could be picked up from some commercial cassettes – buses passing and other extraneous noises which couldn't be heard on a normal domestic machine.

Fortunately, Numa had never lost his fascination with the old disc cutting machines which had sparked his interest in recording. The frustration of being unable to get good LPs cut now rekindled his determination to cut their own. A small advert in the trade press sent them trekking up to Paisley in Scotland where a little firm called Scotia Records was offering an old BBC cutting machine for sale. After they had endured the kindly Scots' hospitality of a huge high tea, they were taken to see the machine and there, standing next to it, was what they were really looking for – an old Neumann cutting machine which its owner also proved willing to sell. It was a mono machine when they saw it but was fully equipped for taking the extra parts to turn it to stereo so they just had to hunt for additional amplifiers. At the time they did not appreciate how good the old Neumann valve amplifiers were, until they bought transistor cutting amplifiers which were nothing like as good. Soon they began to realise that they could actually transfer what was on their master tapes to disc for the first time without too great a loss of quality.

The quality of what was on those original tapes was quite astonishing, for the three men, and Numa in particular, were already revealing their gift for recognising neglected or potential quality performers.

Vlado Perlemuter, aged fourteen.

His peers would not begrudge the pianist Vlado Perlemuter the accolade of being the greatest of these early Nimbus artists. When Perlemuter made his first recording for Nimbus on 26 July 1973 he was nearly seventy, but although he was already 'one of the greatest piano teachers of the century'[1] and 'respected by his peers, and more anxious

64

to serve music than to succeed in his career'[2], his was still not a name widely known to the record-buying and concert-going public. When he was directed that July morning to No. 6, 'a tidy suburban bungalow with red brick ramparts and gold coloured wooden gates'), the process began which was to remedy that neglect. And how painstaking a preparation for this '. . . *miracle, c'est simplement le piano à redecouvrir*'[3], his pianistic journey, had been.

Born in Kaunas, Lithuania on 26 May 1904, he had fled with his parents from a Cossack pogrom to Paris in 1908. Paris was to be his home from then on, apart from the war years. The son of an accomplished lieder singer, he had studied with Cortot, worked with Fauré on Fauré's pieces and, in 1927, spent long and arduous days with Ravel at his home in Montfort L'Amaury to ensure that the accents, pedalling and rhythmic patterns were as authentic as the composer could have wished. Perhaps it was then, as his great advocate Sir William Glock, then head of music at the BBC, suggested, that he deepened 'his own inclination towards the simplest and most faithful treatment of anything that he undertook to play.' Glock had, in fact, given Perlemuter a series of Chopin programmes on BBC radio to which Numa, Michael and Gerald, perhaps because of the poor technical quality of the broadcasts, had listened, unimpressed, at the insistence of Perlemuter's agent, Basil Douglas.

Sir William Glock, former Head of BBC Music, who persuaded Numa to record many of the best Nimbus artists.

Douglas continued to badger them, yet but for a rapidly cooling and uneaten fish on his dinner table one day when the Nimbus trio had forgotten they were supposed to be his guests, Perlemuter might never have become Nimbus's best-selling artist. Ashamed by their lapse, the three men felt obliged to go and hear Perlemuter at the Queen Elizabeth Hall when next invited to do so. Despite the acoustic difficulties of the hall Numa realised within moments that here was a great artist which Nimbus must have and invited him to record Ravel's piano works that summer.

Vlado Perlemuter recording the Ravel piano cycle.

Basil Douglas brought him to Birmingham, insisting that as Perlemuter did not know the Nimbus trio he must come for company and to make sure Vlado was happy and properly looked after. When Perlemuter arrived, he and Numa soon got into conversation in French with Basil hovering around them. Perlemuter turned to him and said, 'What are

66

you doing here still, Basil? I'm fine. Thanks for driving me. You can go now.' Perlemuter made himself completely at home and completed the Ravel exquisitely in three days.

If Perlemuter's Ravel is great, then his Chopin is unique. As Glock, writing in *The Times* in 1973 put it:

> His playing, especially of Chopin, is, at its best, so inspired that it is difficult to listen with satisfaction to the readings of all but a very few of his contemporaries ... His interpretations are, I think, unique and more inimitable than of Ravel. His playing of Chopin is simple and architectural. That is its most impressive feature. There is nothing exquisite or mannered about it. He puts line before detail, large patterns before small, though this certainly does not mean that there is any lack of nuances. It is only that they are of a different order. It is a balancing act, with the important things put first and the others gaining from that.
>
> One remarkable thing about him is that he never grows stale, that after half a century he still engages in slow and humble practice with the left hand of pieces that he has known all his life.

For Gerald the memory of Perlemuter's first Chopin recordings in Birmingham remains movingly clear.

> Vlado did not even think to question our way of going about recording. His recording experiences had been largely in the days of 78s so he didn't think of any other way of doing it. Doing it in bits didn't make any sense at all. You find with people like Vlado that no performance is the same anyway, so it is actually impossible to edit – technically you can, but musically you can't.
>
> The Chopin recording he did for us in Birmingham, particularly the B Flat Minor sonata, was an extraordinary performance. His brother had died not long before and by the end of the funeral march Vlado was in tears. It was an extraordinarily moving performance as was that of the finale that follows. He was like a child after. He ran round to the control room and said, 'My God, I did it all without pedal, I'll never do it like that again. Can I hear it?' Normally he never bothered to come and listen to a play-back at all. There was a famous occasion here when he'd done something that he was particularly pleased with, but he didn't know whether we'd recorded it or not. Michael was operating the talk-back and tape operating. There was a marvellous croaky noise from Vlado, 'Michael, Michael, did you hear that? It was superb' and Michael said over the talk-back, 'Yes, Vlado, we recorded it.' Vlado's reaction was highly amusing. 'You what? You what? You recorded it? (pause). It was not bad.'

In the archives of Nimbus – a maze that makes Hampton Court as straightforward as a Roman road – there lurks a tiny scrap of paper in the hand of this great twentieth-century pianist. It consists of a scrawled out five bars of Chopin's music and one note, a B flat, of one chord, is penned in red with the plaintive caption, 'did I play B natural here?' A perfectionist talking to perfectionists: not to suggest that a bar from some other 'take' be patched on to cover the error but to ask whether the whole piece would need to be recorded again. To watch his total concentration when playing, his complete absorption in the music and his playing of it, his absolute exclusion of anyone or anything else is to understand as you listen why the CDs of his Chopin Nocturnes and of the Sonatas (the latter twenty years after it was recorded) remain Nimbus's two all-time best-sellers.

If Nimbus was impressed with Perlemuter, then Perlemuter was no less enraptured with Nimbus as his letters of the period show. 'Heartfelt thanks for this week of work in the Nimbus family, for having revealed to me not only an exceptional recording quality but for having put in my way friends, an indissoluble friendship, so simply established through the music we love so much . . . *Au revoir*, my good Nimbuses – with luck there will still be meetings on our respective paths which will warm our poor hearts.'

That this mutual trust was a rare feeling for Perlemuter is evident from a note many years later from his agent to the organisers of an American concert at which Perlemuter was due to play. 'I have to tell you that Mr Perlemuter's experiences with broadcasting have been so unfortunate that he decided some years ago never to allow it again. He would insist on your co-operation in ensuring that no attempt is made, either with tape-recorders or more sophisticated equipment, to broadcast or televise any part of his concert. Furthermore, he will need a letter of confirmation from you in this regard. Otherwise, he will not come to Newport.'

Of course, as with any artist of temperament, things did not always go smoothly. Perlemuter was plagued by his *'moments affreux et doulereux''* one of which was the breaking of his hip slipping on black ice outside Nantes railway station in 1985, and there are frequent references to 'my myseries and my torments', depriving him of the strength to make recordings. Perhaps his biggest cause of discontent however, in the early days at least, was that shared by many of the other early Nimbus artists. On 29 December 1976 he wrote: 'Imagine my anxiety at your silence. You know with what happiness and enthusiasm, encouraged by your friendship, I recorded for you. Those sessions were a kind of "testament" for me. But I have heard not a sound, nothing, and could be angry . . . I have willingly redone the arguable or criticised passages. But the thought that works as important as the Ravel, the ballades and sonatas of Chopin, the Liszt Sonata and the Beethoven *Eroica* variations are buried in the deepest recesses of your "files" [boxes] flings me into despair. Tell me something – good or bad – I beg you.'

That letter was written shortly after Nimbus had moved to Wyastone Leys where, at last, they were able to unblock the pipeline and begin to manufacture their own LPs, among the first of which were the treasures in those 'boxes'.

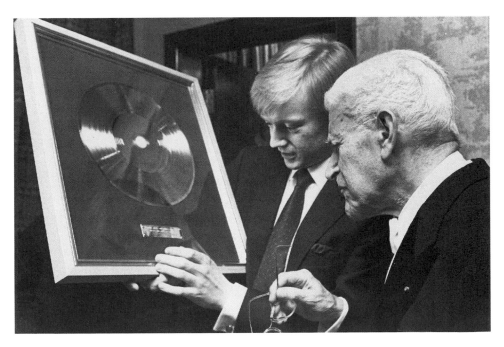

Vlado Perlemuter inspecting his golden disc with Adrian Farmer at his eightieth birthday concert at the Bath Festival.

In November 1986 Basil Douglas wrote tetchily to Adrian Farmer: 'If after all these months you have decided that you don't want to record Souzay, that is for you to say, but although he is a man of the world, with considerable experience of record companies, it will be quite surprising if he doesn't regard his treatment by you as a bit of an insult. Your handling of the matter has indeed been remarkably casual, and for example, I doubt if a message of this importance should have been left to your assistant.'

By and large, however, Nimbus's relationship with Perlemuter and Basil Douglas remained one of mutual admiration and affection and as recently as March 1992, Perlemuter and Adrian were corresponding about 'dear Vlado's wish to make a recording of the Chopin mazurkas.' Perlemuter, who had been made a *Grand Officier de la Légion d'Honneur* in 1991, was still teaching despite feeling 'harassed' by some of his pupils, and still eagerly drawing talented young pianists to Nimbus's attention. Indeed Perlemuter seems indestructible and a letter to Adrian from the impresario who had just staged a 1992–93 season Perlemuter concert in the Teatro Ghione in Italy observed: 'I think we are all very much indebted to Nimbus for the wonderful insight that you have had to record these artists (I am also thinking of Cherkassky as well) . . . I enclose the reviews of [Vlado's] miraculous concert, and we have every intention of his coming back again in 1993–94.'

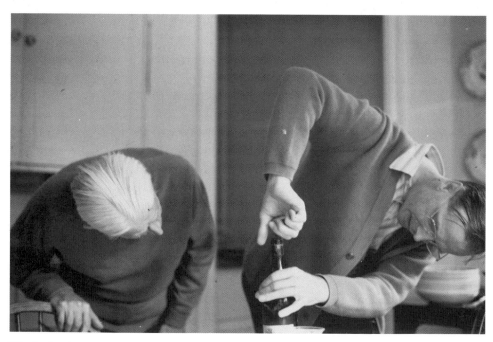

Vlado Perlemuter supervising Michael opening a bottle of 1949 Clos de Vougeot to celebrate a triumphant concert.

70

Central also to the early musical development of Nimbus were two other pianists, Martin Jones and Nina Walker.

It is indicative of the Nimbus priorities and organisation that the earliest item in the voluminous file for Martin Jones is a piece of printed music, dated January 1972 – the *Thème varié* of Francis Poulenc. The follow-up letter on 6 January is a 'Dear Michael Reynolds; Yours faithfully' one, listing the pieces Jones is working on, including the Alkan they were to record many years later. Jones and his wife stayed in 'the small guest bedroom' in April 1972 when he recorded the Debussy Preludes for a fee of £50 plus travel expenses. By June – he was the young artist in residence at Cardiff University at this time – he had begun the Mendelssohn recordings which remain one of the musical landmarks in the Nimbus catalogue, and the salutations between the two parties had become the usual affectionate Nimbus ones. Jones was delighted with the studio piano, which Gerald had thanked him 'for playing better than anyone we have ever had apart from Numa's beloved Nina [Walker]', and attributed it to his good playing. Gerald still believes Martin Jones' Mendelssohn series to have been quite extraordinary. 'He had this miraculous way of starting and stopping tone which is quite unique to him, nobody else seems able to do it.' Of the recordings the *Guardian* wrote, when they were transferred to CD: 'In most ways just as impressive in realism of piano sound are the much earlier recordings made in the 1970s by Martin Jones of Mendelssohn piano music, now beautifully transferred to CD. All three of the set of six which I have now heard are fascinating.'[4]

These recordings, like all the others of these early days, did not see the public light of day until 1977 when Nimbus had begun to press its own discs. (There are only leaflets – catalogues were never even dreamt of let alone printed in those days – of the LPs Nimbus issued but not lists of all the recordings they made prior to their move to South Wales.*)

Jones took happily to the Nimbus working style. 'How nice it is to work in such splendid surroundings and with kind people who are helpful and not always looking at the clock! The conditions we have before we start recording are so much better, enough to make others green with envy.'

Martin Jones was also enraptured with the Nimbus sound which

*Appendix C

he thought 'beyond comparison with other systems.' Gerald had condemned such other systems in a letter to him because 'the orchestra comes off best but the poor soloist does very badly indeed, the essential nuances of a performance get lost with all that mechanical and chemical processing on the way. These essential qualities do transfer very well indeed on tape, provided of course that it is Quadrophonic.'

At this time the BBC were discussing the possibility of buying the Nimbus system but nothing came of it.

As with all Nimbus artists there was the usual waxing and waning of the relationship. After two years of intense activity, supported by friendly correspondence about family life, there followed eighteen months of silence, at the end of which Jones felt compelled to write to ask if he had 'upset the Nimbus management in some way', and obviously thought he needed to put 'Jones' in brackets after he signed off 'Martin'. It is quite possible that his first wife *had* upset the Nimbus management – on the whole its founders did not take kindly to the wives and sweethearts of their artists thus entangled – but by 1978 they were working amicably together again and the relationship was strengthened with the arrival of Adrian Farmer who took on the bulk of the dealings with Jones. Indeed, Nimbus thought so highly of their evermore reputable early protégé that in January 1990 they agreed an annual advance of £5,000 for 4–6 unspecified recordings a year – a long march from the £50 of two decades earlier.

Martin Jones, British pianist, at the time of his recording of the complete Mendelssohn cycle. Jones is Nimbus's most recorded artist.

However the most significant recruit of these early days to the Nimbus family was the pianist – and subsequently celebrated vocal coach – Nina Walker. She was important to Nimbus not only for her own musical gifts but for the effect she was to have on Numa's work. Nina, who had studied under Arrau, was freelancing in 1972 after an arduous two years losing technical stiffness and learning to play with that total ease of her whole body which characterises her playing. She was a little put out when the fruit of all this labour was an invitation from Julian Budden to play some nine minutes of snippets for a programme on Verdi for the BBC. She accepted because she wanted to work with Budden. Nina Walker had, in fact, already been recommended to Numa by Lady Shrewsbury, but as the founding trio always took Nadine Shrewsbury's recommendations with a pinch of salt they took it no further. Then one day Numa happened to be listening to a tenor recital on the radio at the end of which the announcer credited the accompanist as Nina Walker. With a characteristic laugh Nina told me what happened next – another of Numa's twists of fate, in which she also believes. 'The next day the 'phone rang and this wonderful voice said "Miss Nina Walker, this is Mr Numa Libin. I am in Birmingham and I would like to see you." When I asked him why, he said, "Well, we have a nice recording studio here, I heard you on the radio yesterday and I want to meet you because I heard a sound which I recognised." I told him the story of the nine minutes and he told me to come right away. When I protested that I couldn't find my way he instructed me not to drive but to get on the train and get out at New Street where I would see them all standing on the platform waiting for me. I asked, "How shall I know you?" and Numa replied, "I'm the one in the middle with the button missing off his coat," and indeed, that's exactly what he was.'

Gerald vividly remembers Nina's arrival at New Street. 'There was Nina arriving like Anna Karenina, knee-length black leather boots, long black coat and black fur hat. I don't think we ever saw her quite so splendidly turned out again. By coincidence she had prepared *Winterreise*, something Numa had been working on for years. The first thing they did when they got in the studio was to perform the entire work straight through, and that was the pattern of their working.'

Nina was not even sure why she had been invited to No. 6. 'I thought I had gone for lunch, so I took off my coat, had a cup of tea and went into the studio. The piano was open with *Winterreise* on the stand.

Numa smiled at me and said, "Let's do *Winterreise* before lunch and see how we go." I sat at the piano and we were off. It was an extraordinary experience. Although we were almost the same age and our concert paths had crossed all our professional lives and we knew each other by name, we had never met. Obviously we had each learnt our Schubert separately, but we just went through a complete *Winterreise*. That was the first time I heard myself properly with this extraordinary microphone because I had been used to multi-miking with the opera. After that I used to go up once a month and we would experiment with the microphone. This constant experimentation was wonderful. We would do a complete cycle of something which we always recorded straight through each time although because it was experimentation we didn't necessarily use it.'

This was the beginning of an extraordinarily fruitful partnership based on mutual, but not uncritical, respect and on personal harmony. The work the two of them got through was prodigious, recording the Brahms Four Songs, the Mussorgsky *Songs and Dances of Death* in a single day, and the same with *Winterreise* and *Die Schöne Müllerin*.

Nina had just been working with Numa and the young Dutch bass, Jan Kist, when we talked on a bright November afternoon in 1993 and she described the relationship. 'I think the great musical relationships come from great human relationships, come from enjoying each other's company and having minds in tune. He's been very ruthless with me. We don't say everything's nice. We're strong with each other and it's still the same this morning as it was twenty-one years ago. I don't know why, he'll do something and I've already thought of it myself, it's a kind of body language. We make each other fly without doing anything. I just love being with them. It's their whole life; the planning and the desire to do something. Very rarely will you find that all in one place like that.'

Nina was not only Numa's accompanist, until her work with the Royal Opera House made this impossible in the late 1970s, but, from the outset, she became a director of Nimbus, which she remained for many years. This was a unique accolade for the Founders to bestow on any woman for as Numa explained '. . . there is a basic, uncomfortable, no-man's land between the sexes. Great areas for misunderstanding and offence to be taken in a way that simply doesn't happen with your own sex.' But Nina was the special exception so it was not surprising that in

1985, following a break from Covent Garden, she returned frequently to Nimbus for some years to produce many of their solo and chamber music recordings and, with Adrian, a spectacular *Midsummer Night's Dream*. This was a classic example of the total performance approach,

William Blair playing Puck in a complete recording (Shakespeare and Mendelssohn) of *A Midsummer Night's Dream*.

for instead of recording the different elements piecemeal and stitching them together afterwards, as most companies would have done, Nimbus recorded actors, singers and musicians together, with the speech setting the tempo of the music. When it was done they teased Numa by telling him that it was no good and he, typically, told them not to take it to heart for they had done their best. They would listen to it togegher anyway. In fact, it was such a marvellous performance, that Nina, Adrian and the three Founders sat listening with tears streaming down their cheeks and Nina thought to herself, 'yes, that's what we are all after.'

Nina Walker and Montserrat Caballé at La Scala, Milan, 1975.

Nimbus superseded Hermes and the new approach evolved from the old with the registering of the new company, Nimbus Records Limited on 2 April 1971.

Since the beginning of that year the three men had been looking for the right name for their new recording enterprise, even playing with a matrix of letters and cabalistic signs to see what it threw up. Pegasus, Isophon, Axel, Banner, Announce and Amber – the latter objected to initially (though it was registered much later) by a literal-minded registrar on the grounds that as gramophone records sometimes had amber coloured labels it might be confusing – were all considered and rejected. Adopting the name Nimbus was the result not of a search for a dignified intellectual word implying thought or sanctity, but of Numa's impish sense of humour. There was at the time a cartoon strip in a Paris newspaper featuring a Professor Nimbus, who was forever ogling pretty women and whose bossy wife was always hitting him on the head with an umbrella. It was after the henpecked academic that Nimbus Records was named eventually for the very prosaic reason that it was the only one of their favoured names which could be registered worldwide.

Michael was quick to spot that the new company's memorandum and articles did not cover any possible new audio, or visual, or audio-visual format that might be invented in the future and on 18 August 1971 inserted general all-embracing definitions which would one day enable Nimbus to exploit the remarkable new recording media that they have played a substantial role in developing – CD and Video-CD. In March 1972 Nimbus's elegant trademark was registered and Michael, uncannily prescient, registered the new company and its visible symbol in both the European Community and America. The new company was thus all ready to go in 1972 but, despite the wonderful recordings made and stored up in its first four years, not until the family moved to Wyastone Leys on 22 October 1975 could it gather the momentum necessary for its spectacular take-off in the eighties.

CHAPTER FIVE

The first year at Wyastone Leys was frenetic. Restoring the building and grounds, and accommodating relatives (their mother and sister) were substantial enough tasks in themselves, but only diversions from the main objectives. The dilapidated old ballroom had to be transformed into the elegant and acoustically sympathetic studio that served Nimbus until 1992 and a manufactory for the mastering and pressing of long playing records had to be built.

Before they began work, the Founders tried to recruit people from the record industry to help them design their plant but, surprisingly, few seemed ever to have designed an LP plant from scratch. Some

Three exhausted men, Gerald, Numa and Michael, after the completion of the rebuilding of the house and the establishment from scratch of the recording studio and the LP plant.

were overwhelmed by the size of the task, others seemed unable to understand or accept the high quality standards Nimbus demanded. All of them gave up, leaving Michael and Gerald to design the entire layout themselves.

Their task was made no easier by a severe shortage of money, for the banks had refused to lend the fledgling company a sufficient percentage of the equity value of their property to leave them with adequate working capital. As a result, they had to skimp on some equipment in order to buy high quality for such critical items as the steam boiler. They did not want a potential bomb on their hands. One of their economies was to design their own presses which, while they produced excellent quality records, were not always reliable. What these necessities did do, however, was establish an important psychological precedent, giving Gerald, in particular, the confidence to solve Nimbus technical problems with its own designs rather than by buying in ready-made solutions. This approach made Nimbus a fortune in the mid-1980s and still enables the company to open up new areas of business today. Practical experience of trying to meet order deadlines with the manual presses and Michael's careful and perspicacious forecasting – always his forte – convinced them that they would have to automate the process as soon as possible. This involved them in a very useful dialogue with Decca resulting in Nimbus buying two cumbersome and ugly American presses which did the job well. They kept the manual presses for the short runs that soon began to earn them substantial revenue from, among others, the BBC transcription service, whose business they cornered, and the various music libraries that had to have good quality pressings. Nimbus was rejecting 15 per cent of its output, not because of poor production but because they rejected records with which other companies would have been content. Initially this reputation for quality was achieved by word of mouth, stemming from their very first customer. A Norfolk-based organ enthusiast had come to Nimbus in Birmingham to get them to cut masters for this notoriously difficult instrument to press. He was so pleased with the results that, when Nimbus established its own pressing plant, he brought them an order for a run of 500 records. There were only Numa, Michael and Gerald and one electrician to tackle this first order and they, at the same time, were supervising, and often directly labouring on, the building of the studio and the production and sound engineering of their own recordings. By the

Firm finds true groove at Wye Valley mansion

AT a time when major record companies are facing financial difficulties, a small business in South Herefordshire is thriving.

Nimbus Records is snapping up sales in the high-quality record market.

The company began in Birmingham in 1970. But it was not long before it was expanding and seeking new premises.

Four years ago it found the ideal setting for recording distinguished classical music — at Wyastone Leys, Symonds Yat.

Today Nimbus Records not only records top artists and musicians in its studios at the mansion, but continues the production process through to cutting, pressing and distributing the final disc.

Much of the success is due to the dedication of the directors, Gerald and Michael Reynolds and Numa Libin.

Gerald said: "Most of our recordings are with our own artists, although we do offer manufacturing facilities to other producers.

"We are interested more in finding great musical interpreters than merely filling gaps in the record catalogues."

Last year Nimbus Records manufactured half a million records at Symonds Yat.

In the control room are (from left), Mr Reynolds, Mr Numa Libin, and Mr Michael Reynolds, while BELOW foreman Colin Dix presses a record.

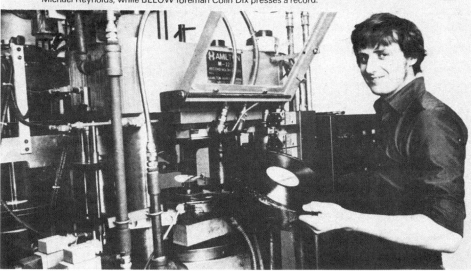

Early press report in the *Ross Advertiser* of 13 February 1980, showing the Founders at work.

time they had pressed and carefully visually checked every record of that first order to achieve 500 perfect copies it was two o'clock in the morning and as they sat round the kitchen table wearily drinking tea, the three men wondered where the customers would come from. They need not have worried. So excellent were the organ pressings that their pleased purchaser was soon busily recommending Nimbus to everyone he came across. Coupled with their own telephone sales approaches to every record company in Britain they could identify, they were soon building up a good clientele.

Their first major customer was Rediffusion, which was licensing all the Supraphon catalogue and issuing it on its own label in Britain. (When they stopped it was a bad blow.) Nimbus persuaded Stephanie Lengauer at Wienberger's to give them a try and she was so impressed by the quality that she brought the new company all her work. Then KPM came down to Wyastone Leys with a particularly important recording and in cutting it for them, Nimbus showed how much could be preserved in transferring to disc. KPM were impressed and transferred their business to Nimbus also.

The new company then made a direct cut recording for a jazz label called Incus, run by Evan Parker. Parker came with his soprano saxophone and his glass-fibre reeds, which produced the most extraordinary noises. He was able to do circular breathing and went on doing it for twenty minutes at a stretch, improvising by using the acoustics of the Nimbus studio to build up a huge volume of sound. It was so deafening in the room that Gerald feared it might blow everything up, but the three pioneers were ready to try anything.

The direct cut was something of a Nimbus speciality. The snag was that to make masters in this way the cutting engineer would have to anticipate the actual sound of the performance by a fraction of a second. Gerald, who cut these discs by hand himself, therefore made himself in a matter of months as much a master of reading a score half a bar ahead of the music as any famous conductor, and thus demonstrated once again his capacity to learn difficult things quickly when sufficiently motivated. The Nimbus team felt particularly happy with direct cutting because it seemed to them the most honest way of recording a performance. It also yielded the best playing quality by eliminating a generation in the transfer process and thus avoiding the degradation involved by having to have an intermediate medium.

Michael Reynolds
adjusting the controls at
the mixing desk.

Gerald Reynolds at the LP
cutting lathe.

Numa's faith in direct cutting and lacquer records was so great that he bought back the company's old LP presses in November 1992 and first direct cutting machine. This was partly out of sentiment and the wish to record his new high voice repertoire by this method in 1994 and partly because, as he said, 'within two or three years' time we will have a small steam generator and make superb 45rpm discs and 78s and people will pay absolutely through the teeth for them. £45 each at least I should think.' If that sounds an outrageous price it should be remembered that the original 78s were selling just before World War I for a guinea apiece. This was about twice the average industrial wage, whereas £45 is approximately a quarter of a week's industrial wage today. Numa's vision of the future for LPs and 78s will be realised if the wishes relayed to Antony Smith, the Nimbus representative, at the independent label producers October 1993 conference, are fulfilled. Several companies told him that the only reason they had stopped issuing their records on LP was that Nimbus had stopped pressing and they could not get the required quality elsewhere.

Just how successful this direct cut approach was is illustrated by the response to Bernard Roberts' Beethoven series. The music critic of the *Sheffield Telegraph* wrote: 'I recently bought the first volume of your projected Beethoven Piano Sonata cycle and felt I must write to you and tell you just how much pleasure and delight your playing has given me. Undoubtedly the superb recording of your piano tone helped, as did the fact that these were live performances – even the few mistakes could not detract from glowing performances that I will return to again and again in future.'[1]

The Observer also observed:

> Its argument, that the music's intellectual cohesion is its greatest virtue whatever Beethoven's intentions, is rather persuasive. The reading hangs together better than Barenboim's.
>
> Perhaps Roberts was encouraged to take this line by Nimbus's direct-to-disc recording process, which (deliberately) cuts out tape editing. Or maybe the unity is partly a result of that process. In any case one has to say that the Nimbus recording is not quite so agreeable as the DGG. Nimbus has pioneered direct-to-disc, as well as the 45rpm LP, and the results have an immediacy which takes a bit of getting used to. Here at least is a record which makes the effort worthwhile.[2]

Nimbus made two other major innovations in the technique of LP transfer, one by accident and one by ratiocination. Gerald had considered for some time that more efficient use could be made of the disc surface by improving the so-called 'varigroove' method of cutting LPs. This required the mastering lathe to narrow the groove spacing when the dynamic demand was small and increase it when the dynamic was large. In this way, not only would the quality of reproduction be enhanced but, because the times at which the groove would be more widely spaced were far fewer than when it would be narrower, more information could be packed onto a 12" disc by getting the grooves to snuggle up together. As a result, by refining the process, Nimbus was able to get onto one side of an LP as much as fifty-three minutes of orchestral playing time, as opposed to the more usual twenty-five to thirty, without any loss of level.

Later on Gerald developed the idea of using a short tape loop of the appropriate interval and measuring the variance between the current sound and the sound in the groove cut previously to improve

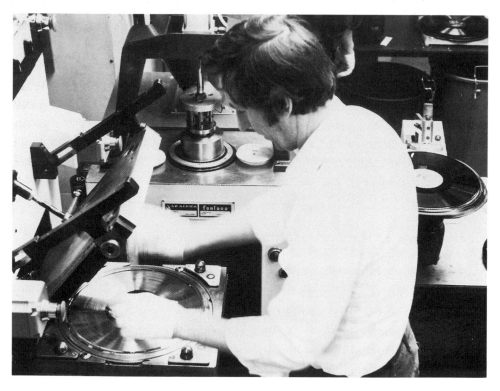

Graham Eddy at a semi-automatic LP press.

Nimbus staff in the LP press shop.

the 'varigroove' method still further. One of the first of many refinements Jonathan Halliday made to the cutting process on joining the company in July 1981 was to convert this tape loop method of anticipation into an entirely electronic one which required only a single run of the original tape to cut the master. By anticipating the dynamic requirements and varying the groove width to meet them more efficiently, Nimbus soon acquired the reputation of giving customers more than their money's worth.

Largely by accident they then discovered that they could achieve significantly better quality reproduction without any loss of playing time. They had recruited Dennis Blackham, an excellent young cutting engineer from the popular music record business. As Gerald, the realist, said: 'We do not approve of pop music and we are not involved in it in our recording activities, but we are not so impractical as not to realise that if we were to rely purely on the classical market we simply would not have a business.' On one occasion Blackham was transferring a piano recording from tape to LP master and left the cutting machine set at the 7" pop music speed of 45rpm when he should have changed it to 33rpm. He came slightly sheepishly to the Founders to tell them what he had done, but suggested that before he scrap the lacquer (the master) they listen to it. They were all amazed at the difference in quality and realised that by combining their improved 'varigroove' and 45rpm playing speed they could deliver both quality and quantity. They found that they were able to put entire Tchaikovsky symphonies on a single LP while retaining the quality of the performance, or alternatively, to give sixty minutes (thirty minutes a side) of harpsichord playing on a single disc or at 45rpm. Nimbus christened this process SAM45 (Super Analogue Master). They also found themselves asked to master and press a great deal of profitable pop material in this format because they could still give about twenty minutes a side. As Gerald observed: 'I don't know how we managed to cope with all these things at once, but at least the LP pressing business was making enough money to give us a reasonable living and finance our music-making.'

Perhaps the most significant piece of 'music-making' that Nimbus did in the pre-CD days, technically and commercially at least, was the recording they made on 22 January 1982 of the Hanover Band playing Beethoven's First Symphony and the First Piano Concerto with Mary Verney as soloist. This was the first Beethoven recording of an authentic instrument orchestra and the start of a long association between Nimbus and the Hanover Band, which we shall look at in greater detail later. It was Nimbus's first location recording; it was the first Nimbus recording for which Adrian was sole producer and it was Nimbus's first digital recording.

The location chosen, after reconnaissance of many possible venues for their acoustic suitability, was St Giles', Cripplegate, where Nimbus was subsequently to make several memorable recordings. Adrian described how he came to be *the* producer on this landmark occasion. 'We all went down together. Numa, Michael, Gerald and Jonathan set up the microphone and so on and then the Founders just buggered off. Just left. And that may have been one of the moments when it all started to change. Clearly they already had the idea that the business was going to develop and that the whole of the music side was going to have less of their attention.'

Adrian's three colleagues were able to walk away not only because they had confidence in his musical and management skills, but because they knew that Jonathan had installed a technical set-up that would produce an unprecedentedly high quality of recording. Nimbus had not itself attempted to make digital recordings before Jonathan's arrival, though as a leader in the production field it had, of course, installed digital equipment in order to process and master the digital tapes sent by its customers. Indeed, its cutting of a disc (Glière's Third Symphony) for John Goldsmith of Unicorn preceded Decca's first issue and was thus the very first digital record published in the United Kingdom. As soon as digital equipment became available, Nimbus tried out Sony's early versions, the first of which was 'not too bad, but not too good either' according to Gerald. The subsequent sixteen-bit system Sony produced 'was awful'. The only remotely satisfactory early digital recording system in the late seventies was that of a small American company, Soundstream, but as the proprietor refused to sell and would only rent out his edit suite on his own premises and Nimbus did not fancy flying to Utah every time they needed to edit a recording, this was ruled out.

Under pressure from the industry, Sony then developed a system based on the U-Matic (¾″) video tape machine. They could convert a digital signal into 'pseudo-video', store it on the video recorder, then take the video and turn it back into digits again. This was an improvement but the results were still not acceptable to Nimbus, who found the sound hard and unmusical.

Soon after Jonathan arrived, Gerald remembers him tackling the problem:

> Jonathan developed a very useful 'black box' (the contents of which are still a trade secret), which in conjunction with an oscilloscope identified the real problem with the early digital systems. This was that around zero volts, rather than being a smooth transition from just above zero volts, through zero to below zero, there was a sudden abrupt discontinuity. If the discontinuity went in one direction the converters were going deaf to signals below a certain level which simply didn't get recorded at all. If it went in the opposite direction then, with low level signals, you got nasty crackling noises which is what we were objecting to. However, in those days the analogue to digital converters were adjustable and Jonathan's 'black box' made it possible to adjust them and obtain a much better recording.
>
> One day Sony brought down to Wyastone Leys a whole table full of Hewlett Packard wave analyzers and other expensive apparatus, but they couldn't measure the actual problem whereas Jonathan's simple

black box showed it on the oscilloscope in such a way that you could see the transfer characteristic at low levels so you could adjust the converters. All the same, we still found it necessary to reset them for every recording as they would drift over a few hours.

Nevertheless, such were the uncertainties at this stage that right up until the night before the recording, Nimbus was seriously thinking of a belt and braces exercise, using its Ampex analogue recording system as well. This was their practice for the first few studio recordings where it was easier to cope with parallel systems. They soon dropped this precaution because, whatever the deficiencies of digital recording, it soon became apparent that it got certain basic things right. It did not suffer from distortion or squashing at high levels and, properly set up, it was satisfactory at low levels as well and captured the bass correctly. Nimbus became rapidly aware that the lowest frequencies were very important to the impression conveyed of the location in which the recording was made, as much of the ambient noise was bass noise. Gamblers by nature, the Nimbus team decided to go for broke on a digital recording at their first location and left the analogue equipment at home.

With the converters carefully set up and adjusted by Jonathan, and Adrian's high adrenalin acceptance of the challenge to make good his first solo production, the Hanover Band recording was such a success that it prompted the usually pernickety *Hi-Fi* magazine to describe it as the first digital recording which actually sounded musical. Even if the returning triumphant recording team did round off the venture by getting snowed in a mile from Wyastone Leys and had to be towed out by a friendly farmer's tractor, Nimbus Records was never again to get stuck in the analogue past.

Another, but by no means novel, ingredient in the Hanover Band success was the Ambisonic sound system* on which Nimbus had

*Jonathan's version of the Ambisonic microphone array – the standard one is manufactured by Calrec, a Siemens subsidiary – uses three coincident capsules: one B+K 4006 omni-directional and two Schoeps Mark 8/CMC 5-U figure of eight. The recording chain used is as follows: Microphone – Gain box – UHJ encoder – Digital recorder.
  The gain box provides phantom power for the microphones and has very quiet front end amplifiers and a stepped-resistor gain control. The output signals are Ambisonic B-format, which is then encoded into two channels, using either an Audio and Design or Calrec encoder. There is no subsequent mixing, compression or manipulation of the sound. Whenever Nimbus records, it uses a full Ambisonic playback system, currently using ATC monitors, Crown amplifiers and an Audio and Design decoder.

already been working by then for nearly a decade and which Jonathan was progressively to sophisticate much further. Ambisonics had been developed in the early 1970s by Michael Gerzon at Oxford University and Professor Fellgett and Geoff Barton at Reading University. It was financed by the British Technology Group and used by Nimbus from the outset. The natural listening process involves for each individual an enormous number of variable inputs according to his response to pitch, tone, volume, direction and so on. To reproduce the live listening effect exactly, therefore, would also require thousands, even tens of thousands, of different channels and speakers. Stereo, with which most people still make do, and then quadrophonics, while an advance on monaural systems, were relatively crude attempts to compromise between the finite possibilities of sound recording and reproduction and the almost infinite number of elements in a live hearing. With either stereo or quadraphonic, to be incorrectly placed vis-à-vis the speakers is to distort the effect quite significantly. On the other hand, the Ambisonic system was designed to create the illusion of omni-directional sound with what was still a relatively small number of channels and speakers. With Ambisonics it is possible to walk about the listening area while still gaining the impression of a realistic relationship with the original source of sound – as one would walking round the back of a concert hall, for example. Multi-microphone techniques cannot achieve this effect so easily since they sample sound at more than one place at a time. Ambisonics is a more 'natural' form of listening and the listener needs only a decoder and two additional speakers to his stereo system to enjoy the benefits of it.

Ambisonics has never been widely accepted on a commercial scale, partly because the price differential to the order of 40 per cent compared with a standard stereo replay system was too great for the ordinary classical music-lover, and partly because the record critics in the leading newspapers and music magazines were not equipped to listen to any recordings in Ambisonic mode. The earlier Nimbus Ambisonic recordings, when encoded down to stereo, were not as technically good, in most critics' opinion, as recordings originally made in stereo. When Nimbus issued its first four LPs they went to four separate reviewers at the highly influential *Gramophone* magazine. All were received well on artistic grounds and all were criticised technically for the quality of the recording. Numa, Michael and Gerald went to see the Editor and

Proprietor of the magazine, Anthony Pollard, to try to persuade him that his reviewers had failed to appreciate the nature of what Nimbus was doing and should adopt a different tack. Pollard firmly and politely told them his reviewers' opinions could neither be prejudiced by pressure from him before they wrote their pieces nor tampered with after they had done so. Nevertheless, Pollard was sympathetic to the Nimbus aims and magazine and manufacturer, while frequently disagreeing over various issues, continued to regard each other over the ensuing fifteen years with mutual respect.

The fact was that the chamber acoustic of the studio salon at Wyastone Leys was something most record critics on *Gramophone* or any other magazine would rarely have encountered in recorded form before, though they would have been perfectly familiar with the actual sound encountered in a live chamber performance. Not associating it, however, with the recorded format, they did not, therefore, respond favourably to the Nimbus acoustic and recording technique. Accustomed to recordings made either in dead studios or cavernous concert halls, their ears did not readily attune to the sound produced in the much larger and livelier studio at Wyastone Leys. *Gramophone*'s reviewers of those first four records commented: 'Though very accept-

Mike Lee, the first commercial director.

able, the tone of the recording is not as three-dimensional as with . . .'; '. . . a rather hollow sounding environment and with too much surface noise.'[3]

When Nimbus Records were listened to on Ambisonic replay systems as they were, for example, by the technical critic of *Gramophone*, they were enthusiastically received, but these good opinions were insufficient in commercial terms to outweigh the scepticism of critics who had never even heard Ambisonics.

The impression is partly psychological, of course, and the balancing of the audio technology employed with the way the human mind receives, processes and analyses sound, particularly non-verbal sound, might be called the science of psychoacoustics.

The skill in that science developed by Nimbus over more than twenty years has been an important element in the high quality of their recordings and it was to bring the whole technology within their immediate control when they bought all the rights to the Ambisonic system from the British Technology Group in June 1990.

However, if the quality of the Nimbus product met with widespread, if by no means universal, approval from the outset, the same cannot be said for either the customer service or the marketing. As Webb commented in his book *The Quest for Quality*: 'Product quality was achieved at Nimbus in the early days and word about it spread informally among the music companies which were the major customers. Other aspects of quality at this time were decidedly open to criticism, notably customer service and delivery. Happily, the market's requirements were far less exacting than they are today.'

This criticism Gerald accepts as justified. 'The record industry is a funny industry with everyone, apart from the very biggest companies, working from hand to mouth. The production people want to re-educate the customers to longer lead times, but I'm afraid the industry just doesn't work like that and in the early days we let a lot of people down because of delivery deficiencies. Mike Lee was the one who brought the idea of customer service to the company, whereas we tended to insist on product quality but perhaps did not give as much attention to service as we should have done.'

Customer service and delivery times certainly improved significantly from the time Mike Lee joined in 1979 and when Nimbus was pressing

91

large volumes of CDs in the mid-eighties its reputation for rapid, punctual and efficient turnaround was as good as any in the business, largely as a result of his management skills. As Webb wrote of him, 'he would set a standard on an aspect of operations and then see that it was met.'

On the marketing side, while things did get better with the appointment of various marketing specialists, such as Roger Bateson in the late eighties and with Adrian's increasing interest in this aspect of the business, they never improved to the extent evident in customer support. The situation was probably fairly summed up by a leading Nimbus artist:

> Since the musician's livelihood depends on their ability to market and give proper accounts it can be very frustrating when they don't. They don't seem to be interested in promoting the records they've produced for you.
>
> The benefit of them not having to make money and therefore able to record things purely on their musical merits is great but the disadvantage was the complacency. The excitement lay in the doing and the making; the selling was unimportant.
>
> You have to keep badgering them for discs, for example, for selling them and in the end you run out of steam. With most people you have a dialogue but with Nimbus it's very difficult.
>
> Most of the other artists I know who have recorded for Nimbus have the same story as I have; a flush of enthusiasm and then declining interest.

Today Nimbus has three attractive catalogues covering the three major streams of its output, in contrast to those early LP days when no catalogues were printed at all and the company simply sent review copies of records to various magazines and hoped for a response. Nimbus also now undertakes its own UK and US distribution with a corresponding improvement in the take-up of its records by the retail outlets.

In the summer of 1988 Adrian sent one of his executives, Antony Smith, to scout around record retail outlets in Britain's major cities to find out how Nimbus was perceived. To their dismay, many of them barely recognised Nimbus and its records were often unavailable. When Nimbus took issue with its distributor, Target Records, it was assured that this was the best that could be done with the material available. Attempts to remedy the situation in conjunction with the distributor were not successful and it became apparent that to achieve any significant improvement Nimbus would have to tackle its own sales. Antony therefore set out in a transit van loaded with posters and supplies of every one of the then approximately 150 titles in the Nimbus catalogue and approached the retailers direct. In the first three months this one-man operation had achieved equivalent sales to that of the distributor's entire team. A second representative was taken on and later a third and the British success was taken across the Atlantic and the same approach adopted in America.

Early publicity was often good, largely as a result of the efforts of Numbus's PR consultant, Eugene Beer whose broadcasting connections were excellent. For example, he got the new company coverage on BBC's *Tomorrow's World* because of its technical innovations and novel approach to the philosophy of record-making, and saw that Martin Best's first record, *The Dante Troubadours*, was covered on Kaleidoscope and won the Edison Award.

One of the first records to be pressed at Wyastone Leys was the last recording to be made at the Birmingham studio – a commendable capture of a vanishing age of piano playing. Youra Guller was already eighty-one and, says Gerald, 'undoubtedly the greatest pianist Nimbus ever recorded'. She came on the recommendation of William Glock and the introduction of Hugues Cuenod to record for Nimbus in Birmingham in 1975. Cuenod warned Nimbus that 'Guller had an extraordinary talent for making friends and an equal talent for losing them.' However she remained friends with Nimbus until her death in 1980.

Guller had been an infant prodigy who appeared to have completely seized up technically early in adult life. She rebuilt her technique and embarked during her adult career on a Far Eastern tour, in the course of which she vanished into the back streets of Shanghai for eight years – possibly on a protracted drugs binge. At one stage – she had been extremely beautiful as a young woman – she had decided to be an actress and sought a career in Hollywood where she took up Spanish dancing, principally upon the dining tables of her friends which did not endear her to them. This she did both to display her talents and because she was afraid of the ravages of old age which she had seen destroy her friend, the pianist Clara Haskil. Fortunately she threw off the corrupting effect of both drugs and Hollywood and re-emerged in the 1950s and 1960s to give a noteworthy series of concerts in London.

It had been Nimbus's intention to record her playing the Chopin mazurkas, for which she had a great reputation, but when she arrived Gerald was quite shocked.

Youra Guller, Romanian pianist, in her eightieth year doing her last recording, the last to be made in the Birmingham studio.

The first thing we had to do was to feed her up for a couple of days because she was extremely poor and living in sad circumstances in a little flat in Geneva. Her timetable was crazy; she'd get up at lunchtime and have breakfast, tea-time she'd want lunch and she had a passion for lamb chops. The first couple of days were just feeding her up and getting her physically ready to play. Our piano tuner was on standby, of course. He was tearing his hair out wondering what was going on. She did spend a little desultory time in the studio trying to play these mazurkas and we thought, this really isn't very good. She was blaming the piano and generally being a bit difficult and then we said, this isn't

94

going very well, why don't you play something that you've known for a long, long time? Go back to things that you've known years ago. And she suddenly said, 'I have been a silly girl, this is a beautiful piano, it's just me. Right, now I'll play some Bach.' And so she did.

She did the Liszt transcriptions of the Prelude and Fugue in A minor and Fantasy and Fugue in G minor and this huge sound came out. Some Bach enthusiasts are horrified with this huge romantic approach to Bach but it does communicate all these things from the dim recesses of her early years. The neural pathways opened up again as if they had never been closed. We became very close friends. She very much wanted to make another recording for us but she was too frail.

We eventually persuaded Erato to licence us the recordings she'd made the year before, the Beethoven sonatas op. 110 and op. 111. The 111 is an amazing performance.

Her rhythmic control was absolutely rock steady. When there was obviously a new statement, she had the courage to wait, to pause and wait, before making it. The trouble with some of the young performers is they feel impelled to fill every gap. Her performance of sonata 111 is absolutely amazing; it seems to go on forever, and you want it to go on forever because she has the courage to say this is a new statement and to make space before it happens. We've generally had more success with older performers because with the wisdom of years people gain that courage.

It was not just the old warhorses who benefited from Nimbus's enlightened approach to music and recording in those early days at Wyastone Leys. Martin Jones continued to produce excellent work. As one critic wrote: 'Martin Jones sketches in light and shade beautifully, taking care to stay well within the confines of understatement, saving the fireworks for the complex, innovative Debussy to come later in the series.'[4] Nor have Nimbus recorded anything more purely entertaining than his saucy five CD renderings of all Percy Grainger's tongue-in-cheek piano works.

During this early period Nimbus also discovered John Wallace, with whom they were to have many successful collaborations. In 1977 Peter Goodwin had set up a brass quintet, Equale, for the brass players of the Philharmonia Orchestra with John Wallace on the trumpet. They sent a tape to Nimbus and despite the fact that Numa 'always loathed brass' he had self-knowledge enough to recognise his limitations and leave the judgement to others.

The two brass quintet recordings Equale made with Nimbus, a mélange of bits and pieces and Wallace's arrangement of Couperin's *Les Bacchanales* were not a commercial success, but then the company hit on a richer vein by inviting Wallace and the horn player Michael Thompson to record the Haydn trumpet and horn concerti on a single disc. This was a more expensive project, promoted by John Waites, President of the British Horn Society, and which he sponsored to the tune of £5,000. This was a substantial sum for those days and covered the costs of the orchestra, but although the money was welcome the endless dialogue on how the project should be accomplished made for a troublesome sponsorship. The recording itself is a delight, and its most valuable by-product was the establishing of individual relationships between Wallace (and Thompson) and Nimbus and the creation of the Wallace Collection, a series of a dozen recordings of different brass and orchestral pieces covering most of the recognised trumpet repertoire and many hidden gems as well. These proved both commercially and artistically successful due to the synergy between Wallace's enthusiasm and virtuoso playing on the one hand and Nimbus's recording methods and willingness to experiment on the other.

Scotsman Wallace, the third generation of his family to be a professional brass player, has always been an enthusiast from the day, aged seven, when his father brought home an old cornet for him to play on, right through his long career as principal trumpet in the Philharmonia. In Nimbus he found equal enthusiasm and fell in quite happily with their method of working.

> I really like the idea of doing things as a whole performance but other people don't. Nobody else records like that and you get compared with everyone else who's been put together very carefully in sort of two bar sections but those recordings are quite a false likeness, they're like a film of a play. Everything is cut to make an idealised version in the normal recording but hasn't the atmosphere of the play-like recordings of Nimbus.
>
> There are some people who've got super-human type reputations from their recordings, but they're just the same as everyone else in the flesh, they make mistakes, they play wrong notes.
>
> It's very difficult to record the trumpet with one microphone because the trumpet tends to dominate the other instruments. When we did the Haydn, for example, I had to stand at the back of the orchestra but I think this gives the trumpet a much better sound than when it is close-miked.

Nimbus also accepted that trumpet playing, because of its physical demands, was a little different from other kinds of solo performance and compromised with Wallace to a small extent on the matter of 'no editing'. This became more difficult once the conventional repertoire had been quite fully explored, because the more freakish pieces require sustained high tessitura playing, which is extremely hard to keep up without error or loss of tone.

Wallace's greatest pleasure in working with Nimbus has been their unusual response to the artist's own enthusiasms with regard to repertoire. 'I've come across all sorts of things that would make marvellous CDs, but there's nobody like Nimbus around who'll take a chance on it. Other companies, like Chandos, say "yes we'll do it but only if we get backing." Nimbus is absolutely amazing. Some people get put off by their high-handed attitude and their great opinion of themselves, but they aren't half generous when it comes to putting their hand in their pocket and doing things they believe in or doing things for their artists that cost them a fortune, and they'll never get the money back.'

Wallace accepted the considerable pressure under which recordings were made and enjoyed his relationship with Nimbus's producer, Alan Wiltshire, with whom he worked out an effective partnership. 'Alan liked to do everything very fast because he felt he was only going to have so much time at Nimbus before his hour-glass ran out' – as indeed it had.

By March 1990 financial pressures were making it difficult for Nimbus to accommodate all Wallace's ideas, particularly the more grandiose, and he asked to be released from his exclusive contract.

As I understand it, you now feel I should concentrate on what I do best for Nimbus – and hence we have this recital disc together with Simon in June – which I'm looking forward to.

Larger projects with The Wallace Collection, you said you could not justify on the grounds of cost.

Given this, I must inform you that the *exclusive* relationship which we have enjoyed these past three years will have to come to an end. The Wallace Collection must be kept busy – if it loses momentum then it would be very easy for all the work of the past four years to come to a grinding halt. All that energy expended for nothing.

Both CBS and Collins Classics have been chasing me for some time now about the group and, finally, because I must keep my group working, I've offered Collins the repertoire which you did not want to do – The Pictures and Wagner. In addition, Collins have signed a contract with Maxwell Davies as a conductor and composer. They have asked me to record the Trumpet Concerto with PMD [Peter Maxwell Davies] and the SNO [Scottish National Orchestra], and since this is another project you did not want to do, I've said yes.

It has been difficult for me to have to take these practical business decisions because I have very positive feelings of gratitude to Nimbus for a recording relationship which stretches back to 1979. But I hope you can see my point of view, and hope that this development does not prejudice our June recording.[5]

John Wallace, trumpet player, who was the one man who could make Numa laugh (according to Numa, who hated the trumpet).

Adrian replied promptly with the usual Nimbus generosity towards its artists. 'I was very happy to get your letter and to agree with all that you suggest. I hope that the recording ventures will be very successful for you all and that success will free your mind and give you time to do the best of your work for us. You have Numa, Gerald, Michael and my goodwill, both personally and commercially, and I look forward to working with you again. Our exclusive contract will now be regarded as having lapsed and so you are free to record the repertoire which we were not wanting.[6]

Wallace remains a Nimbus artist and continues to record for them.
A young artist of the LP days who did not survive was the talented
Russo-German 'cellist, Christian Hocks. He had changed his name to
the even less pronounceable Alexander Michejew, but too late to change
the name on the sleeve of his first recording for Nimbus, the Kodály solo
'cello Sonata, which was easily his best performance, and Bridge's Sonata for 'cello and piano. The Kodály, in particular, he obviously loved and
understood, as a letter to Numa in April 1978 shows. 'The tonal range of
the instrument is even extended (by lowering the two lower strings from
C to B, and from G to F sharp, that is a half-tone). This means that all the
incredible possibilities of this piece were discovered by Kodály, who did
not base his work on any forerunners. One can say without exaggeration
that it is one of the most difficult pieces in the 'cello's repertoire, and
also one of the most fascinating ones.'[7]

To hear this recording is to understand why his tutor, Pierre Fournier,
described him as 'surely one of the most talented 'cellists of his generation.' Numa congratulated him warmly at the time of the record's
issue.

> Do not worry about your recording date, it is unchanged – 14 to 19
> January with Parsons, God willing, if we are not blown up, if you do
> not lose your 'cello, if you do not go off with Lenny Bernstein (this is
> a joke). Of course we are delighted to tell you that your record has
> come out quite magnificently and in our opinion is sensational.
>
> We are sending you with this letter twenty records and hope
> that although you are not narcissistic you will listen to them in
> wonderment, because, by God, it is a remarkable performance.
>
> As I have teased you enough I shall not send you my undying
> love and affection, but rest assured of my sincere friendship and that
> of Michael and Gerald.
>
> All my love to you, and do not do anything horrible to your hands.
> Yours, Numa[8]

But Michejew proved difficult to work with and after a number of
recording fiascos in the intervening years the musical relationship was
terminated by Adrian Farmer a decade after it began.

> The time has come for me to tell you that Nimbus does not wish
> to plan any further recordings with you. Although the havoc of the
> LSO sessions has mercifully passed from my mind I have no reason

to expect that similar problems would not occur should we resume a serious relationship.

You have both shown me personal kindness and for that I thank you but our musical collaborations have been too mixed a blessing and it is my wish that they should end.

My decision is quite final, it has taken me a long time to arrive at it and this is the view shared by my colleagues.

I would be happy to remain a friend but not a collaborator.[9]

Michejew replied heatedly, and Numa, while standing four-square behind Adrian's decision, tried, as he often did, to soothe the wounded amour-propre of the artist.

I read your letter with great surprise. First of all I must say that I have absolute faith in my Head of Music.

I do find it very sad that two younger men, both of whom are intelligent, both of whom I admire, seem to be at loggerheads. Rest assured, my dear, that I think your Kodály unaccompanied work is the very best thing I have ever heard in the 'cello repertoire and your performance is very, very great. Also I have real fondness for you – as I am sure Adrian Farmer has too. I can only add that, when the time comes, we should be delighted to see you again. However, may I suggest that you try to make your peace with Adrian? And I shall make the same suggestion to him.

I should like to add a further word of advice. I believe you should now look into the possibility of re-recording the repertoire you did with Nimbus with another recording company; we shall in no way object.[10]

Adrian also made his peace, as Numa had suggested, and the relationship ultimately ended on a much more friendly note. 'Having given what I hope is honest reflection on the content of my letter to you I would ask you to accept my apologies. The tone and manner of my letter was abrupt and without compassion for you either as a man or musician. I have no pride in my correspondence although I remain certain of my intention which was that you should be free to record with other companies.'[11]

Like the first Michejew recording, the majority of Nimbus LPs were not only musically successful but contributed to the company's growing prosperity. Paradoxically, this prosperity, by giving the Founders the freedom to look for new developments, together with a chance telephone call, sealed the fate of the very LPs that created it and replaced them with an entirely new recording medium.

CHAPTER SIX

Numa had kept in close touch with Geoff Barton at Reading University over the development of Ambisonics and Geoff would give him the latest titbits from the audio-visual world. One day, in the summer of 1981, he casually suggested that Numa might be interested in having a look at 'a new audio compact disc read by a laser that Philips are developing', and Numa took up his suggestion. The 14 bit Philips disc of the time did not sound as good as professional tape equipment but watching that first primitive CD demonstration, Numa had one of those instinctive visionary moments which characterised his critical decisions. Brushing aside any hesitations and doubts on the part of his colleagues he there and then categorically committed Nimbus not only to the new medium but to being the first in Britain to manufacture it. The decision could have been like those earlier decisions to adopt natural acoustics, single takes and Ambisonic sound – more than arguably right in principle but commercially relatively unfruitful. This vision was of a different order and its pursuit quite transformed Nimbus Records from a respected, but nevertheless small, manufacturer in the LP field to a place in the top ten of the world's CD manufacturers.

One leading figure in the music magazine world has an interesting theory as to why Nimbus was first into the CD market.

> On the one hand you had the big record companies which were commercially hard-driven and whilst technically they couldn't lag too far behind the game, they had no reason to involve themselves in the latest developments. They were managed by people who were not real music lovers. They were not sitting at home at night playing their records and recognising the inadequacy of something. But the people who did listen closely to the music, their companies weren't large enough for them to see how the benefits of the new technology could apply to them. Nimbus was a different kettle of fish because it had people who could recognise the benefits of the new technology to music *and* had the means to apply them. This is why they went into CD. The quality of the pressings of the major companies was

deteriorating quite significantly, they were under commercial pressure but could not increase the price of the product in the market place so they had to cut costs by making the record thinner and not worrying so much about imperfections – after all a pop record didn't have a very long shelf life – so Nimbus were able to fill the vacuum. Nimbus's records were more expensive than those coming out of EMI or Polygram, but the quality was there so they were beginning to make good profits. It was, therefore, a bold as well as a farsighted step for them to recognise the impending demise of the LP market and gear up standards even further by CD. As a record company with its own manufacturing facility, directed by musicians and audio engineers, Nimbus was probably unique, certainly if considered apart from the international conglomerates. Nimbus directors recognised in CD the record buff's dream and, with the financial resources they had behind them, committed themselves to the new medium at a time when the large companies were reluctant even to release on CD let alone invest in a manufacturing plant.

In January 1982, through their contact with the UK Managing Director of Sony, Nimbus received an invitation to visit Japan at Sony's expense. Sony had already agreed to pool patents with Philips by this time. The atmosphere at Sony greatly appealed to the Nimbus team, not only because the Japanese were open about their research and eager for Nimbus to start making CDs (there were only two CD plants in the world at that time, one in Japan and Polygram's in Germany), but because they felt at home with the improvisation and shortcuts with which Sony were trying to solve the problems. They had seen all this before in developing the Nimbus LP plant. Gerald and Jonathan were thus encouraged to think that they might master the technology themselves.

It was a very different story at Philips to whose research department they were reluctantly admitted a little later in the year. There money was being thrown around on a much larger scale in a more orthodox development programme. Had Nimbus visited Philips first they might have been so daunted as to have dropped the whole idea. As it was, the price Philips were asking for their CD mastering lathe, £1.5m, was completely out of Nimbus's reach. Nevertheless, in March 1982, Nimbus signed a licence agreement with Philips to manufacture CDs to the specification laid down in the Dutch company's 'red book' of performance standards. The licence itself did little more than refer to the various patents and certainly gave no information on the making

102

Signing the CD Manufacturing Licence with Philips at Eindhoven, Holland.
Left to right: Numa, Dr Jonathan Halliday, Michael, CIA van Acker and
JJGC van Tilburg of Philips, Gerald.

and operating of a master CD lathe. Philips was gently rubbing its
monopolistic hands together at the thought of the sale of mastering
equipment they were about to make to Nimbus. But in signing the
licence Nimbus were not playing it quite straight, for they had omitted
to mention, quite legitimately, until after the deal was done, that they
intended to manufacture their *own* mastering lathe. But if Nimbus had
not told the whole truth to Philips, Philips were equally economical with
the truth towards Nimbus, for they assured them that they controlled
all the patents to the technology at the very time that Eindhoven was
involved in litigation with Thomson in Germany over who really had
the rights to CDs. A spate of consequential cases were to arise in which
Philips settled with such patent disputants as Discovision and left their
own licensees to fight their own cases. The licensees in turn found they
were defending themselves against patent claimants on the one hand
and counterclaiming against Philips – a firm that seems to employ more
lawyers than engineers – on the other. Nimbus was to dissipate a great

deal of energy, money and time, particularly Jonathan's all too scarce time, in such disputes over the next ten years.

Nimbus's decision to go it alone was astonishingly bold for so small a company and one whose experience of bank financial support had not been very happy. But by using their savings together with a £30,000 grant from the Department of Trade and Industry and a loan of £30,000 from the NRDC/British Technology Group, they designed and built the mastering lathe in ten months for £150,000. Philips had taken many millions of pounds, a large development team and six years to produce theirs. This must have been one of the best investments NRDC ever made as they recouped it many times over in royalties before the contract expired in 1987. Not only was the Nimbus mastering lathe cheaper and more quickly available – Philips were quoting an eighteen month delivery time – but it was a far superior piece of equipment for many reasons.

Who better to tell its story than Gerald Reynolds, one of the two brilliant minds which gave it birth.

We started from scratch, from first principles, to develop our own system. We'd had to learn how to make CDs as we went along because there was no external expertise. Although we'd had the experience of making LPs and certain things like the printing and electroplating were common to both sides, injection moulding was new to us, metal deposition was new, sealing the discs with lacquer, that was new, and all these processes are inter-related; if you don't get one right you can't get the next one. On one occasion we had the horrifying experience of discovering that all these layers of materials peeled off a batch of discs we made. Firms coming in after we had paved the way were able to purchase equipment that did a lot of the tasks for them which we had to design and make up from scratch. But the way that we did it meant that we had far more information and understanding of the processes and could develop a more sophisticated plant which we are now in a position to sell to the industry.

As far as mechanics were concerned, which was my main respon-sibility, we decided to keep all of the optics stationary in the mastering lathe. This was the heart of the system. The only part we wanted to move was the turntable carrying the glass master. This was the opposite of other people's designs where the glass master remains stationary on its axis and the optics move across it, which is less stable and more difficult to control. It was easy to find rotary air bearings to carry the turntable but we were struggling to find a linear air bearing to carry the whole assembly on a kind of sledge. It was very difficult because linear bearings tend to be far less stiff and accurate than rotary ones. At this point Numa came up with a piece of lateral thinking and said, well why don't you stop beating your head against that wall and simply use two lots of rotary bearings, one for the turntable and one for the traversing of the turntable so you have a pivot rather like an elbow. Once we got that idea we decided we wanted to use viscous damping to control the movement of the turntable as it moved laterally to create the spiral track. It moves very slowly, some eighty minutes to move an inch-and-a-half or so, and to do that with really high precision we decided to have very heavy viscous damping. With a linear damper this means if it's viscous enough to give you enough control, you have a problem getting the piston back to the beginning again. You have to open the valve and let thick oil through and this creates all sorts of problems of leakage and friction-free pistons, etc. Once we went for a rotary bearing to give the pivotal motion for the disc, we were able to introduce a rotary damper. The first version was really like a continuous ring of variable capacitors in an old-fashioned radio. This meant we could use the very heavy damping it provided to move across the programme area then unclamp the outer part of it and move it freely back to the beginning again. Thus the damper was moving round part of an arc and then round another part and so on. This got over the damping problems as well.

The Philips system, using two parallel linear bearings, suffers from something they call wobble as a result of them not always being perfectly in parallel. Because they could not introduce our type of viscous damping they had to rely on a mechanical lead screw to move the optical parts. Even a highly precise lead screw is not perfectly smooth as you get fluctuation corresponding to the pitch of the screw.

Most designers today understand digital but not analogue, but because Jonathan is an extremely gifted analogue designer we had an analogue approach and looked on digital as simply a special branch of analogue design. This meant that the servos he used to control the speed of the turntable relative to its radial movement used analogue circuitry, which is inherently smooth and does not produce any abrupt changes like the digital circuitry which other people use. The trouble with doing it by counting pulses is that you get discreet step changes. So with a digital approach you can't get infinite resolution which is absolutely smooth. With analogue, therefore, we had a built-in advantage and could use the full tolerance within the CD specification, which is why we can get side lengths of 77/79 minutes without sacrificing the quality of the disc, whereas people like Philips don't like to do more than 74/75 minutes with their system.

The precision of the mechanics, and the smoothness of the analogue solution to the electronics, meant that the Nimbus/Halliday lathe had so much control over the slow movements required (less than half a millimetre a minute) that it could achieve the very small track spaces which would enable Nimbus to provide double and even quadruple density on their CDs to their great future advantage – an advantage denied their competitors.

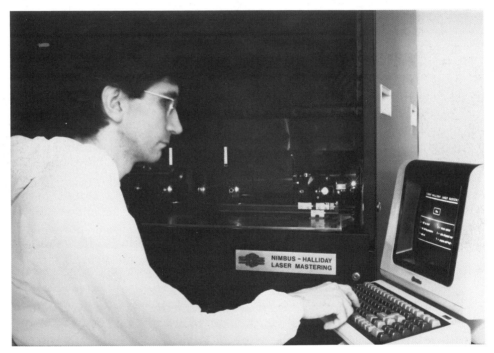

Dr Jonathan Halliday at Nimbus's first CD laser mastering machine, 1984.

In the Nimbus Manufacturing CD Plants today in Cwmbran, South Wales and Charlottesville, Virginia, you would scarcely recognise the off-spring of the early LP manufacturing at Nimbus or, indeed, of its more immediate progenitor, the first CD plant at Wyastone Leys. When CD manufacture began in 1984, many of the processes were manual, for example the polycarbonate discs which carry the basic information on a CD, were plucked from the mould by an operator using a little rubber sucker on the end of a stick, because Jonathan had rightly pronounced the first robot unsafe. Today, they are removed by a sophisticated and efficient robot arm.

The three most critical factors in CD manufacture are the accuracy of the original master, the process of moulding by which the core of the CD is impressed and the cleanliness of the working environment in which the process is carried out.

Numa and accompanist and fellow director, Nina Walker, dressed in clean room gear.

So much of the quality of a finished CD depends on the error-free precision with which the master is made. It starts its life as a blank disc of a special glass 24cm in diameter and 6mm thick (these dimensions should not be confused with those of the finished CD which correspond to the working area of the master – 12cm – and are only 1.2mm thick). This must be as symmetrical, smooth and as nearly without flaw as is humanly possible. Before the glass is treated, it is cleaned in de-ionised water and dried. The disc, after being primed with adhesive, is coated with photo-resist, a light-sensitive chemical. The 0.13 micron coating is only one-eighth as thick as in the similar process used to coat wafers in the semi-conductor industry and has to be absolutely evenly applied to an area almost seven-and-a-half times greater. The coated disc is baked in a curing oven for forty minutes at 80 degrees centigrade and, when cool, tested by laser scanner for any surface defects – failure rate is between 1 in 20 and 1 in 10.

107

This pristine and virgin glass disc is loaded into the mastering lathe, as is the master tape of the music or speech to be impressed. The information on the tape supplied by the record company now has to be translated into a form which can be read and reproduced by the domestic CD player. The blank master disc is rotated and moved laterally in such a way as to produce a uniform spiral movement relative to the fixed laser beam to which it is exposed. The laser beam is turned off and on literally billions of times (4.3 million pieces of information a second), thus leaving a pattern of dots and dashes on the disc surface which have been alternately exposed and unexposed to the laser light.

The laser-exposed disc is then developed in a process not very different from photographic processing. The exposed areas are dissolved by the developing solution to form pits in the surface of the disc while the unexposed areas are unaffected and provide the 'shoulders' between the pits. Great precision is required in both exposure and development to ensure accuracy in the required size and shape of each pit. This pattern of intermittent exposure is the CD version of the digital signals on the original master tape translated by the highly complex encoder in the mastering lathe.* Of course, if there are faults in the original tape, such as 'dropout', they will be faithfully reproduced on the CD so the prudent manufacturer carefully checks each incoming tape before mastering. Although the quality of master tapes is improving, largely due to the use of Exabyte 8mm tape cassettes, errors still occur, for which the CD manufacturer does well to avoid the blame.

In most lathes the mastering is carried out in real time, but the Nimbus/Halliday lathe is already capable of 2.8 times real time and is being developed to achieve faster copying times still. The original glass master would clearly make but few impressions before it became distorted and useless. From it, therefore, there has to be produced a more durable metal master for mass production of CDs. The challenge presented by achieving mass production of this microscopic process is great. To give but one measure of the difficulties involved the track of a CD is almost eighty times smaller than the track of an LP and is only 1.6 microns wide. As higher densities are demanded the precision required will be even greater; four times density requires pits half as small and tracks half as wide and this is already being achieved at Nimbus.

*see Appendix B

Metal masters are created by a process similar to that by which children 'grow' crystals in a bowl. The glass master disc is now vacuum-coated with nickel so that it will conduct electricity. Then, by electroforming, a 0.3 to 0.4mm additional layer of nickel is 'grown' on the glass master and subsequently separated from it. From this negative image of the master a positive master is grown. From this final positive master a number of metal stampers with the negative profile, i.e. with bumps where the original glass master had pits, are made which will then make identical depressions in the mass-produced discs to those produced in the master disc. Each stamper can produce tens of thousands of CDs and each original master many stampers.

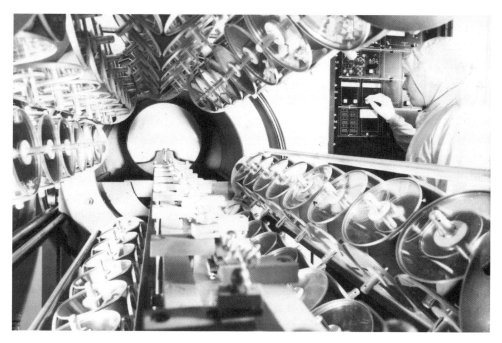

Batch metalising of CDs.

The stamper is placed in one half of the mould of an injection moulding press in which the opposing mould face is a permanent, smooth, highly polished surface. A very pure raw polycarbonate, chosen for its combination of rigidity and translucency, is heated for four hours at 130 degrees centigrade and then piped direct to the press to avoid the risk of distortion from the expansion of intrusive moisture. If the polycarbonate were to solidify with even a minute amount of stress

109

in it the laser in the CD player, which reads the pits through the plastic side of the CD, would be split or polarised (bi-refringence). This would make it read two contradictory messages and create faults in the sound reproduction as a result. The lasers in many cheaper players are not particularly accurate so the manufacturer has to allow a considerable margin for reading error as well. The hot polycarbonate is injected into the closed mould in as little as a tenth of a second. It forms and cools a polycarbonate disc, complete with centre hole and uniform edge, carrying accurate copies of the millions of pits in the CD master, every five or six seconds.

The 836 'megabytes' of information on a standard 12cm CD are impressed upon the usable surface area of approximately 86 sq cm, some three-quarters of the total area. That is to say on every square millimetre there are some 97 'kilobytes' of information. A tiny speck of dust, a grain of pollen, let alone anything so substantial as a human hair in the materials of the disc, can therefore blot out from the reading laser a significant amount of information and cause faults in the reproduction of the speech or music encoded upon the disc. To avoid these problems, the whole manufacturing process is carried out in a clean area in which the workers are completely covered in protective clothing apart from their hands and faces. There is also a positive air-flow over all the critical parts of the production line itself. Playback in the domestic CD player is not effected by subsequent dust or scratches on the surface of the mass-produced discs. Because the laser reads the pits through the thickness of the disc such defects are out of focus and not translated into signals which might distort the sound.

A robot arm extracts each moulded disc from the press and places it on a spindle which conveys it along the production line. As the discs are put onto the spindles, a stream of cold air is directed onto them, to harden them more rapidly. The disc is next picked up robotically and passed into a small coating chamber. Here, a solid block of aluminium is the reservoir for the millions of individual molecules of that metal – chosen for its cheapness and high reflectiveness – which are deposited evenly on the surface of the polycarbonate disc by an atomic bombard-ment process, known as 'sputtering'. (The 'sputtering' is effected by beaming a gas plasma created by passing 30 amps through argon at 600 volts.) This provides the reflective mirror without which the laser light would simply pass through the impressions on the plastic surface without reading the information. It takes 3½ seconds to coat the exposed areas of the disc (the centre and edges of the disc are guarded from coating as the aluminium is hard to seal securely otherwise). This is almost twice as fast as the presses can turn out discs, so two presses feed one sputtering machine.

The Leybold Sputtering machine has to be cleaned out, offline, every eighty to one hundred and twenty thousand discs and part of the production management skill of Nimbus is in timing all these maintenance operations so that, with the minimum of spare machinery, the production line is never at a standstill.

On many CD production lines if any one stage in the line gives problems, the whole line has to shut down. So Nimbus prefers a flexible approach, with separate buffer stations between presses, metallisation chambers, lacquer machines and label printers, so that discs can be stored in the event of a problem downstream or the printer set up for a new title without stopping the line. Each stage is faster than its predecessor so that it can catch up on upstream hiccups and not waste production time. Just prior to the 'sputtering' stage, each production line has an ingenious back-up capacity to enable it to handle the disc output of any of the other presses in the event of a breakdown of that production line. The discs from the interrupted production line are loaded onto a spindle adjacent to the working line and whenever a gap occurs in the flow of plastic discs, one of those from the secondary spindle is picked up and placed in the gap. This is not necessarily at regular intervals and the sequence of insertions is recorded and passed down to the far end of the production line so that, as the finished discs come off, they are appropriately allocated to the correct output line. So, except in very rare cases of error from human intervention, lovers of Bach are spared the irritation of listening to the Beach Boys, and vice versa.

Because the aluminium coating is very far from durable, it has to be protected to ensure the longevity of the CD. This is done by a machine which picks the discs off the line, places them on a spindle, deposits a small measured quantity of liquid resin round the centre of the discs, disperses it evenly over the surface by centrifugal force, passes it under ultraviolet light for the resin to be rapidly hardened and then deposits the finished CD on the appropriate stack to await printing. The durability scare about CDs (see Page 43) related to discs in which the solvent-based lacquer was hardened by hot air. The criticism did not apply to those in which ultraviolet light was used as the hardening agent, the method Nimbus employed from the beginning. Nimbus later tested hot air, but stuck with ultraviolet, another example of the company's talent for making the right technical decisions long before the methods involved become the approved orthodox solutions of the industry as a whole.

Printing can vary from a simple, black, basic text and pattern to highly elaborate three-colour printing off the latest Kamman colour press. The discs are then electronically inspected for faults. The automatic testing apparatus checks a disc every three seconds by rotating it rapidly for scanning by a radial laser beam to detect any 'scratches, dishes, or pin holes': the bright specks of light you can see on some early CDs if you hold them up to a window or an electric bulb. These automatic tests are supplemented by the eyes of skilled testers who can sometimes spot faults missed by the machines.

The test sorts the discs into passed and failed and, if the reject rate is above 3 per cent, the checking operator will check the whole batch visually. In any case, the failures are continuously computer analysed so that if any particular fault is showing consistently it can be remedied in the production line. Rejection rates at Cwmbran are now below 10 per cent, which compares with the rejection rate of some 50 per cent a decade earlier when manufacturing began. KPM, investigating the company for Robert Maxwell in 1988, were critical of the then reject rate of 20 per cent, failing to recognise, as *Classical Music* did not, that 'Nimbus prides itself on the fact that it rejects discs which other companies would be quite happy to market. It is this pursuit of perfection in all it does that has given Nimbus its international reputation for high quality.'

From the production area, the finished and printed discs are sent out for insertion into jewel cases – as the somewhat fragile containers for CDs are called in an attempt to enhance the perceived value of the CD – for the insertion of printed material and the attachment of any special sticky labels, etc., and onward dispatch to the customer.

At the time of writing, the Cwmbran plant of Nimbus Manufacturing, with thirteen presses, has a capacity of 135,000 discs a day, on a three-shift system and works pretty near the limits of that capacity most of the time under the watchful eye of the Production Manager, Anne O'Beirne.

Numa Libin, as he was then known, *c.* 1960.

Michael Reynolds, *c.* 1960.

Nina Walker, Numa's long-term recording partner and accompanist.

The exterior of the studio extension in Birmingham.

The interior of the Birmingham studio.

The ruined ballroom at Wyastone before conversion into the chamber music studio.

The chamber music studio in all its glory.

Aerial view of Wyastone Leys.

This would be challenging enough were the production going out in very large batches but, in practice, most runs are for less than 1,000 discs. The very nature of the pop music business in particular, requires extremely rapid turn-around from the receipt of the master tape to the delivery of the finished CDs. Thus, in the course of twenty-four hours, the masters may have to be changed as many as 150 times to fulfil 150 different orders. Even though a skilled operator can change a master in as little as two minutes this still means that for over 20 per cent of the day, one machine is not producing CDs.

The process in the American plant is, *mutatis mutandis* for the different conditions of the American market, the same.

Co-ordination of the various activities is also vital to keeping up the level of output. This is ensured by a combination of efficient administration and energetic progress chasing. A team of eight Customer Service assistants divide up, between them, responsibility for particular groups of customers. The assistants, utilising a computer-based critical path programme, allot the incoming requests of their particular clients to the next available slot in the production process. In the event of a customer having a crisis demanding a particularly short turn-around, then the critical path can be juggled to accommodate him with an ease and rapidity which would have been quite impossible with so many different customers on a manual system. The accumulation of this data constitutes the complete matrix of production activities which the Progress Chaser on each shift has to ensure are planned, co-ordinated and carried out. There is a very real sense of team spirit between all those involved from start to finish of the process, who recognise that Nimbus's strength in the market place has been very largely built up on the quality of the service it provides its customers. Although, in the Nimbus/Halliday mastering lathe, the manufacturing side of Nimbus once had the technical edge, these lathes are now being made available throughout the industry and, indeed, today provide Nimbus Technology & Engineering with its principal current source of profit. The technical and quality standards with which the company gained its early, strong foothold in the market, are now considered the standard and normal requirements for any CD manufacturing plant.

Without the Nimbus/Halliday mastering lathe, Nimbus would not have got the flying start ahead of its competitors nor gained the technological lead in the CD and CD-ROM fields which it enjoys today. So much of both firms' current success stems back to that first mastering lathe which Gerald and Jonathan had designed and, with Roger Jones's help, built by the end of 1983, less than ten months from the licence agreement. They cut the first master in December by a prodigious effort which Roger remembers well.

> On the first lathe, Jonathan and Gerald very much burnt the midnight oil. When I came in the next morning I'd have a list of components to make. When we went to CD from six o'clock onwards until say eleven or twelve at night I was very much involved in doing the plating for Jonathan. Then Mike Lee asked me to get the factory up and running. We spent all hours of the day and night, weekends, running one press, experimenting with the lacquering, printing, metallising, maintaining the kit during the night so we could start work again in the morning. We started with an empty building. We had no experts to whom we could go and say 'we've got this problem, will you help us?' It was a new industry, and it was very tight money-wise.

The new factory in the shadow of the house.

The Nimbus team probably re-read with some pleasure the rather arrogant letter from Philips recommending Nimbus to buy its mastering lathe because 'we very much doubt you could make a laser mastering system.' Nimbus has continued for almost a decade to be the only CD

114

manufacturer in Europe other than Philips to produce its own mastering equipment.

Heath Robinson would have been in his element with the development trio as they devised equipment – Jonathan, optics and electronics; Gerald, mechanics and Roger, machining parts – for the various stages of pilot production and setting up of the first factory at Wyastone Leys. They made an ingenious coating machine which lifted the glass master out of the trough of photo-resist on a guitar wire – which would break from time to time with rather messy results. They had to find ways of coating the master with nickel to produce a metal negative master then a positive and then a metal stamper to go into the mould for mass production. However, they had no moulding machine of their own on which to produce CDs, for although they had ordered one for delivery in November 1983 this was greatly delayed.

In July 1984, suspicious that the Continentals were ganging up to prevent a British CD manufacturer beating them to the draw, Numa successfully beseeched General Electric Plastics to fill the missing link in the production sequence and sell Nimbus its second-hand laboratory press for £104,000. This became the first production

Celebrating the purchase of the first CD moulding press, 17 July 1984.
Left to right: Gerald, Numa, Michael and Mustapha Moyedi of General Electric Plastics, Holland.

The delivery of the CD press, 1 August 1984.

machine in the UK while the Wyastone Leys factory was still waiting for its new Krauss-Mafei presses. Although Nimbus had been the first to order, Krauss-Mafei delivered first to Sonopress in Germany. Not that there were not snags, even with the stop-gap remedy, for the GEP press had been cross-wired when being re-set up so that the robot arm would not extract the stamped discs from the press. It took the Nimbus engineers several days to track down the problem and in the meanwhile the discs were extracted by hand with a rubber sucker on the end of a stick. In remarkably short time all the problems were solved and the CD production line began to roll. To make a CD they put a blob of resin on the centre of the master, squashed it down with a sheet of perspex, hardened it in 'UV light' and 'hoped to God that the resin, once cured, would stick better to the perspex than to the nickel and come off on the right side.'

That this manual process was a little hit and miss is attested to by the fact that to fulfil their first order from the BBC for fifty CDs of a concert from Aldeburgh they had to make several hundred. Roger Jones remembers those early heady days with justifiable pride. 'For the first fifty discs we actually manufactured about 250. Down there at shop-floor level we didn't have time to get blasé or romantic about it, but really it was a little bit of history.'

The team produced its first playable CD from the laboratory in May 1984 at a time when there were only a few thousand CD players in Britain. The figure for 1983 was only 19,000, but the floodgates were opening fast and by 1986 this was up to 530,000. Even before they had proved that they could do it, orders for CDs were flooding into Nimbus by April 1984 at a rate which clearly showed that they would rapidly have to push up their planned output of 30,000 CDs a month to 30,000 CDs a week.

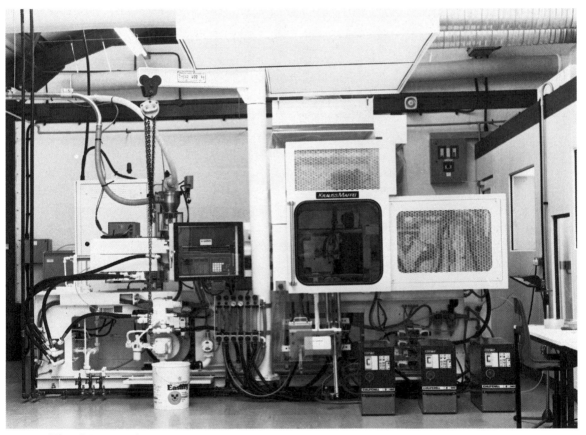

The CD press fully operational and making its first discs (the first CDs to be pressed in Britain), 22 August 1984.

By tragic coincidence Michael and Gerald's mother, who was living at Wyastone Leys with them, died on the night of the first CD production run, but while Numa 'sat with the dead' and experienced a disconcerting 'out of body' experience floating above the corpse, the pressing team, including the two brothers, worked on in the new factory nearby.

On 22 August 1984 the first mass produced CDs in Britain came off the Nimbus production line.

Dr Jonathan Halliday holding the first disc.

Gerald, Numa and Michael, holding another first disc.

But technically superior music records were not the only product of the Nimbus/Halliday mastering lathe's ability to produce discs with 2–4 times the conventional information density upon them. The information industry itself, not unnaturally, seized upon this idea of condensed data storage medium with glee. A single 12cm CD-ROM (Compact Disc Read Only Memory) can store 2.4 gigabytes of information; the equivalent of 2,000 floppy discs. Emil Dudek, employed for the second time by Nimbus in 1987 as technical assistant to Gerald, has been the driving force behind Nimbus's great success in this field since the company, somewhat speculatively, embarked upon CD–ROM under his guidance.

The idea of CD-ROM had been hovering around in Nimbus for some time but there was nobody suitable to do anything about it because Nimbus always employed on a whim. They weren't really interested in CVs or technical background but looked for personality traits, aptitude, ability to learn and so on.

I was without an immediate position and I asked what they were doing about CD-ROM so I found myself, with half an assistant, technical head, sales person, everything. Brand new product, brand new idea, still technically limping along and I think only at somewhere like Nimbus would they do something in a situation like that where they'd say, here's a new market, here's some money, go and get on with it. The only monitoring I got was the stuff I deliberately forced on them; there was complete and utter trust.

One of my first days at Nimbus I was told we were one of the very few sites in the world where you could walk in, sing into a microphone and walk out with a disc, so I thought the implication would be nice if everything could be done the same way with CD-ROM.

After burning his fingers by buying a CD-ROM software package 'from a man in a garage in the United States who had written what looked like very good CD-ROM programmes and was willing to sell in exchange for Nimbus clearing his credit card bills of $60,000,' Emil realised that 'software was a different animal and had to be sold differently.' In the end he settled for commissioned software only, working hand in hand with major clients to solve the problems encountered in large contracts. For Emil, software was a means to an end, the end being to secure lucrative CD-ROM pressing contracts for Nimbus. Today these can involve literally millions of discs. In this he was warmly supported by Gerald who 'had a great way of taking the available data and making extremely logical decisions, which made him so easy to work with. He was always there, was fast and responsive. We ended up with 75 per cent market share in the UK because we were everywhere and helping everyone and doing everything at very considerable expense in marketing. To start with we made a huge loss.'

Luckily the development coincided with Nimbus having the profit-generated cash to back it. Nimbus also made the point of demonstrating to clients that CD-ROM was not just an appendage of the CD music pressing side but an autonomous operation, housed in its own separate building. Very large contracts in the UK were won with firms such as Abbey National, British Telecom and Rover and Nimbus Manufacturing still holds 65 per cent of the UK CD-ROM market and CD-ROM accounts for 10 per cent of its pressings. As in other branches of CD, price competition is fierce for the multi-million disc contracts to be picked up throughout Europe. Nimbus's dominant market share in the UK and substantial presence in Europe was won by their emphasis on service to the client. The profitability of Nimbus's UK CD-ROM activities relies as much on this element as on the fact that, in relation to its size, the UK is one of the most highly developed CD-ROM markets in the world. By contrast, Nimbus's CD-ROM operation in the USA from 1987 onwards chose to be software-led, with expensive software packages and top-heavy administration and until it changed tack under a new manager in 1992 incurred heavy losses as a result. However, the importance of the CD-ROM development in the UK was not just its substantial contribution to profit but that it proved to be a significant additional attraction for investment at the very moment when Nimbus's survival depended on securing fresh finance.

Numa after the deal with British Telecom to put all British telephone directories onto a single CD-ROM.

121

CHAPTER SEVEN

Nimbus, as a purely recording company, was inevitably slow to take off, doing no trade at all until its third year when turnover reached the dizzy heights of £163. Three years later, in 1977, it was still only £1,375. Losses had accumulated steadily from just over £5,000 in 1972 to almost £107,000, with a corresponding deficit on the balance sheet of just over £64,000 in 1977, the year following the move to Wyastone Leys and from then on the whole financial process began to accelerate rapidly. In 1978, turnover rose to £92,000, more than doubling the next year to over £190,000, reaching £280,000 in 1980, £384,000 in 1981 and £534,000 in 1982. While 1978 saw still increasing losses, almost £114,000, by 1979 this had turned to a profit of nearly £52,000 and although profits fell in the next three years (£23,000, £6,000 and £4,000 respectively) as the Founders invested in new developments, the pattern had changed very significantly. The year of commitment to CD saw a very substantial re-financing, already referred to, and a healthy-looking balance sheet with shareholders' funds nearing the half million mark.

The pressings side of the business, subdivided into Nimbus Pressings, showed a similar pattern with losses mounting to a peak of £82,000 in 1980, falling to £13,000 the following year and turning round into a profit of over £11,000 in 1982. The developments on the pressing side were funded largely by loans from Nimbus Records which reached a peak of £236,000 in 1980.

In 1983, as part of the general tidying up and re-financing package, Handsworth Wood Properties, the Hermes Development Company and Nimbus Records Pressings were consolidated into the Nimbus Records group by a series of share swaps. By 5 September 1983 the company had an ordinary share capital of £366,074, there were £123,674 cumulative redeemable £1 preference shares and £66,000 cumulative participating ordinary preference shares, together with a £116,000 loan from the Midland Bank and a £300,000 overdraft facility from Lloyds Bank. Significantly, now that the banks were seriously involved, Nimbus had to adopt a more formal approach to business than before and, for example, instituted service agreements for key personnel (the Founders, Jonathan, Adrian and Mike Lee) for the first time.

By January 1984 it was clear that additional finance of at least half a million pounds would be needed by early 1985 to fund the CD expansion. Turnover topped half a million again in 1983 and 1984, and by 1985 had jumped to almost £1.8 million. Not unexpectedly, with the expansion into CD, losses of £115,000 and £168,000 were incurred in 1984 and 1985.

Already, on 1 March 1984, the Nimbus Board had minuted that there would be no competition in the UK for at least twelve months. In the event almost two years were to elapse from that first production run in August 1984 before Britain's second CD factory opened – and that was Nimbus's own at Cwmbran, a few weeks before EMI opened up at Swindon. No wonder Nimbus was confident in the spring of 1984 that the two banks which had cautiously supported their venture into CD manufacture would help them find not only the £100,000 by which

Jim Drennan of Midland Bank Industrial Finance, subsequently Chairman, with Numa in the newly constructed factory.

they had already exceeded their planned expenditure, but the additional half million which would be required to see through the next stage of the development. Lloyds, which had provided an overdraft for the new plant, had been Nimbus's bankers, even if rather parsimonious ones, since its first Birmingham days and Midland, which was now the largest shareholder in Nimbus having taken 27.5 per cent of the shares in return for its total investment of £490,000, had appointed a non-executive director, Jim Drennan, to the Nimbus Board. In December 1985 Nimbus poached Drennan to take the role of Chairman (Numa became President). Additionally, a grant of £50,000 was received in June from the Department of Trade and Industry which also helped a little with cash-flow problems. Within two years this confidence in Nimbus's future prospects had been amply justified.

The *annus mirabilis* was undoubtedly 1986 with a fivefold increase in turnover to £9.3 million and a profit before tax of almost £2¼ million (£1.5 million after tax). Shareholders' funds stood at a healthy £2.3 million with capital expenditure of over £4½ million.

This phenomenal period of growth culminated in April 1987 with the bestowing on the company of the Queen's Award for Technological Achievement. As Edward Greenfield wrote in the *Guardian* at the time:

> The Queen's Award ... has just been awarded, amid well-deserved official fanfares, to what always used to be described as a small company, Nimbus Records of Wyastone Leys, Monmouth.
>
> With extraordinary enterprise, courage and technical skill it was Nimbus and not any of the big companies that three years ago produced the first British-made compact discs, with only the big Polygram plant in Hanover competing at the time in Europe.
>
> Nimbus is now producing 20 million CDs a year, with exports valued in millions. What has tended to be forgotten in all this expansion is what first established Nimbus's reputation: its recordings.

But for two or three years at least the good times were over. Although turnover rose to almost £23 million for the fifteen months ending 31 December 1987 (the significance of the fifteen months will become apparent later), operating profit margins were down from over 27 per cent to under 7 per cent – largely as a result of a collapse in the ex-factory price of CDs. There was a staggering 50 per cent increase in

124

the general costs of the business due to rapid expansion at Cwmbran and the start-up in America which also accounted for a jump in capital expenditure to just under £12.2 million. From being highly profitable the company incurred a loss of £436,000 in this period and could certainly not have survived without a massive injection of external finance which its disapproving bankers were no longer willing to provide.

Another way to measure both the rate of growth at Nimbus and at least the partial source of its problems is to look at the number of employees. Until the move to Wyastone Leys, apart from the directors themselves, there were never more than one or two others involved until 1977 when LP pressing began. Even then, there were barely more than half a dozen employees until the development work on CDs started in 1982. In 1983 twenty-one people were employed and in 1984, twenty-eight. In 1985 the number of employees doubled and in 1986 was four times higher than the previous year. This had more than doubled again to 460 in 1987 and a wages and salaries bill of £162,000 in 1983 had become one of £7.8 million that year.

In 1983 the three family directors between them had drawn only £21,000. By the end of 1987, with the various external appointments, there were eleven directors costing the company £260,000 a year. By mid-1987 a combination of tough competition and the consequent introduction of new labour-saving technology entailed laying off 110 people. In September that year Nimbus decided it had to bring all UK production under the single roof of the more modern plant at Cwmbran and, despite the efforts made to redeploy them, almost the entire Monmouth workforce, 140 people, was made redundant in October.

For the past twenty years Nimbus has been like a Hawaiian surf-rider speeding exhilaratingly but dangerously forward under the curling lip of a great comber of financial disaster. A sixth sense of anticipation has kept it precariously balanced and ever accelerating towards a successful beaching. In the CD business manufacturing supply and demand have been like unsynchronised sine waves that coincide only briefly as they cross each other.

The demand for CDs* grew from 20 million in 1984 to 140 million in 1986 and to 1,163 million in 1992, the last year for which figures are available at the time of writing.

*Owing to differences in the way singles have been enumerated it is necessary to omit them from figures for all three audio media. This does not effect relative trends significantly.

Even in 1986 CD output had barely attained a fifth of LP sales and a seventh of the dominant cassette format. CDs were then taking some 8 per cent of the audio market. Three years later they passed LPs and were getting on for half cassette sales. Another three years and CDs had overtaken cassettes in Europe and America, but although CDs held some 35 per cent of the world market with 1,163 million discs, an explosion of demand for cassettes in Russia and China (350 million between them) and the Third World put cassettes, with 1,603 million units well ahead again – for the time being at least, until the new markets switch to CD, as China is already doing with Nimbus's help. The unfortunate long playing record languishes now at 9 per cent, which had been the level of CDs a bare seven years earlier. The equally inevitable, if much regretted, demise of Nimbus's 'own label' LPs is mapped out in a series of memos.

The factory coming up to full production of 15,000 discs per day.

NEWSLETTER

Nimbus Records announce 2nd Compact Disc Factory

Nimbus–a greater CD production

The planning of Nimbus' second CD manufacturing plant is now at an advanced stage. It will be built alongside the first CD Factory on the company's Monmouth Estate by incorporating and extending an existing complex of buildings.

The new facility is expected to be ready for production to start in the summer of 1986, and with an additional twenty presses this will raise the total production on the Monmouth site to twenty-five million compact discs a year.

Explosion of demand

The present CD plant began twenty-four hour continuous running in July. The introduction of non-stop production has come earlier than Nimbus envisaged, but it has been necessitated by the explosion of demand for CDs worldwide.

Nimbus will be celebrating its first year of CD production on September 13th, and by the end of October expects to have reached the full production capacity of six million discs a year.

view to stable block

An artist's impression showing the proposed second CD Manufacturing Plant looking towards the stable block.

L-R Gerald Reynolds, Dr Jonathan Halliday, HRH the Duke of Kent, Michael Reynolds, Mike Lee and Count Labinsky

Private visit of HRH the Duke of Kent

The Directors of Nimbus were pleased to show His Royal Highness The Duke of Kent the Compact Disc Plant and Recording Studios on the Monmouth Estate during an informal visit on the 3rd of July.

Nimbus to end LP issues

From August 1985 new issues from Nimbus' own label of classical recordings will be on compact disc only. The superiority of CD as a listening medium and an abrupt loss of interest in LPs are the main elements in hastening the end of simultaneous new releases.

Nimbus is experiencing an unprecedented high level of demand for its own recordings on CD, whereas, worldwide sales of Nimbus LPs in the last six months now represent only a fraction of total sales, with some major overseas territories ceasing to trade in LP issues completely.

The high quality LP custom pressing service which Nimbus has offered over the past eight years is however still in demand and there are no immediate plans to close the Analogue Factory.

A 1985 press release.

Gerald (*left*) and the Duke of Kent on a private visit on 3 July 1985.

In January 1985 the Board noted that the LP side of the business had made almost exactly twice as much money during the month as had CDs; £130,000 compared to £67,000. Nimbus announced: 'From August 1985 new issues from Nimbus's own label of classical recordings will be on compact disc only.'

'Nimbus will be celebrating its first year of CD production on September 13th.' And in the October News Letter they stated: 'The high quality LP custom pressing service which Nimbus has offered over the past eight years is however still in demand and there are no immediate plans to close the analogue factory.'

By March 1986 the Board decided to close the LP side completely and transfer the remaining employees to CD, and in April that year the last LP to date was pressed at Nimbus – for the time being at least.

It is an interesting indicator of the loyalty the family, and Numa in particular, is able to command that, albeit in widely different roles today, from gardener to receptionist, development managers to quality inspectors, virtually all the members of that small early LP pressing team are still with the company.

This astonishing growth in the new medium would seem to indicate

128

The staff at the changeover period from LP to CD production.

a potential gold mine for all those concerned in the manufacture and sale of CDs but a look at the increased *value* in CD sales over the same seven-year period shows this to be far from the case. Whereas the 285 per cent increase in volume in the three years of CD production from 1986 produced a 220 per cent increase in value to $7,187 million, the 117 per cent growth in the next three years yielded only a 44 per cent increase in value by 1992. Although CD volumes had risen nearly eightfold in the preceding seven years, revenue had little more than trebled.*

The reason for this is not hard to see when the demand pattern is matched to that of manufacturing capacity. From 1984 to 1986 demand comfortably exceeded supply and Nimbus, as the sole UK manufacturer until mid-1986, was the principal beneficiary of this state of affairs. In May 1985 the Nimbus Board was minuting that they could take no more orders until the spring of 1986, shortly before the company's new 40,000 sq ft factory and office at Cwmbran, some twenty-five miles from Monmouth, was expected to be open.

*see Appendix A

Cwmbran, the new factory.

Towards the end of 1986 it was apparent that the balance between demand and supply was about to be sharply reversed. Not only were new independent plants about to come on stream but a number of major record labels, such as EMI, were due to open their own in-house production lines. By 1988 almost two-thirds of European CD pressing was in-house, and although Nimbus continued to be the major player in the 'free' sector, its market share fell from 45 per cent in 1988 to 21 per cent in 1992. In the early days, Nimbus pressings from the UK were being supplied to many countries, including America, but by the early 1990s its customer base was virtually confined to the UK.

In 1984–85 all the major labels, even those like RCA that had access to group-owned pressing facilities, had been pressing with Nimbus either on an ad hoc basis or under contract. The most important of these contractual deals from Nimbus's point of view was that struck with Virgin in October 1986. Virgin was to have most favoured nation status in return for bringing its work to Nimbus and a minimum 400,000 CDs a month. It also invested in Nimbus by taking up one million pounds of £1 non-voting redeemable preference shares at 10 per cent. Within a couple of years Virgin was falling so far short of its minimum commitment that Nimbus was even contemplating legal action. However,

CD injection moulding machines at the Cwmbran factory.

because Virgin in turn had been flexible about interest payments and redemption of shares, this was fortunately never pursued.

What the full order book of 1985–86 had done was to give Nimbus the confidence to go ahead with the opening of the new factory at Cwmbran built with the aid of a Welsh Development Authority grant of £1.5 million phased over three years, but otherwise financed entirely out of profits. Understandably perhaps, the enormous success of the early CD years generated a certain euphoria at Nimbus. With the decision to expand into the largest potential market of all, the United States, by building a plant there, Nimbus was incurring risks of a new order of magnitude. The American venture perfectly illustrates the ingredients, the strengths and weaknesses of Nimbus as a business, combining as it did an astonishingly perceptive vision of where future opportunities lay with a breathtaking readiness to undertake very high financial and commercial risks; ends were clearly perceived but means were sometimes rather blithely assumed to be forthcoming. Nevertheless, the US venture not only became cash positive within three years – quick for an overseas investment in America – but was an important element in attracting the interest of Robert Maxwell.

Readers who have followed the Nimbus story thus far will not be surprised to learn that, while the decision to go to America was a waking vision appropriately discussed by the Board, the location of the plant itself was the realisation of one of Numa's vivid dreams. One day in the early summer of 1986 Numa came down for breakfast to announce that he had 'seen' the location of their new factory in a dream. 'I saw a clear vision of green luscious grass, a range of mountains, a lake. I said to Jim Drennan, then Nimbus Chairman, "it's in Virginia, go and find it, that's where we have to go and build our factory." I said "go immediately." He asked "what part of Virginia?" I said "I don't know, but there is a range of mountains." ' A more than a little sceptical Jim Drennan was dispatched at once to America to find such a location and to his credit, and everyone's astonishment except Numa's, he had done just that within a matter of weeks at Charlottesville in Virginia.

The American factory in the shadow of the Blue Ridge Mountains in Virginia.

Guildford Farm in Greene County, Virginia was more a manor house than a farmhouse and was built by the Early family in 1820 – at the same time as Wyastone Leys itself. Its colonial-style exterior and beautiful dark wood panelling at once appealed aesthetically to the Nimbus family and, more importantly, matched very closely Numa's vision. The 264 acre estate was bounded by a mountain trout stream, the poetically named Swift Run River, with enticing sandy beaches and deep pools for trout and swimmers alike. The long driveway was flanked by trees, a pretty, small lake and a riding ring. The house looked out across rolling grassland to the Blue Ridge Mountains. Its peacefulness was one of its main attractions, the only sounds being the squeaking of the buzzards and kites. No wonder the family told the *Richmond Leader*, 'Guildford Farm will be a home for us [because] we live and work in the same place. We would not travel thousands of miles to set up a plant in an industrial park.'

Numa exploring new technology in Virginia.

Nimbus was an equally attractive proposition to the people of Greene County, which had only sixteen manufacturing jobs, for it was about to bring another 260. Within six weeks an entire planning process, including a public inquiry, had been completed, which would have taken twice as many months in England. Gerald was delighted with the American 'can do' approach.

The contract was completed in November 1986 and shortly before Christmas the family decided to visit their 'second home'. After several delays en route they were finally flown into Charlottesville, but not until Numa had threatened to wreck a diverted plane with his umbrella when the airline tried to make them travel the last sixty-mile lap in a truck with the 'damned crustaceans – lobsters to you ignoramuses' with which they had flown so far. It 'never, well hardly ever' snows in Virginia, but it did that Christmas, three feet of it, and the family was quite willingly compelled to spend Christmas in their new home. Despite the wintry start, the adjacent new factory had been completed by the following September.

The problem was that this £10 million expansion was bitterly opposed by Nimbus's largest shareholder, Midland Bank, who declined to finance it despite Nimbus's punctual repayment of all the bank's loans. Midland Bank's discontent ran so deep that by the end of the year the bank was making serious noises about freezing its financial support altogether and in March 1987 its former representative on the Nimbus Board, the record company's chairman, Jim Drennan, resigned. In July 1986 Richard Branson, who was about to commit Virgin to press its CDs with Nimbus, wanted to buy out Midland's 27½ per cent stake, but the family, and Jonathan in particular, were hostile to the offer and at Jonathan's suggestion asked for £15–£18 million. This was overpriced, of course, but still indicative of Nimbus's burgeoning value at that time. Not surprisingly, nothing more was heard from Virgin after that but twelve months later Nimbus may have been wondering how wise their rejection of Branson's offer had been.

At the same time profits from CD pressing were rapidly diminishing in the face of much stronger competition and indeed a ruthless price war as some of the 'big boys' began to make silly offers to the record companies in an attempt to drive rivals out of business. In autumn 1988, the busiest time of year for CD pressing, Polygram in Hanover, for example, offered to press for ten pence a disc less than the lowest alternative quote any record label had been offered, *whatever* that might be. The Koreans were making similar unrealistic bargain offers. Nimbus had been comfortably able to charge £1.85 a disc from 1984 to almost the end of 1986. Between January 1987 and December 1988 alone, prices fell by 60 per cent and by 1992 this price had steadily fallen to between seventy and eighty pence.

Profit margins were sustained to a greater extent at Nimbus, whose prices were 10–15 per cent higher than those of their competitors. It was Nimbus's contention that superior quality and service enabled it to charge higher prices, and the Peat Marwick review of the company previously referred to did attribute the price differentials to customer loyalty. Certainly all the second division music majors and the largest independents – Virgin, Telstar, Island, Pickwick, Chrysalis, A & M, K-Tel, etc. – relied heavily on the Cwmbran plant (and most of them still do), and even the giants such as EMI and RCA would use it to cover hiccups in-house. Now the original wide gap between Nimbus's high standards and the industry average had narrowed considerably and high quality was now the *sine qua non* for any manufacturer. Competition became focused on price and quality of service.

Pressing success was also thought to be in part due to the 'spin-off' from the reputation and newsworthiness of the record label. The official line was that: 'As the company has sought to expand its manufacturing operations, it has been greatly supported by having in its own label, a flagship visible to the industry and domestic market which links corporate identity with innovation, quality and reliability.'

One former senior executive challenges this view. 'It was always believed within the business that the record label had a considerable effect on our ability to sell custom pressing to other record labels but, in my opinion, that wasn't true, but it did give us an inside knowledge to what is needed in a record label. A great many customers within the pop world didn't even know we *had* a record label, anyway.'

Whatever the reasons, the facts are not in dispute. Although by 1988 Nimbus was still number nine in the world's CD pressing league (higher if in-house pressings are excluded) with 19 million CDs of the 451 million produced by the top nine companies, by mid-1987 it was in deep financial trouble.

It is reasonable to ask how Nimbus got into such a mess in so short a time when its shrewd and intelligent Founders were keenly aware of the new, bitterly competitive climate in which they had to operate. Ian Webb put it kindly in his book, *The Quest for Quality*: 'If Nimbus's performance in its area of operation is universally accepted as excellent, its attitude towards formalised business-planning is, to say the least, haphazard . . . decisions tend to be taken informally at lunch or over dinner. This is a company that has no financial director.'[1]

The magazine *Financial Decisions* for November 1987 took a similar view:

> Nimbus is a small technology-driven company with excellent credentials and a proven track record. In the difficult times ahead, a clue to its weakness may lie in the words of its non-executive director, Peter Laister. Asked about the company's internal structuring, he says, 'I think the answer is, it is different. But it works. It is certainly different to a large organisation.
>
> 'I think there is a lot more personal individualism in the company and a lot more individual commitment, which works. I think they [Labinsky and the Reynolds brothers] do an extremely professional job of running the company. In growing so quickly, they haven't always done enormous, great big planning exercises or reviews.
>
> 'They've looked at the market and they've said, "Well, we need to do this," and they've done it. Now, as they are growing in size, of course, they are having to adopt more of the practices of a larger business.'

With its banks unwilling to help, Nimbus was compelled to seek new sources of finance to pay for the US expansion to which it was now contractually committed, and that meant a higher profile company with high profile directors. A near neighbour of the family at the time was Sir John Harvey-Jones who lived near Ross on Wye, a dozen miles away. Having retired as Chairman of ICI, he was sufficiently intrigued to accept an invitation to join the Nimbus Board, introducing in his wake a few weeks later, Peter Laister who had recently retired as Chairman of Thorn-EMI and was advising Robert Maxwell on new media matters as a member of the Board of Maxwell Communications Corporation. Mixing Numa and his Nimbus Board with Harvey-Jones was like mixing sodium and water, or, as Sir John put it more restrainedly in a note to me in which he declined to comment in detail on his brief relationship with Nimbus: 'I would not wish to do anything which could in any way harm, or reflect badly on the company and I do wish it every success. But suffice it to say that our styles of working really did not gel.'[2]

136

The crunch came when Sir John set up what he thought was a suitable deal with City financiers for the funding and restructuring of the company only to have it rejected by the Founders. Unfortunately they were unable to contact Harvey-Jones to inform him before he heard from the bankers in question and handed in his resignation in person with an impassioned outburst. Harvey-Jones, whose arrivals at Nimbus Board meetings the receptionist delightfully described as 'a whirlwind followed by a flowing tie', whirled out of the critical meeting hotly pursued by Numa, who the same eyewitness describes as 'doing a swan dive down the stairs in Sir John's wake.' Harvey-Jones helped restore Numa to his feet but the precarious equilibrium of the relationship had been more permanently upset and he did not return. This was perhaps less surprising than that the family should have been 'shocked by his unexpected resignation.'

Harvey-Jones told Peter Laister, who had only just accepted a directorship but not yet attended his first board meeting, what had transpired, presuming that he, too, would wish to resign. However, Peter felt that this would not be an honourable thing to do, particularly at a time when the resignation of another distinguished non-executive director might well put paid to all hope of Nimbus raising the money it now urgently needed to survive. Peter not only remained on the Board, but within days of his appointment found himself addressing the Press on the company's behalf, Numa being in no state of health to do so, and the rest of the family feeling themselves less well-qualified. A degree of calm and confidence was restored and shortly afterwards, because Numa felt Nimbus needed a high profile Chairman while seeking additional financing, Peter took over that role and Numa once again became President. Towards the end of 1987 Peter headed up the drive to re-finance the company at the start of what he describes as 'the most exacting and time-consuming part-time directorship I have ever held.'

If these turbulent events were primarily significant in terms of the financial survival of Nimbus, we must never lose sight of the fact that the Nimbus family made money to make music, not music to make money, but the change in the size and nature of the organisation inevitably also meant a change in its relationship with its artists.

CHAPTER EIGHT

The transition to CD and the consequent great change in the scale of operations was bound to have a considerable influence on the family's relations with Nimbus artists. The Founders soon had virtually nothing to do with the practicalities of the music-making because they were far too busy running what was becoming an increasingly complex business. They were experiencing that traumatic and extremely difficult transition from a small family business to a much larger one that would usually have been run on corporate lines, but at Nimbus was not. Although Adrian and Nina took on the musical role very effectively in the early years of CD, Nina returned to the world of vocal coaching by taking up a senior post with the Royal Opera House in 1987 and Adrian became more and more involved in marketing and the international side of the business. Excellent music producers and executives were appointed, such as Alan Wiltshire and Sylvia Strange, but the performers were now two steps removed from the trio at the heart of the Nimbus ethos. As Jonathan said, 'going to CD changed the style of Nimbus. It was relatively relaxed in the first years, there was time to have tea on the grass and to spend a lot of time with each of the recording artists who came to Wyastone Leys so that each recording was an event in its own right. It involved everyone. But once we were producing more than 50 CDs a year for our own record label this was not possible.'

It was thus increasingly difficult, with so many newly contracted performers, to maintain the three basic rules of Nimbus recording – natural sound, the single take and minimal editing. The changing relationship between Nimbus and the great violinist Oscar Shumsky, as revealed in their correspondence, illustrates these difficulties well, besides encapsulating more eloquently than other artists were able to do the arguments against the Nimbus approach.

Oscar Shumsky, born of Russian parents in Philadelphia, was already, at the age of seven, playing concerti with the Philadelphia Orchestra. Its conductor, Leopold Stokowski, described him 'as the most astounding

Oscar Shumsky, Russian-American violinist.

genius I ever heard.' He was the youngest student ever accepted by Leopold Auer, a protégé of Fritz Kreisler, and he became, in David Oistrakh's view, 'one of the world's greatest violinists.' However, his talents were soon largely diverted to conducting and teaching at Juilliard, the Curtis Institute and Yale, among other places. He became what the *Milwaukee Sentinel* described as 'another grey eminence whose gifts exceeded his stardom.' It is fair to say that the rediscovery of Shumsky as a player of genius in his later years was partly due to the recordings Nimbus made with him, the Mozart violin concerti in D and A and the six violin sonatas of Ysaÿe.

When the Ysaÿe was released in 1983 one reviewer wrote: 'Nor should string lovers miss another Nimbus special (2137) this time Ysaÿe's six solo violin sonatas, played magnificently and very musically by the Russian violinist and teacher Oscar Shumsky. This is a Nimbus scoop, recorded with tremendous care and integrity, while the performances are among the handful of records I will often dip into and often enjoy.'[1]

Adrian Farmer went for the first time to hear Shumsky play early in September 1981 and wrote to his agent a few days later.

> As discussed both with yourself and Eric Shumsky [Oscar's son] I enclose both details of a proposed contract and some recordings.
>
> First let me say again how much I enjoyed Mr Shumsky's playing, it was a great joy to hear music being made rather than the chromium-plated nonsense which so often passes for performance at the moment.
>
> The catalogue is not large since we are only interested in performances and performers who have something of their own to contribute. Mr Shumsky is without doubt such an artist and I would welcome a collaboration with him. The recordings which you kindly sent to me are a travesty of the unique sound and wide dynamic range of Mr Shumsky's playing and it is important that disservice be corrected.[2]

Negotiations took a year, but on 18 October 1982 Shumsky was contracted to Nimbus and he clearly enjoyed the forging of the good relationship with Adrian Farmer which followed the recording of the Mozart concerti.

In the same month Shumsky was explaining to his putative accompanist for a Nimbus recording of the Brahms Hungarian Dances, Professor Frank Maus, how Nimbus went about a recording and was full of praise for the single microphone technique and the minimal 'interference' by the engineer. But this was, to a degree, already lip service for Shumsky was clearly egotistically concerned to make sure Maus did not overdo the piano part which, in the Joachim version to be recorded, can overshadow the violin. Since Nimbus left the responsibility for balance to the players nothing could be done to re-emphasise the violin part if it were swamped during the recording and, in an earlier letter to Adrian[3], fulsome with praise and pleasant reminiscence of their first meetings, he had already hinted that Maus might need to be reined in because of the brightness and volume of his playing.

Signs of strain began to show in September 1983 and although the

Oscar Shumsky recording a Mozart violin concerto. Jan Pascal Tortelier conducts the Scottish Chamber Orchestra. Producer Adrian Farmer is distinguishable by his lack of instrument.

exchange of letters on Shumsky's proposed recording of the Brahms Violin Concerto is friendly enough it contains his first fairly tentative challenge to Nimbus's technical approach, on this occasion the question of the single microphone technique in an orchestral context.

The work now under consideration was the Brahms Violin Concerto in which again Shumsky was worried that the violin part might be lost playing against an over-enthusiastic orchestra given its head by a conductor seduced by the richness and momentum of the orchestral score. He flattered Adrian, for whose high standards and 'bat's ears' he had already expressed his admiration, in the hope that this would induce him to give way on the principle of not 'miking up' the solo instrument since Shumsky himself in this instance shared the view that the orchestra should not be 'shushed'.[4] Adrian, of course, was not seduced.

At about this time a casual comment by Shumsky's agent Richard Apley of Ibbs & Tillett, who happened to be sitting next to Adrian on a plane flight, made Nimbus suspicious that Shumsky might be thinking of recording with another company without letting them know. While he was not precluded from doing this by his contract, clearly conflicting recordings of identical or similar repertoire could have had an adverse impact on Nimbus. This suspicion seems to have been voiced rather forcefully to Shumsky who wrote twice, on 31 October and 10 November directly to Numa to try to mollify him, but without yielding his ground. The great violinist was, however, genuinely concerned about the effect such disputes were having, not only on his own time and energy (he was preparing for an important Elgar concerto live performance) but on Numa's health and he and his wife, Louise, a great favourite of Numa's, continued to express their affection and respect.[5]

In a side swipe at Adrian, Shumsky implied that the problems were all no more than misunderstandings which arose from the younger man's failure to communicate (a not entirely groundless complaint!) and his poor judgment – an accusation subsequent events proved to be much less well founded. Nevertheless, he acquiesced in the proposal that in future he stick to the solo violin or violin/piano repertoire in his future recordings for Nimbus, although he continued to presume that a proposed recording of the Bach concerti with the Scottish Chamber Orchestra would take place, a presumption in which he was not to be disappointed.[6]

Numa was partially, but only partially, placated and his response was to suggest again that they confine themselves to non-orchestral works.

> Having received both your letters I take note of what you say about poor judgement. I can only tell you that I do not in all sincerity feel that there was any poor judgement on our part. I feel pretty vehement about the whole episode, and saddened by the nonsenses that have occurred and interrupted what promised to be a very fruitful relationship.
>
> Out of real frustration I suggested, as an act of desperation, and possibly bad temper, that we limit our work in the future to solo fiddle and piano accompanied work.
>
> There is much more that I could say, concerning the wisdom of playing with musical inferiors, etc. etc., but why, why, why should I bother? It sometimes seems that I must always be the proverbial drop of water on the stone.
>
> Were you not the great artist that you are I know perfectly well what I would have done: to have sent the whole thing to blazes; to have said 'no more'. But for the great affection that I have for you and especially for Louise I would most certainly have done that.
>
> I count loyalty to be absolutely paramount, and without it there is, I assure you my dear Oscar, no possibility of any continuing relationship between anybody.
>
> I remain your sincere friend.[7]

Then, in typical Numa style, he made an emollient telephone call on New Year's Day which seems to have had the desired effect to judge from a letter Shumsky wrote on 6 January[8] in which he was particularly excited by the prospect Numa had just held out to him of recording the Elgar concerto with the Royal Philharmonic – though nothing eventually came of that idea.

Early in 1984 (the letter is undated) Shumsky challenged the second Nimbus rule – minimal editing. He had been listening to the tapes of the Brahms Hungarian Dances and was evidently unhappy about the unedited results.[9] He argued that no musician ever gives a flawless, mistake-free performance and that it would, therefore, be quite legitimate to edit out mistakes from a recording in which they would be perpetuated every time the record-buyer played his performance. He argued that while the audience at a live concert might pass forgivingly over a mistake, the auditor of a recording would be reminded irritatingly of it every time he played his record. This was both a little obtuse and unrealistic since for all but a few professional musicians, the interval between playing of any one recording tend to be fairly lengthy. Moreover, he had obviously either missed or deliberately ignored the Nimbus argument that such editing destroys the spirit of the performance and that in correcting wrong notes, to excess at least, the soul is cut from the performance also.

Shumsky, in asking for editing, argued that works in which his performance had been extensively edited were none the worse for that and concluded by protesting (again with some justice) that he should not have to worry about money matters but be left free to concentrate on music-making. As we shall see later, Nimbus stuck to its belief that you either issue a performance largely as it was given or scrap it altogether.

On 22 March Shumsky wrote complaining that he had no written reply to his letters, a fairly common complaint from Nimbus artists, particularly once the small management team faced the pressures of an explosively expanding CD business, and in any case was disinclined to engage in contention, something they often avoided by ignoring it until it went away. Shumsky was not unsympathetic to the stresses being experienced by the Nimbus family and, with Louise, still expressed genuine concern for their welfare.[10] He wrote again on 5 April to complain more heatedly, and again with some justice, that he had not been accorded the courtesy of even a one line reply.[11]

Ironically, Adrian had at last written to him that very day, a letter which in effect terminated the contract with Nimbus.

You will find, as we have done, in listening to the Bach, that some aspects of the performance, mainly intonation problems and the failure of yourself and the orchestra to move in the same direction, are rather distressing. You will imagine that it is possible for me to correct these things by editing, but, as you said in your first letter to me, we do not, indeed, see eye-to-eye on this point and I will not, repeat not, for any artist, bend the rules on this subject, nor do I take well the suggestion that since you got away with it on your (other) recordings you will get away with it on your Nimbus recordings.

When I first heard you play in London I was very, very truly 'knocked out' by your playing, your intensity, your ability to be unaffected by the praise or blame of your audience and critics. It is my sad experience that, for whatever reason, I have watched this very special strength leak away in the pursuit of fame.

You will not agree with this, I do not expect you to, but this

The Maxwell deal in a very brief lull in between storms that had already begun. *Left to right*: Kevin Maxwell, Mike Lee, Dr Jonathan Halliday, Michael Reynolds, Gerald Reynolds, Adrian Farmer, Stuart Garman (Nimbus Company Secretary) *Front*: Numa, Robert Maxwell.

The four
seasons at
Wyastone
Leys.

William Boughton conducting the English Symphony Orchestra in the Symphony Hall, Birmingham.

The Haydnsaal at the Esterhazy Palace, Eisenstadt, Austria. Adam Fischer conducting the Austro-Hungarian Haydn Orchestra who, under exclusive contract to Nimbus, are recording all the Haydn symphonies, a project which should be completed in the year 2000.

Roger Jones (engineer), Gerald and Jonathan outside Buckingham Palace after receiving The Queen's Award for Technological Achievement, 1987.

Gerald Reynolds – the photographer caught!

Dr Jonathan Halliday: scientist, businessman, lawyer.

Numa relaxed and in charge.

is the reason why I feel our association cannot continue.

You made two marvellous recordings for us, Ysaÿe and Mozart, for which I will always be grateful. I hope that you will go on to make more such recordings which will justify the legend that goes with your name and I hope that by releasing you from any obligation to us, you will, in the performing time left you, find a company better suited to your wishes.

Numa asks me to thank you, and especially to thank Louise, for the good that we have shared and tell you that he is well, but not as well as he would like to be. The CD project, as you perhaps will imagine, has drained all our energies since it is a most colossal undertaking for a group, a very small group of already very tired men who, in order to safeguard what little grace we can keep, have to remove from their lives any activity, business or personal, which has ceased to be a joy to us.[12]

As Adrian put it to the manager of the Scottish Chamber Orchestra the next day in a letter cancelling the proposed recording, 'there are certain matters of artistic policy which have not been settled between the artist concerned and ourselves.'

On 18 April, Shumsky replied indignantly to Adrian's letter convinced that he was being deliberately insulted. Despite disclaiming any intention of being drawn into what he regarded as a slanging match he penned a considerable line in insults himself and concluded with an extravagant expression of pleasure in severing of his relationship with Nimbus.[13]

Adrian was determined to have the last word.

It is not well done for you to express such hearty relief at the severance of our relationship, it is a hollow trumpeting and far below the level of awareness you should ask of yourself. The path of acceptance and understanding of why we have reached this point can only be blocked for you by your outburst of vitriol – which is most misplaced and unacceptable.

You could, with simple statement, have said that you believed me to be wrong and reasoned this without abuse. But you did not, and the vile manner of your answer reveals the inherent pettiness of your nature – which you have left very late to overcome.

Once again I wish you a contented and fruitful continuation for your undoubted talent. Do not think that I do this in order to prove that I am a better man than you and possessed of a saint-like patience, for I am not. Indeed, I am maddened by your bullish expectation that you will have everything your way and in your time, and in so thinking have

145

ruined prospects of wonderful music-making. But, I am not unaware, even in my anger, that you are a considerable artist and I must and will always continue to pay homage to those gifts the fates have given you – even when you do not.[14]

And there, unhappily for quality music-making, the relationship ended, apart from a sad postscript half a dozen years later about the Brahms Hungarian Dances which Nimbus had decided not to issue but of which they still had all the various takes. Richard Apley wrote to Adrian: 'Oscar Shumsky has asked me to approach you, to see if Nimbus would consider selling him the tapes of the Brahms Hungarian Dances. I know that you had grave reservations about various things.'[15]

Nimbus granted the sale: 'In consideration of the attached cheque for the amount of TWO THOUSAND FIVE HUNDRED pounds . . . NIMBUS RECORDS LTD. . . . cedes all rights, claims and ownership of the Master Tapes of "21 HUNGARIAN DANCES FOR VIOLIN AND PIANO BY BRAHMS-JOACHIM" to OSCAR SHUMSKY.'[16]

Another great older artist whom Nimbus virtually rescued from oblivion and with whom also they eventually quarrelled was Shura Cherkassky, but while Shumsky at least had a case to argue artistically, Cherkassky really had no grounds for his complaints.

Cherkassky was almost seventy when he signed up with Nimbus in the autumn of 1980 to begin a series of recordings about which the critics were to rave on both sides of the Atlantic. In fact, despite a concert debut aged twelve in a command performance for President Harding, Cherkassky did not enjoy such a good reputation in his native USA as he did in Europe (and in London in particular, where he now lives), until the Nimbus releases of which the *Baltimore Sun* wrote: 'Cherkassky's career blossomed in Europe in the 1940s but never reached the same hue in this country. Then a few years ago, a British recording label asked Cherkassky to record. The result so far is five compact discs that are selling rapidly and rejuvenating Cherkassky's career in the United States.'[17]

His first agent, Andrew Green of Ibbs & Tillet, was repeatedly appreciative on Cherkassky's behalf for Nimbus's support: '. . . we would always want you to have first choice [of repertoire] because of your particular commitment to him.'[18] 'It is marvellous to see that your commitment to Shura is so strong.'[19] '. . . this series of recordings amounts to the largest recording project Shura has ever embarked upon. History is being made all the time!'[20]

That was certainly the view of the critic of the *Ham and High* on 13 May 1983.

> Shura Cherkassky is one of those fascinating artists who bring the same vivid involvement to Stravinsky and Rachmaninov, as to Morton Gould or the smaller pieces of Mendelssohn or Tausig.
>
> I thrilled to his recording of Mussorgsky's *Pictures at an Exhibition* on Nimbus, and now the label has followed up this success with Stravinsky's three *Petrouchka* movements in the solo piano version (45018) superbly and dramatically performed.
>
> They are backed by a side of delicious encore pieces ranging from a finely articulated account of Mendelssohn's E Minor Prelude and Fugue and a charming account of Debussy's first Arabesque to Morton Gould's Boogie-Woogie Etude and Rimsky-Korsakov's *Flight of the Bumble Bee*, the first played with a tongue-in-cheekiness and the second with quicksilver prestissimo fingering in which every note has a place. Not to be missed.

Shura Cherkassky, the Russian pianist who had a long and fruitful relationship with Nimbus.

In July 1985 the *Sunday Times* was no less enthusiastic about two more Cherkassky/Nimbus releases. 'Unlike some recent piano recordings that are dazzlingly close here are two hour-long recitals which capture the acoustic ambience of a concert hall in which the listener sits at a more comfortable distance. Cherkassky's playing is, it need hardly be said, as brilliant as usual . . . two typical recitals by a magnificent pianist are perpetuated.'

Cherkassky himself echoed these sentiments in a November 1986 interview with *Classical Music*.

> 'Certainly there are no signs of age in his playing – much to the delight of Nimbus. After a lifetime at the keyboard which has spread records around Deutsche Grammophon, Eurodisc, HMV, Decca and ASV, Cherkassky is now a frequent visitor to the Nimbus HQ at Wyastone Leys where he is recorded in a style befitting a high-Romantic whose pianistic roots stretch back via his teacher Josef Hofmann to Anton Rubinstein.
>
> 'Nimbus is especially good for me,' says Cherkassky. 'They have an estate, so you don't feel you're going to a building where there's a red light here, a green light there, and lots of cold-blooded machinery. They say: "Play like it's a concert – it there's a wrong note don't worry about it." '
>
> Cherkassky feels that the Nimbus Schumann *Kreisleriana* and Chopin B minor scherzo recordings (NIM 5042) capture his playing at its very best.

But only eighteen months later the relationship had soured a little, partly over royalty misunderstandings*, and Cherkassky was reluctant to go back to Wyastone Leys as he felt the atmosphere would make it difficult for him to play as well as he would wish.[21]

In April 1988 Leonard Bernstein had written to Cherkassky about his latest Nimbus CD, 'My Dear Shura, What a joyful experience I have just had listening to your recording of *Touches*. I've never liked the piece so much as I did listening to your performance – and *what* a performance! You made me revive my old idea of using it as a movement of a large piano sonata. Lenny B. P.S. I am so sorry to have had to miss your Chopin concerto last Sunday. I was glued to my composing desk.'[22]

Cherkassky sent a copy to Adrian and Nimbus shared his pleasure,

*Because the first year's royalties had been paid on all discs placed with wholesalers following a major marketing campaign in the USA, they were large. However, in the second year the wholesalers' 'returns' from this drive had to be offset, as was customary, against the royalties earned in the second year so payments to Cherkassky were consequently much smaller.

but in a letter that showed that there were strains in the relationship.

> Leonard Bernstein's praise of your performance gives me as much pleasure as I hope it does you and is, once again, an endorsement of the special things that have come out of the relationship between Nimbus and Shura Cherkassky.
>
> I was disappointed that you did not come to make the recording and I hope that the awkwardness between us will soon pass. The label and our lives will be much poorer without you and, even though you feel that I have betrayed your trust*, you will not find a greater champion in the record business than myself.[23]

By October Adrian's impatience was unmistakable.

> Time is passing and it is my wish to know if you intend to return to Wyastone to work with us as before. The piano is here, we are here and you still have work to do. It would be careless after so long to waste these crowning years of your life without making more recordings, and you must admit that you never had as successful a recording partnership as the one you have with Nimbus.
>
> However, it is not my intention to lecture you. Do what you want, and in the knowledge of our continued affection for you whichever you decide.[24]

This impatience was not ill-founded for a reason which Adrian tactfully conveyed to Cherkassky's agent, Christa Phelps-Barnard, rather than to the artist himself: 'Time will not, unfortunately, preserve his powers forever.'[25]

The root cause of the trouble was money. It is hard now to discern whether Cherkassky or Ibbs & Tillet were the source of the dissatisfaction, and neither Cherkassky nor his agent were willing to talk about their relationship with Nimbus, nor even to permit their correspondence to be quoted. Although Cherkassky was new to their catalogue, Nimbus agreed a not ungenerous £500 per CD advance in the opening 1980 contract, but Ibbs & Tillet were pressing for improvements from the outset, failing to distinguish sufficiently between the advance – nearly always paid very promptly by Nimbus to all their artists as soon as a recording was made – and royalties which were calculated in arrears and about which Nimbus were sometimes dilatory, not from meanness but from muddle. By the summer of 1987 Cherkassky was using Nina Walker as a channel for his niggles about money and Ibbs & Tillet had joined in by mid-1989. Over a dinner in October that year, Cherkassky,

*A forgotten birthday had sparked this tiff.

Christa Barnard and Adrian seemed to have sorted the problem out and, considering the relatively modest sales volume to be expected, agreed a good advance of £3,000 for two CDs to be recorded over a three-day period a month later.

Within three weeks things were going sour again, and Cherkassky's agent had to inform Adrian that once more the pianist refused to return to Nimbus.[26]

A week later she was pressing Nimbus somewhat peremptorily to resolve the impasse with Cherkassky by giving definitive answers to various questions connected with his proposed recordings.[27]

Only five days before the recording was due the final straw came from a slightly embarrassed Ibbs & Tillet under pressure from Cherkassky who was now refusing to return to Wyastone Leys unless he had advance payment in his pocket.[28]

Numa was deeply upset by this behaviour, and not without some justice for, as we have already seen, most of Nimbus's artists felt that the company played very fair with them over money.

No more is heard of Cherkassky at Nimbus until a rather sad coda in 1991 when the Nimbus Contracts Manager, Don Trend, was objecting to the BBC and Decca trying to reissue Cherkassky/Nimbus repertoire. He also notified Ibbs & Tillet of the steps he had taken. 'Recordings made for broadcasting purposes within the five year exclusivity can never subsequently be made available as commercial records within the full period of copyright.'[29]

Nimbus had felt obliged to protect its position by threatening various legal actions and Cherkassky became agitated by the situation. Still wishing to restore their friendship with Cherkassky, Gerald wrote both to explain and to let the pianist know that rather than upset him they would drop any legal action. Sadly, the message could no longer be direct but had to be passed through Ibbs & Tillet.

It has come to my attention that the recent correspondence concerning the BBC and Decca has upset Shura.

The issues we raised were part of a bigger dispute between all record companies and the BBC and was never intended to become a personal matter between Nimbus and Shura.

Please assure Shura that it has been our sole aim throughout to protect the value of his unique recordings. To remove any impediment to the resumption of the cordial relations with Shura we will be dropping all legal actions.

150

Please pass on to Shura fond regards from us all and let us now all work to ensure that the celebration of Shura's birthday is a great success in every way and that includes the promotion and sale of his recordings.[30]

Nimbus has fallen out with some of its individual artists, almost always, as in the cases of Shumsky, Cherkassky and Michejew, over what Numa or Adrian regarded as breaches of the family code of ethics – musical or financial. The dissident performers may simply have got too big for their boots – or at least the size of boot Nimbus was prepared to supply – or the breaches may have been caused by clashes of artistic temperament, for we should not forget that three of the family were themselves also well-endowed with that commodity. On the other hand, many artists (Roberts, Wallace, Jones, Best, Perlemuter, among many others) have sustained long relationships and, in many cases, more than two decades of mutual loyalty and support. It is significant that most of the breaches occurred in the late 1980s when Nimbus had become large and wealthy and its Founders and inner family were mostly preoccupied with running the business. In any case, for Nimbus, the late eighties had largely become the age of the orchestra. They were also the era of Robert Maxwell.

1

2

3

4

5

6

7

8

1 Marta Deyanova, Bulgarian pianist and
 now Mrs Gerald Reynolds.
2 Tim Souster operating the electronics for
 Equalisation.
3 Adrian signing up Sir Michael Tippett.
4 Soulima Stravinsky, son of Igor, who
 recorded his and his father's piano music.
5 Amaryllis Fleming with her five string
 Amati 'cello.
6 Cyril Smith and Phyllis Sellick, piano
 duettists.
7 Cis Amaral, editor of the magazine
 Performance with pianist, Claudio Arrau.
8 William Mathias, composer, with Numa.
9 Alfredo Kraus (left) and Raúl Giménez,
 his sometime pupil, at the Nimbus piano.
 Both tenors recorded with Nimbus.

9

CHAPTER NINE

Nimbus, with the help of Peter Laister, had been vainly seeking financial support in the City only to find, as so many have found in approaching the paralytically timid British venture capital sector, that the deals on offer provided neither sufficient funds to solve Nimbus's short-term problems, nor sufficiently attractive terms for the Founders to persuade them to accept outside control yet still continue to dedicate their lives to making the business a success. Then, by another of those chances of fate which Numa vowed governed both his destiny and Nimbus's, Robert Maxwell sent Peter, who was his media adviser, on an abortive trip to America to look at a potential CD takeover target. Reporting back to Maxwell that the US deal was not worth doing, Peter offered to introduce him to Nimbus, in which he could acquire a far better company for a far smaller sum of money. Maxwell, never one to bother with such niceties as due diligence until after a deal was done, and then only as an excuse to renege and lever better terms for himself, liked the sound of what he heard, particularly of Nimbus's successful pioneering in CD-ROM, and made an offer on 30 September 1987.

> This letter records our intention to acquire 51 per cent of the share capital of Nimbus Records Limited ('Nimbus') on the following terms:
>
> We will pay a price of £29 million . . . £25 million . . . for new shares . . .
>
> Nimbus will . . . warrant . . . pre-tax profits of the Nimbus group for the year ended 31 December 1989 will be not less than £15m . . .
>
> . . . up to £3m . . . shortfall multiplied by 0.5;
>
> . . . between £3m and £9m . . . shortfall multiplied by 1;
>
> . . . shortfall exceeds £9m, no further compensation . . .
>
> BPCC will be entitled to receive the aforementioned compensation by way of an issue of further ordinary shares in Nimbus, credited as fully paid . . .

BPCC will undertake not to procure any changes to the Board of Directors of Nimbus ... without the consent of two-thirds of the Directors ...

In the event of ... a substantial change in the shareholding of the company, the present directors will be entitled to acquire (at market value) 75 per cent of the music label ...

... land and buildings at Wyastone Leys ... sold to the vendors (and) ... lease to Nimbus ... non-residential part of the buildings ... rent free ...[1]

Once the offer had been made and verbally accepted, Maxwell then embarked on his standard tactic of delay. This entails avoiding actually signing a deal until the target is on the very brink of collapse and then making a very much less attractive offer to be signed more or less there and then, if the victim is not to go under.

Numa admitted he did not realise this at first. 'I didn't then understand the delaying tactics. When he procrastinated I said, "Look Bob, everything is settled so why the fuck are you doing this? One reason, as you know, there is going to be a stock market crash that will knock something off the price. If you do that in three years you'll be dead." One thing Jews don't like is being cursed. I didn't win, but then he didn't either.'

At a meeting on 20 October (in the wake of the 'Black Monday' London stockmarket crash), Kevin Maxwell, representing MCC, put the far less palatable deal on the table, only sugaring it by assurances of CD-ROM business, audio CD deals with the Eastern Bloc, other promises which never materialised and the usual flannel about a smaller slice of a much bigger cake. The Founders, with Kevin on the telephone to his father, were given literally a few minutes to decide whether to accept the new terms or have Maxwell walk away.

Under the new proposals MCC would take 70 per cent for only £20 million (not £25 million) in new equity investment and £4 million paid to the Founders for part of their shares as before. The deal still included a punitive 'ratchet', which would have slashed the Founders' share of the equity even further if applied, unless Nimbus delivered profits of £15 million for the year ending December 1989. To this they could hardly object, since in the euphoria of 1986, after they had made over £2 million profit in the first nine months of that year, they were themselves forecasting profits for 1987 of £13.7 million (in fact they made a loss of £436,000).

The deal did, however, contain a pre-emption clause by which both parties had to offer their shares to the other before selling to third parties and offer them at the same price as an outside deal. It also included, in rider 22, the right to buy back control (75 per cent) of the music label after two years. Additionally, it still secured for the Founders the re-purchase of their cottage and Wyastone Leys with its estate.

The terms, even as revised, were not really bad in the critical situation which Nimbus was in, and in any case, as Numa observed, 'On the Maxwell deal we had no option. Our lawyer said that he was the most horrible man who would cause us heartbreak and would ruin us. Because of this, Stuart Garman's shrewdness and our own instinct, we put in the pre-emption clause and the right to buy back the label. The Maxwell deal was Hobson's choice because Lloyds would not give any money. It was Lloyds Bank, may they rot in hell. The genesis of our not being able to grow bigger was the mean, unimaginative, ruinously stupid Lloyds-bloody-Bank. (And you may quote me on that.)'

Numa's fulmination at Lloyds Bank, while heartfelt and understandable, was perhaps a little severe in the circumstances. The bank that did benefit was Midland which received £6 million for its 27.5 per cent holding which it had bought for only £66,600.

The Nimbus press statement concealed both the relief and the misgivings of the Nimbus family over the deal, and quoted Numa as saying, 'We are delighted to have struck a deal which has brought such a meeting of like minds. The blending of our mutual interests will assure our continued growth in technology and the arts.'[2]

The meeting of the 'like minds', at which hands were shaken on the deal, was an occasion that none of the living participants is likely to forget. Peter Laister, whom Maxwell confirmed as Chairman of Nimbus, recalls it vividly.

> Maxwell didn't really meet them until the deal was done and that was a day I shall never in my life forget. Numa, Michael and Gerald came up and waited in my office which was in the next building to the Maxwell building and you had to go through the news floor of the *Daily Mirror* to get from one to the other. My secretary plied them with tea and was a bit surprised by the exacting demands for the tea; hot water with a whiff of tea in it. Then Numa had to lie down as he was in a state of collapse and we waited and waited and waited. The meeting was scheduled for 4.30

pm and much later the message came, Peter can you come over now? Gerald and Michael and I virtually had to support Numa and walk him, with his arms draped over our shoulders and feet trailing a bit behind, through the whole of the *Daily Mirror* newsroom. The journalists were not at all phased by the sight of three people carrying a fairly inert body through their newsroom. We went up to Bob's private suite, which looked more like something out of a film extravaganza than a private room, where we were ushered in by the butler. It was a magnificent set of rooms. We sat down in the slightly gaudy and strident colours and champagne was brought in and Numa was parked in a chair in a state of collapse. Then in comes Bob Maxwell, running late, in his white towelling dressing-gown which came to just above his knees and showing his great, big, hairy legs and he had nothing on underneath. He comes in booming 'Glad to meet you Count Labinsky' and said all the sort of things that only Bob could get away with. He could have enormous charisma when he wanted to – just as Numa had. It was hilarious, the meeting between this huge giant in a pair of old slippers and white towel dressing-gown and Numa who had to be hauled to his feet to say hello. The deal was struck, hands were shaken, and that was it. It was extraordinarily bizarre in these surroundings, one man in a state of collapse and the other man in a state of undress.

Peter Laister, immediately appointed Chairman.

157

Numa also remembered the occasion: 'At the first meeting with Robert Maxwell I found him charming although I knew he was a liar. I was amazed he was so fat. I was amazed that he had a very big cup like a miniature chamber-pot on the desk and round the rim in gold letters "for a very special person", and I thought, oh, I don't think I like the look of that. He was walking around, looked me up and down and said, "yes, I know all about you." I said, "Do you?" He said, "Yes, I know, I can tell that you've got good Russian blood." I replied that I hoped that it was good and I knew it was Russian, as long as it wasn't Polish I didn't mind.'

The bonhomie could not disguise the mutual suspicion. On 11 November, only four days after the deal was actually signed (this was confirmed by a vote of an extraordinary general meeting of Nimbus Records Limited on 22 December), Nimbus directors, who now had Kevin Maxwell ('a sneak' in Numa's opinion) nominated to their Board, had asked for Maxwell's assurance that he would not use his majority stake to oust them or swamp the Board with his own nominees. Maxwell duly sent them an utterly meaningless comfort letter.

> You have expressed concern that MCC might wish to use its powers, as majority shareholder, to appoint or remove directors arbitrarily.
>
> Continued prosperity . . . and technological advances . . . primarily depend on the continued involvement and motivation of yourself and your Board.
>
> We have agreed that I should write this letter (which we all accept cannot be legally binding) to you to reassure you of our intentions in this respect . . .
>
> . . . The decision to appoint further directors and the removal of directors will *ordinarily* be decided by a majority of two-thirds of the Board of Nimbus. The circumstances in which MCC would envisage using its powers as a shareholder to change the Board would be where the integrity or personal commitment of any Director of Nimbus was in question or where the trading or financial position or prospects of Nimbus were, in MCC's reasonable opinion, being prejudiced to an extent where changes were felt to be unavoidable.[3]

That the letter did nothing to prevent the usual MCC attempt to steamroller newly acquired companies is evident from a note, unusually signed by all three Founders, sent to the MCC lawyer, Debbie Maxwell (no relation) on 26 November. 'The intention to adhere to Mr Robert Maxwell's offer ensuring continuity of management control . . . was perfectly clear . . . Any change now is contrary to the spirit and the letter of both agreements. We cannot move on this point.'

Numa had often fervently expressed his appreciation to Peter following the deal with Maxwell for saving Nimbus from bankruptcy, fear of which had ceaselessly haunted the Founders for the past six months. They were to have much more to thank their Chairman for, particularly in the next two years when he acted as a buffer and mediator between the two larger-than-life personalities involved and the two very different commercial styles of their organisations. Right from the outset he had warned Maxwell that he was dealing with a very different commercial animal from the kind to which he was used. 'It will only work if, basically, you leave it alone, it's not one of your ordinary businesses where you can have your usual habit of putting your people in and riding rough shod over everyone from day one. It's an ailing child and we'll have to get it through its sickness and then let it grow up, which it will.' And to his credit, eventually, he did.

This was not advice that a man like Maxwell, initially at least, could easily digest and the usual stream of memos giving instructions, from who could have cars to who could have outside line telephones, followed. Both these, incidentally, had to be personally agreed by Robert Maxwell. He tried to fire the person at Nimbus responsible for giving a car to Nimbus's new Financial Director, MCC appointee Howard Nash, only to discover it was Gerald, whom he could not sack. Then he tried to fire Stuart who had initiated the arrangement and the family, abetted, as so often, by Peter, flatly refused to take any notice of the demand.

Howard Nash, once he had joined Nimbus, gave his undivided loyalty to his new employer in the abstract and to the family in personal terms, despite a stream of memos, mostly from Kevin Maxwell, to him and to Stuart, insisting that 'the reporting priority and responsibility is *first* to the centre.' The MCC style of approach is well summarised in a later memo from one of the numerous MCC Head Office officials to Howard. 'As you are aware we are holding a Controllers Meeting on 18 September at which Basil Brookes will be in attendance. Following Basil's remarks at earlier Controllers Meetings, if your accounts have not been signed by that date, the Controllers Meeting could be your last activity with MCC.'[4]

Howard was on the receiving end of another piece of MCC bullying when he was suspended for a week by Kevin Maxwell for failing to report to the Maxwells that the Nimbus Board, without reference to the MCC directors, had replaced an extremely expensive hire agreement for the use of company cars by buying them – the subject of a Maxwell veto. The Founders defended him vigorously.

Nimbus paid £900,000 a year in so-called management charges for these peremptory intrusions and for little else of any practical value. As Peat Marwick later observed, 'we understand that MCC does not provide significant Head Office services.' Most of the deluge of paper was at best irrelevant: invitations to football matches and race meetings and other down-market events as hospitality occasions for Nimbus (and at worst a distraction and waste of management time); requests from Robert Maxwell personally to know how many copies of a particular issue (containing nothing of any relevance to Nimbus) of *Global Business* the company had circulated; memos on what graphic artists they should use; endless press releases about Robert Maxwell himself and quite unrelated to Nimbus activities. Despite the shareholders' agreement that it should be otherwise, MCC imposed very low limits on the sums that could be expended by Nimbus without authorisation by a Maxwell director. All dealings with Comecon were to be through MCC, all international flights during the Gulf troubles were to be personally authorised by Robert Maxwell, and so on.

By late 1988 the relationship had reached its nadir with a file of anti-Maxwell jokes and hostile reviews of Maxwell biographies, freely circulating among the staff at Wyastone Leys at all levels.

> Restrain me, I am about to have an impulse. Although no one can restrain Maxwell, not even himself. He does everything by the seat of his large, well-cut pants but, despite being the head of Britain's largest printing business, he still tends to intervene in any and every takeover bid and remains something of a joke.
>
> Maxwell is no ordinary megalomaniac, never finding the easiest way to achieve anything. He has expended all the moral capital he once had through his early 'struggles'. Even when he has been right he has been unconvincing. His deviousness, his bullying, have seen to that.[5]

MCC was always quibbling, but was usually ignored or sent a fairly tart reply as when the dollar gained against the pound from the price at which the takeover valuations had been made and it tried to adjust the calculations. Stuart Garman commented that since the world's banks could not control the movement of the dollar, Nimbus could hardly be expected to.

More formally, Stuart noted in an internal memo on 20 September: 'The shares of MCC now stand at the same level as they did four years ago ... Indeed, the rate at which MCC purchases other companies at what are seen to be excessive prices, the more the "shine" goes off the shares.'[6]

On 27 October Numa was warning staff in a stern memo: 'Any communication with or from Maxwell Communications Corporation ... should be noted and copied to me. Failure to comply with this request will be deemed to display a lack of loyalty to myself and my fellow directors. I am sure you will understand that there is no room in Nimbus for divided loyalties within your work.'[7]

Numa recalled the early period all too well:

> For the first three months, practically every other day Maxwell was on the 'phone saying do this or do that and I said, look you run a newspaper but you know nothing about a record company. He wanted to use the *Mirror* to advertise all the Nimbus records so I told him he was not going to get the hoi polloi buying Nimbus records. We were talking about high communication in arts which is always a minority interest, unlike his football nonsense. He said, 'what's wrong with my football nonsense?' So I said, 'It's common like you. You're only doing it so you can wear that silly American hat and you can go parading around and trying to run, looking even fatter than you are and making a fool of yourself.' And that didn't go down very well. So he made puffing noises at me. I said 'You can puff at me all you like,' and he hung up on me and I've never been hung up on. So I rang him back and told him, 'No one hangs up on me' and slammed my 'phone down. I was upset. After the first three months he stopped interfering.

Numa, in the words of Peter Laister, 'continued to call Maxwell a "blackhearted bluebeard" – which of course he turned out to be – but his money was actually saving the company for them.' No one was so rash as to contradict Numa's view and the antipathy between the two men remained unabated.

It was almost inevitable that these two forceful and extrovert personalities should quarrel, and Maxwell's response was to let it be known that he would be willing to sell his stake in Nimbus knowing full well that the Founders could not afford to buy it – and to exaggerate his usual practice in delaying all payments until well after their promised date.

The impact of this latter tactic was being painfully experienced by Nimbus in connection with its US expansion in particular, as Gerald tried to get across to another of the MCC intermediaries.

> I explained to Richard [Ainsworth-Morris] that we had about eight key suppliers, any one of whom could shut down the plant if they ceased supplying, and also we needed the cash for next week's payroll. If the cash was not available for next week for a) our key suppliers and b) for payroll, that could bring the plant to a grinding halt. To miss payroll would be devastating for confidence of our staff and to delay further payment to our suppliers (Mark Galloway is running out of excuses) would be very dangerous. Any rumour of difficulty in paying our bills would be extremely damaging under the existing climate in the CD business in the States, which is already very nervous.'[8]

It must be admitted, however, that Maxwell had good reason for his displeasure with Nimbus, reason forcefully confirmed in a report to him on the company in November 1988 from Peat Marwick.

> The true cost of producing each disc [i.e. Nimbus's 'own label'] was estimated to be £3.71 in 1988. This is a marginal model and excludes factory overheads and contribution to administration and management costs. Yet the selling price per disc in the USA was £3.08 (at an exchange rate of $1.86) during the same period. Hence every US disc was sold at a net loss of 63p. Currently the US accounts for at least 60 per cent of total sales.
>
> The commercial viability of individual products is not thoroughly assessed.
>
> Due attention has not been paid to marketing/sales . . .
>
> . . . The introduction of adequate management information systems and an overhaul of existing pricing mechanisms needs to be undertaken urgently.
>
> Nimbus in the UK requires considerably more management time and financial support from MCC if it is to be kept within the Group. Nimbus suffers from a lack of commercial professionalism . . . MCC should only commit its management time and financial support if Nimbus is to become a key platform from which to develop CD-ROM activities. Ultimately it is difficult to conceive how this relationship could be made to work on an effective and profitable basis. The pessimistic scenario (see Part II of this report) envisages losses of £3m greater than predicted in Nimbus management's budget.[9]

Peter told the Maxwells the report was superficial and misguided in its analysis – as, indeed, it proved to be – and that MCC, and

Robert Maxwell in particular, had created much of the problem by ignoring his warnings and delaying payments for new equipment. It was to clarify this amorphous situation that MCC, through Peter and with Nimbus's agreement, had appointed Howard Nash as Financial Director at Nimbus. Within a few months, as Peter Laister commented in a note to Maxwell requesting Howard's appointment to the Nimbus Board, 'Nimbus controls and reporting systems improved out of all recognition since he started.'

Numa recorded in a file note the telephone conversation with Maxwell that followed on Maxwell's receipt of the Peat Marwick report.

RM: KM [Kevin Maxwell] is off.
If you can't make a profit with your current capacity why add more?
NL: Very short-term view, Robert.
RM: Can't have these losses; won't tolerate losses. Four million, I hear.
NL: Well, you will have to. There are losses and you made over half of them – 3.0 million of them.
RM: What! No point in quarrelling amongst ourselves. I won't tolerate losses. If we are to have losses I shall have to sell my holding.
NL: Robert, how is your health?
RM: Frightfully busy.
NL: I am sure you are used to that. You told me I had to get used to my pain.
RM: Have to see what the final figures are.
NL: More than four million.
RM: We'll see. Goodbye.
Not a heated conversation; just insistent on not tolerating losses.[10]

In the small hours of the following night Numa received a sequence of more disturbing calls in different male voices on his private line asking whether it was true that Maxwell was about to fire the entire Nimbus Board and what he felt about being sacked. Numa put the telephone down without comment, noting that he was 'very cross' and suspecting London reporters. If the callers were Fleet Street journalists then they had probably been put up to it by Maxwell himself, but, as it was on a private line, it seems more likely to have been Maxwell stooges trying to 'put the frighteners on', or a disgruntled employee. Whatever the source, in January 1989, Maxwell put Nimbus on his 'for sale' list, paradoxically at the very time evidence was just beginning to accumulate that the financial causes of his dissatisfaction were being significantly reduced.

Nimbus, too, went public in that month with its disappointment at the Maxwell deal. 'Unfortunately the benefits and anticipated synergy between the two companies have not been achieved and therefore both parties are seeking alternatives.'[11]

Nimbus dressed the decision up as best it could to its employees in January 1989.

> Mr Maxwell's decision, which was mutually agreed, comes at a time when there is an unprecedented mood of optimism and buoyancy in the CD market and when Nimbus is at its strongest ever in terms of orders. During the period September to December 1988 (a peak period for the CD industry) our orders were nearly 21 per cent higher than for the same period in 1987.
>
> This is an exciting time for Nimbus and we believe that the withdrawal by Maxwell Communication Corporation provides us with new opportunities. We are now in discussion with a number of industry partners and financial institutions to find a new investor to support our programme of growth and expansion.[12]

Again, on 26 June, Nimbus management had to make a staff announcement denying rumours – by now, in any case, unfounded – that MCC was selling its Nimbus shares.

Nevertheless, the process of fence-mending had begun, with Nimbus appealing to both Maxwell's paranoia and his overweening vanity. 'We wish to make it clear that we want to support your position in Nimbus and do not wish the enfranchisement of the Virgin preference shares to interfere with this. We therefore undertake to vote with you on any matter where Virgin might seek to use their voting rights to the detriment of the interests of either you or us. We are sure that you will act in the same spirit.'[13]

Then they invited him to be the narrator in *Peter and the Wolf* at a concert to be given in the Albert Hall! 'Dear Mr Maxwell, re. *Peter & the Wolf* and *Carnival of the Animals* Count Labinsky has asked me to make the arrangements for your narration of the above two works and to write to you giving you the various details relating to their recording.'[14]

Maxwell gleefully accepted the invitation, and Adrian admitted that the thought that he might actually make the recording 'had us worried. By God, it had us worried!'

But not as worried as Nimbus losses had got Maxwell.

Although the Maxwell injection had greatly brightened the balance sheet – net assets of over £19 million; shareholders' funds, almost £16 million – by the end of 1987 the losses for the fifteen-month period to 31 December exceeded £3 million. By March 1989, the next fifteen-month accounting period, they had almost doubled to £5.7 million; net assets had dropped to £9 million plus through writing off the revenue account deficit; investment and shareholders' funds were down nearly £2 million. Nimbus bitterly attributed half its loss to March 1989 to Maxwell's inordinate delay in making funds (authorised in February 1988) available for the new plant needed in the USA until late 1988 and so missing the peak production season – US sales were only $316,000 to the end of that year. Maxwell was not one to admit that he might be even partially at fault and continued actively to look for a buyer. Indeed he instructed Peter Laister to find one.

Once more Peter's diplomatic skills came to Nimbus's rescue. In a long and carefully argued memo to Maxwell on 8 May he put the case for deferring the sale of Nimbus, although he had secured an offer from Electra.

> Your brief to me on Nimbus was to arrange a sale of the MCC 70 per cent in Nimbus . . .
>> It is clear that it is a poor time to sell a group such as Nimbus . . .
>> Nevertheless, I have achieved a firm offer.
>> Electra [would] purchase the MCC shareholding for £1 (and invest) £7.5m; £2m as straight equity, £3.5m as redeemable pref's and £2m as short-term loan . . . close to commercial interest rates . . . the Virgin Pref's be repaid first and the balance set against Lloyds' debt.
>
> The broad debt situation at Nimbus is:
>> there is an £8m debt with Lloyds (out of a possible £10m facility);
>
>> Virgin's £1m preference shares are now due for redemption;
>
>> US debt approx £1m (over covered by asset security).
>
> The poor performance in 1988 was due to three factors:
>> America was in a start-up situation;
>
>> The market-place was extremely depressed by the temporary over capacity, typical of an electronics growth market in its early stages;
>
>> The delay in ordering the automation equipment for UK and USA cost £3m.

Automation is essentially complete.

The Marketplace has begun to stabilise with growth outstripping capacity . . .

American recovery . . . the bottom has been reached and further modest expansion of the American plant will take it above its break-even level.

Overall losses are very much under control . . .

The Nimbus mastering technology has now been expanded to produce a CD-ROM disc pressing at 4 × existing density i.e. from 0.6 gigabytes–2.4 gigabytes. This technology appears to be 1–2 years in advance of the capability of any other manufacturer . . .

On the key issue of cash for 1989–90 – the UK will be cash +ve – the USA will be negative at $2.5m but including $1.75m of new capital expenditure to bring the US plant to planned capacity.

1990–91 should show both profits and cash +ve operations in the UK and USA. Broadly they approximate to a total of £4m PBI (£2.7m PBT) and positive cash flow of £4m.

. . . I would recommend:

Do not accept the Electra offer in its present form;

Continue support of Nimbus against revised forecasts . . . cash flow as above;

Repayment of the Virgin preference shares jointly by Nimbus/Maxwell;

Continue to seek a partner . . . [15]

Michael, the other supreme diplomat at Nimbus, also played his part in influencing attitudes at MCC by a careful and rational explanation of how Nimbus had got into trouble and how it was proposing to get out of it – a very different response to the usual brusque dismissal of MCC queries and complaints.

The overriding feature of 1988 for this company has been the effect of competing compact disc pressing plants having over-capacity . . . even though the volumes of CDs increased. . . . This over-capacity has produced drastic reductions in manufacturing plants.

Since January 1989 prices have begun to firm up in Europe and Nimbus has achieved increases from all its UK customers . . .

The company has undertaken a major capital expenditure on automating the production in UK and installing additional lines in US . . . achieving the planned cost savings.

... great strides have been made in producing 4 × higher density of information on CD ... up to 2 gigabytes and video up to one hour's duration ... a new solid state blue laser will be required – to be developed and produced by the Japanese. In the meantime the company is making prototype replay equipment to meet immediate demands.

This period saw a major increase in sales in America with seven discs in the Classical and Crossover Charts and Nimbus was voted No. 7 Classical Label, ahead of RCA and Philips in 1988.

(It won the following awards): The Koussevitzky Award for contemporary composers on record; The Venice Planetarium Fund 'Music and Life' prize for the high artistic and technical quality of its CD recordings; the 'Diapason D'Or' was awarded to several recordings including the latest from Vlado Perlemuter.[16]

These approaches obviously had the desired effect and Maxwell decided to stay with Nimbus on certain conditions. Peter prudently got Maxwell to confirm the deal by an authorising signature on Nimbus's copy of Peter's note setting it out.

I am greatly appreciative of your response on Nimbus. With this renewed support I am confident that Nimbus can make the progress and contribution you would expect.

... I have now cleared with the Founders their willing acceptance of all of your conditions. ...

I would appreciate your signing a copy of this note to allow me to use it as your authority. ...

On the question of share ownership Nimbus Founders acknowledge that MCC will rescind the ratchet outlined in the original agreement. Nimbus also fully accept that in return for all of the support outlined below, a re-adjustment of share ownership to 75.1 per cent MCC and 24.9 per cent Founders will take place with immediate effect ...

Nimbus Sale — Nimbus to be retained
Review in 1–2 years.

— 6% general award July 1st, 1989
Directors to forego increase.

MCC and Nimbus to purchase Virgin Pref Shares and pay-up interest in ratio of shareholdings. Interest to be repayable (MCC £750,000 Capital + £116,000 repayable Founders £250,000 Cap + £38,500 repayable). Agreed.

167

Equipment purchase at SHAPE auction on June 27th–28th.

Cash within existing budgets and latest forecasts for UK and USA to be supported.

Productivity has risen by over 50 per cent in the past year.
[This is a] different outlook to that presented to MCC by the consultants in November 1988!
— reject Electra bid
— continue to seek an Industry Partner (US or Europe)
— sell or float in two years' time. . . .[17]

Despite the change of heart, Peter was still having to badger Maxwell for overdue funds nine days later. 'The working cash situation is now becoming desperate and some suppliers will withhold deliveries next week thus causing additional losses at the plant. Request the budgeted and scheduled transfer of $250,000 to the US Bank by the beginning of next week.'[18]

Part of the process of reconciliation between Maxwell and Nimbus had also been the agreement of Michael and Gerald to facilitate the redemption of the £1 million Virgin preference shares, for which Virgin had been pressing to the point of litigiousness during the summer of 1989, by personally re-purchasing a quarter of them together with the accrued interest. The rationale for this was succinctly set out in a note from Nimbus's redoubtable lawyer at McFarlanes, Nick Thomas.

It is clearly difficult to justify Michael's and Gerald's purchase of a proportion of the Virgin Preference Shares in purely short-term financial terms, since it is highly likely that those shares are presently worth less than par and there can be no certainty as to when Michael and Gerald will be able to recover their investment or, even, obtain a return on it.

What the purchase of the shares does, however, is to facilitate an agreement with MCC whereby, as a *quid pro quo* for helping to resolve the 'Virgin situation', MCC is prepared to modify the ratchet so that it does not operate to maximum effect (which it would otherwise do), thereby, on a medium- to long-term view, improving the position of the minority shareholders. . . .[19]

In fact, as Stuart Garman faxed to Nick Thomas on 11 October, the ratchet was to be completely replaced by a revision of the shareholders' agreement which gave Maxwell 75.1 per cent of the Nimbus equity, in other words unblockable control. (So long as the Founders held 25 per cent or more of the shares they could prevent special resolutions being passed at General Meetings to their detriment, for example imposing a dividend policy or altering the Articles of Association.) It must be recognised, however, that had he stuck to the original ratchet he would have been entitled to some 80 per cent. The balance sheet was also restructured at the same time to remove the large revenue deficit and Nimbus was all set to embark on the recovery of which signs had already appeared by August 1989 when the pressing plant sold a million units – double the budgeted figure. Despite a price increase on 1 September, November sales reached £2.4 million and continued to rise, so the total by the financial year end had reached 30 million discs (12 million in North America) placing Nimbus as the sixth largest supplier in Europe and the second in the UK, behind only EMI. As the supply/demand cycle oscillated once more on the demand side of the balance line, major customers became anxious lest Nimbus be unable to supply them. However, thanks to the earlier decisions to increase capacity and automate production lines the company was able to reassure them. More important from Nimbus's point of view, with the hardening of prices, production lines that had been barely breaking even when running at full capacity in May 1989 were now able to operate profitably and generate a positive cash flow in the latter half of the year.

The financial trend on the pressings side continued to improve steadily and for the twelve months ending March 1990 were 63 per cent up at £26.5 million. Sales by volume rose 54 per cent in the UK and 80 per cent in the US in that year against an overall market growth of 40 per cent. All of this an obviously mollified Maxwell made much of in the MCC annual report for 1990. He did not live long enough to witness the even more spectacular growth of 1991 with turnover rising to £31.6 million (however, not quite the £37 million Maxwell had somewhat euphorically forecast) and an operating profit of £2.2 million, which cut the year's overall loss to a mere £111,000. The employee level in that year repassed its previous highest level to 654 and continued to rise to 694 the following March, when a turnover of £38.4 million gave rise once more to net profits, this time of £681,000.

By 1990 Howard Nash had not only introduced a more realistic, or rather rational, accounting policy for the record label by writing off recording costs for each recording over a three-year period but, for the first time in the company's history, was able to quantify the losses of the music-making side of Nimbus's business at £581,000, £578,000 and £1.106 million for the three years. Had these losses not been incurred the company would have returned a profit much sooner and much more dramatically and one wonders how aware Maxwell was of this element in the Nimbus accounts. Since he rang Numa at Christmas 1990 to bestow his 'official blessing' on Nimbus for being 'just about the only company in my Group to make a profit!', he was by then clearly not discontented with the situation. Whether he had been or not would, of course, have been entirely immaterial to the Nimbus family for whom the sole *raison d'être* of making money was to make music.

Therefore before we go on to consider the impact on Nimbus of the sudden demise of their principal shareholder, we must return to the music-making of the 1980s.

CHAPTER TEN

The switch to CD and the diversion of effort to the building up of the manufacturing and technical side of the business caused a slight, but temporary, slow-down in the rate of release of recordings. In the last four years of LP production, 1982–85, output of LPs had gradually decreased as the number of CDs grew, as the following table shows.

	CD	LP
1982	4	15
1983	8	14
1984	10	10
1985	17	1

From October 1986 all new releases were on CD format only. Although most were also made available later in cassette form this was never a very popular medium with Nimbus Record buyers and by the end of 1992 still represented less than ten per cent of all sales.

By 1987 CDs were being released at fifty to sixty a year. Not all these were new recordings as, in keeping with the Nimbus policy of not deleting back issues from the current catalogue, many of the best were re-issued on CD. The critical approval which greeted the majority of them when heard in the new format fully justified the decision.

One of the impressive things about Nimbus is the impact its music label has made on the music world by sheer quality rather than volume of output. In the eight-and-a-quarter years of CD production up to 31 December 1992 – the last date for which figures are available in January 1994 – Nimbus Records have sold less than 2½ million discs all told. Only one has topped the 30,000 mark, Volume I of Perlemuter's Ravel, three more are over 25,000 and only six more over 20,000. Of the top ten records, four involve Paco Peña and guitar music, three are of Perlemuter's piano playing, two of the English Symphony Orchestra and one *Prima Voce* record of Caruso. Only forty-six CDs, a little over 11.5 per cent of the total number of titles in the catalogue, have sold more than 10,000 copies and a dozen still show under 1,000 copies each. Total sales currently run at between 400,000 and 500,000 discs a year. Many of these are from back catalogue issues and, as a result, Nimbus sales compare favourably with those of the major companies.

However, the main emphasis in a 'family' so dedicated to quality musical performance was the making of new recordings. Almost coincidental with the start of work on CD was the signing up of the troubadour, lutenist and singer, Martin Best in January 1981.

Best fell in love with the idea of singing to an instrument when he was six years old, when Arthur Kingsbury came to his house and sang the 'Raggle Taggle Gypsies, Oh', accompanying himself on a guitar bedecked with coloured ribbons. A series of cheap and basic guitars later (he paid £6 for his first at the age of fourteen), Best went to the Guildhall School of Music to acquire technique, despite 'finding the repertoire of the classical guitar very dull.' He went to the Segovia School in Spain and then lived in a hill village where he 'learned at first hand how it was to live in a community that sang.' Next, by now with lute and guitar equally readily coming to hand, he joined the Royal Shakespeare Company, where John Barton trained him in writing lyrics, setting them to music and organising programmes of words and music. He started with the Hollow Crown and then devised nine or ten other programmes with Terry Hands, Patrick Garland, Trevor Nunn, Peggy Ashcroft, Judi Dench and others.

Now he had Shakespearean song, troubadour songs, English folk songs and Spanish folk songs. Touring America he was exposed to other traditional music of a different sound and began to think of himself as a modern troubadour; a journeyer through these different cultures.

Best's first recording contract had been with Argo. His first major contract was at EMI where he was given a big budget and experimented with mixing medieval music and rock together. This should have been exciting, but Best felt so insecure that he was unable to resist any of the producer's suggestions, most of which he disliked, and the flavour went out of the project.

However, virtually the first recording Best had made was with Grosvenor Records, a tiny company in Birmingham, and it so happened that Numa had heard it, liked Best's singing and decided to record him one day. When that day came in 1981 Best paid his first visit to Wyastone Leys.

The whole atmosphere at Nimbus was one that I responded to. First of all it was very beautiful. Their approach to recording and to being a record company was organic with the way they wanted to live and I responded to that. I also responded to their anger. I liked the way that Numa would flail out at the record industry, I could relate to that. I like dealing with people who have strong idiosyncratic approaches to things. I didn't enjoy the experience of the commercial scene with EMI very much and the Nimbus approach was a wonderful moment because I could go right back to my roots. The first record I made for Nimbus in 1981 was, I think, the first record ever made devoted to one troubadour. And when they said 'we do things as performance, we don't like editing' I was absolutely thrilled because one of the things that got me down with my previous recordings was the editing. I like to record in a place that has some sort of spiritual resonance; a country house, a church something like that. The music I do comes out of an ambience which has a historical resonance. Buildings that are used for a human purpose are the ones I like to make music in, so going into the ballroom to record was just wonderful. I said, at last I can just sit down and sing and make a record.

That first recording, *The Last of the Troubadours*, was issued on LP in 1981 and won the Edison Award. It was re-issued on CD in June 1983. Best has gone on to make half a dozen more recordings with Nimbus, including *Songs of Chivalry* and *The Dante Troubadours* and *Gramophone*'s Christmas Record Pick of the Year in 1988, *Thys Yool*.

At the other end of the decade Nimbus started an equally successful relationship with the Medici Quartet which was signed up in 1986 and its first recordings, the Ravel Quartet in F with a Strauss coupling and then the Debussy Quartet in G Minor coupled with Shostakovitch Quartet No 8, were released in the summer of 1987.

After the first recording session Adrian wrote to Nicholas Curry of Seven Muses, the Quartet's agent, to express Nimbus's pleasure and hopes for the new association.

> We are delighted that our partnership has begun with such promise and we have the greatest admiration for the professional and musical standard of the Medici which produced such excellent results.
>
> In your letter of 21 October, you hoped that our first sessions with the Medici would be the beginning of many visits to Nimbus resulting in a fruitful partnership.
>
> We are indeed interested in discussing, without prejudice, the possibility of an exclusive contract for a period of five years with option to renew.[1]

Martin Best with his lute, leader of
the Martin Best Medieval Ensemble.

Paul Robertson, leader of the Quartet and keen psychologist, replied in a letter to Numa: 'The 4tet has now got a marvellous new 2nd fiddler who actually enjoys music – so we all enjoy ourselves a lot more as well, and the old one, was he pushed or did he jump? I'm still not sure, perhaps he just fell. The interesting thing is that I discover it doesn't really matter. Incidentally, many thanks for the formal welcome which is much appreciated.'[2]

These first recordings were well received, in America as well as in Britain, as this typical review testifies:

> First of all, congratulations to Nimbus for pairing the Debussy Quartet with something other than the Ravel Quartet.
>
> Not only is the hackneyed pairing avoided, but the choice of an alternative is inspired: the brooding Quartet No 8 of Shostakovich.
>
> Nimbus, as serious record collectors already know, is one of the most technically advanced of the small independent classical labels. It was among the first companies to embrace compact discs exclusively, and this clear, sparkling specimen shows they did the right thing.[3]

174

The praise for the technical quality of the recording must have been a pleasing change for the Quartet after the rough handling its Elgar Piano Quintet made for Meridian a few months earlier had received at the hands of magazines such as *Gramophone*. The Nimbus recordings must have fallen sweetly on other ears, for in November 1987 Curry wrote to report an important conversation to Nina Walker, the Quartet's producer at Nimbus. 'Ursula Vaughan Williams would like you to consider his [Ralph's] Phantasy Quintet, for string quartet and viola, which, as far as she can tell, has never been recorded, and which is a superb work.'[4]

Nimbus's great achievement with the Medici was the recording of the complete cycle of Beethoven Quartets. The project got off the ground most ingeniously through a highly original ploy by the Quartet to win themselves time to rehearse for recording instead of having to play concerts. In October 1986 they gave a series of recitals at the Queen Elizabeth Hall with the aim of persuading invited members of the audience to sponsor one or more quartets and have their names associated with them at live concerts and on the records thereafter. Half a dozen were quickly taken up and Nimbus itself sponsored all those which did not eventually find a patron.

The cycle was recorded over two years, but from opus 74 to the end in a mere two months in 1989 – as one member of the Quartet David Matthews remarked, 'Nimbus doesn't edit so you put in everything plus, and that is knackering. It's great; it's exhilarating, but you pay a price for doing that.'

Professor Paul Robertson, leader of the Quartet, described the process by which Nina Walker became almost a fifth member. 'She's a great lady,' says Robertson. 'She drove us into making these enormously big statements, huge statements, statements that you didn't know you had in you, but which are actually in the music. It shatters your world. It's not cosy stuff, not when you do it like that. It's devastating.[5]

The usual ups and downs were less marked than was customary, Nimbus's only quibble being when Medici brought along an outsider who might be representing them, and Adrian, whose cherubic countenance and amiable manner sometimes concealed an acerbic pen, objected.

> I am obliged to tell you that Nimbus would not wish to continue to act as the Medici Quartet's recording organisation should you decide

to formalise your relationship with Nick Franks.

The ill-informed comments that were directed at Nimbus during those few hours have successfully undermined the trust built up over the last period of years.

Nick Franks explained himself to be acting only as the Quartet's mouthpiece. If this was so I can only conclude that it was your agreed intention to see how far Nimbus could be pushed. I trust you now have a clear answer.

I believe that Nimbus has been one of the few organisations consistently prepared to support the Quartet and that you are in error with your present stance to us.[6]

The Quartet also wanted to be allowed to make recordings of work they performed in connection with their 'residency' at Lancaster University, as Robertson wrote: 'I am not at liberty to be a primarily emotional creature anymore – bailiffs at the door (this is unfortunately not figurative) have an extraordinarily bracing effect.'[7]

In principle this permission had already been agreed earlier in the year as Robertson explained to Adrian:

Fortunately, I have had an opportunity to speak in person with Numa, Michael & Gerald, and they have listened and responded with all their customary kindness and understanding.

They have generously agreed to release us to record independently a number of projects from Kingston Polytechnic and Lancaster University.

It is my most earnest wish, and that of my colleagues, that the exceptionally happy relationship, both artistic and personal, which we have always enjoyed with you all will be nurtured and cherished in the future as it has been in the past.[8]

Nimbus only asked that a 'by permission of Nimbus Records' be included on any such recordings. But, in a way that Nimbus entirely understood, the Medici wanted in the end to be in charge of their own label with control over venues, engineers and producers. Robertson explained their reasons in an article in *Classical Music* on 14 November 1992. 'It is rare in this profession that you are a truly free agent, and in the end our feeling was one of frustration. Nimbus were as good as any record company are likely to be, but they didn't bother with the kind of marketing or publicity that we felt was necessary. Ultimately, that is damaging to our careers. It was a distillation of a life's work and we didn't do it just for it to appear on CD – and then not be promoted.'

Numa with Welsh composer Alun Hoddinott, whose piano sonatas and orchestral works Nimbus recorded.

The farmhouse near Charlottesville, Virginia bought as Nimbus's American headquarters.

Planning for the American factory in the boardroom at Wyastone Leys.

July 1990.

October 1990.

November 1990.

January 1991.

March 1991.

May 1991.

The building of the Nimbus Foundation's Performing Arts Centre.

May 1991.

August 1991.

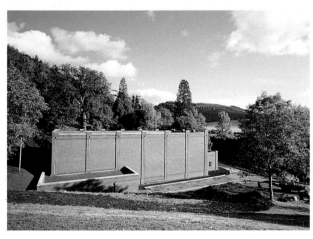

October 1991.

December 1991.

December 1991.

Complete and opened May 1993.

A happy Count Labinsky in his fulfilled dream of a concert hall.

HRH The Prince of Wales in the house at Wyastone Leys to open the
Performing Arts Centre, May 5th 1993.

The completed Wyastone Leys estate in 1993, showing factory, house and Performing Arts Centre.

In response to this Numa sent a generous message that 'He was pleased to hear of developments in your personal and professional life and hopes that things continue to prosper. As long as no complete Beethoven Quartets are recorded ... he had no objection to your going ahead and naturally hopes that it is a great success.'[9]

Best and the Medici must suffice in a book of manageable length to exemplify Nimbus's smaller scale works during the first CD decade but there were, of course, a number of other notable recordings – Martin Jones, Paco Peña etc. – in a decade dominated by orchestral work.

The latter end of the decade saw two other important developments with which we shall deal later, *Prima Voce* and the World Music Series, but generally speaking the period was dominated at Nimbus by orchestral works.

When the horn player and authority on old instruments, Dr Horace Fitzpatrick first contacted Nimbus about the Hanover Band in 1981 the band was in a parlous financial state – a state of affairs which was to persist in greater or lesser degree throughout the next decade during its exclusive recording relationship with Nimbus. Without the wildly generous scope and nature of the record company's financial support in the course of making twenty-seven CDs and twenty-one cassettes covering no less than forty-one major works, the Hanover Band would not have survived another ten months, let alone another ten years.

At first Nimbus hesitated a little, but Fitzpatrick's Sunday telephone call on 22 November 1981 to say that 'if Nimbus withdrew the Hanover Band would cease to continue in existence' touched the right chord and a deal for the first recording of the Beethoven First Symphony and First Piano Concerto, to which we have already referred, was made. Five days later one of the founders of the orchestra, Caroline Brown, effectively its joint manager with her husband Stephen Neiman, wrote to Numa about the proposed recording. 'Dr Fitzpatrick and I will be sending very precise style sheets to Adrian. I understand there is a move afoot to get Monica [Huggett] billed as the Musical Director. I think they had better form their own orchestra if they want that issue to get through. Thank you, Numa for guiding me through this, however painful.'[10]

Fitzpatrick duly supplied the 'style sheets' which in great detail explained how the band endeavoured to reproduce the original orchestral sound with its lower pitch, its intimate chamber music approach, its late eighteenth-century feeling for tempo and its 'dramatic address to rhythmic accent and dynamic colour which eyewitnesses describe in Beethoven's own performances.' Fitzpatrick was delighted with the results Adrian obtained. 'Please accept our thanks and congratulations on your brilliant production of the Beethoven record with the Hanover Band. Musically and psychologically you were in complete control; without your tact, judgement and firmness we would never have finished in time.'[11] (No wonder he wanted the team to record Leopold Mozart's Hunting Symphony complete with hounds and shotguns, which, sadly, it never did.)

Monica Huggett, the leader of the orchestra, which in contemporary terms meant effectively its conductor – an invention of a later and vainer age – amply had what Adrian called, 'that disgruntled energy necessary for any successful artist', and though the five-cornered relationship between leader, managers, patrons (mainly the Verneys), the musicians and Nimbus (also very much 'a patron') was never an easy one, it was clearly fruitful and remained so when Roy Goodman replaced Huggett in 1986.

The critics who reviewed that first Beethoven recording over the next twelve months were as delighted as Fitzpatrick.

> The most original Beethoven yet recorded.[12]

> This new digital issue coupling the First Symphony and the First Piano Concerto (Nimbus 2150) puts us in a new generation of authentic performance.
>   The recording made in St Giles' Cripplegate, is excellent, just big and atmospheric enough, and the Nimbus surfaces are as immaculate as ever.[13]

> Here Nimbus have used the Sony PCM 1610 two-track digital recording system although this particular 1610 is unlike any other machine in the series Sony have supplied to studios. It has been extensively modified by Dr Jonathan Halliday of Nimbus to eliminate a number of unwanted audible products which they have managed to trace to specific sections of the circuitry. This alone merits an article in itself, so suffice to say that if you haven't been enamoured by digital recordings so far, this one should not be lumped with the rest of the 'porridge'. Clear your mind of any preconceptions and just listen for yourself.

And that sort of immediacy of expression and contact with the listener does not come from excessive retakes and editing to remove the last tiny blemish. (If you don't believe me ask any orchestral player who has endured the 'patchwork' process of putting together a recording.)

In truth I hear little or nothing that does need editing from these performances, unless of course you really do find the odd tap of a bow on a front desk wholly objectionable (in which case you probably find Beethoven unacceptable too!)[14]

This marked a change in tone by many critics towards Nimbus's recording technique and philosophy as manifest in their orchestral recordings. Made in naturally reverberant surroundings, these did not attract the criticisms which many had made of the solo and chamber performances recorded in the 'lively' studio at Wyastone Leys.

The contract to record all the Beethoven symphonies which followed naturally on this success in March 1982 was to win much additional kudos for both band and recording company over the next five years. Though the quality of the individual symphony recordings is rather variable, the boxed set when it was completed was named Record of the Year in 1989 in *Fono-Forum* and the Fifth, under Monica Huggett, was described by the *New York Times* as follows: 'The most exciting, daring "original" Beethoven performances to emerge on disc thus far come from the Hanover Band on Nimbus. [These] are the most revelatory original-instrument performances of this repertory yet recorded.' These were very much qualities brought to the orchestra by Huggett, their volatile leader.

The *Pastoral* reached the Number 13 spot in the US Classical Billboard ratings chart soon after its release.

Both financial and musical relationships between the two bodies were to prove equally uneven. The first stumble, inevitably, arose over the thorny subject of editing on which Adrian felt he had to lay down the law in a lengthy exposition to Caroline Brown on 6 July 1983.

I believed that we had fully established the ground rules of our relationship, and find that I was mistaken. This is to clarify beyond doubt the way we wish to continue and the reasons why we have stuck by the Hanover Band through difficult times. Nimbus is only interested in making recordings of performances which communicate as powerfully as possible the spirit of the music. We have no interest in building up a library of definitive renderings that have had all their

179

errors removed and are consequently not in fact performances given at one moment in time. This is a fundamental and immovable philosophy.

Our editing policy will continue to be minimal; we will save a great performance which momentarily comes off the rails and look sympathetically on slips or noises which seriously threaten the flow of musical thought and intensity. That is the extent of it.

You must remember that I can only work with the notes you play and there are places where you never did get it right! However, I was resolved to look at them again and with that in mind asked you to provide some indication of places where substantial correctable errors occurred. You have taken severe advantage of this suggestion in the very way in which we had hoped you would not. You would have us go against the idea of performance, to correct minuscule slips, the outcome of which would be a note perfected porridge bearing no relation to the magnificent recording that you have made.

To be blunt – the few corrections I made (and was happy to do so) have already made the Band sound better than they were, even in its present modestly corrected state it is of a total quality which

Monica Huggett, leading for Mary Verney in the first Beethoven piano concerto with the Hanover Band in their first recording which, on 20 January 1982, was Nimbus's first orchestral and first digital recording.

Geoff Barton and Jonathan Halliday in the control room for the first Hanover Band recording using digital equipment.

is actually beyond the competence of the Band to reproduce in a live concert.

We cannot indulge you over the matter of edits. Whether you trust our judgement or not is up to you, but final editorial control rests with us.

I know that none of you believe it but it is true and must be said again and again until it becomes part of everyone's soul – editing only improves the notes, the more important quality of communication is absolute and cannot be improved by cutting it up.[15]

Obviously the message got through for the subject disappears from the agenda from then on and when Roy Goodman came to record the highly original Beethoven *Missa Solemnis* made in the Great Hall of Birmingham University, his editing request was modest and limited. 'Perhaps there is one thing you could change ... It is the very first note of the *Agnus Dei* – the timps are really too early – making either myself or Ben Hoffnung seem incompetent!'[16]

A quarrel with Goodman, but not an abiding one luckily, later arose in November 1989, sparked off by Nimbus's characteristic lack of communication. It opened with a fax from Goodman on 25 November:

Hello! I am Roy Goodman – one of your artists!

   Firstly – why do I see CDs in the shops of recordings I have made for you, before I have received a copy myself??? . . .

   Thirdly, why can I not receive a cassette copy of the last main edit of each recording I made for you???

   A great supporter for many years,
and, I hope, for many more,[17]

This was followed by a contrite one the next morning. 'In the hope that this message will reach the same destination as the fax which I sent last night – I would like to apologise for the aggressive tone of that message. I was not feeling quite myself, and I am afraid that I slightly lost control.'[18]

Adrian apparently made a conciliatory reply for on 27 November Goodman faxed, 'I must have been in a bad mood – thank you for a kind reply!'[19] and the quarrel had blown over.

Not so easily dismissed was the disagreement which marked the parting of the ways between Nimbus and the Hanover Band.

In June 1990 Hyperion, a rival record company, approached the Hanover Band with a proposal to record all the Haydn Symphonies over four years with a major advance which would remove the Band's perennial cash flow problem for the time being and give respectability to its unattractive balance sheet, the state of which, the band claimed, had earlier cost it the sponsorship of American Express. Nimbus had already embarked on its slower paced project to record all the Haydn Symphonies with the Austro-Hungarian Haydn Orchestra so had neither space in its catalogue nor cash in its budget for such a proposal, although it had already recorded Haydn Symphonies 101 and 104 with the Hanover Band in March 1987. Nevertheless, Nimbus was reluctant to see a rival series, particularly from an orchestra with which they were so closely associated.

To get into perspective both Hanover Band's almost frantic eagerness to accept the Hyperion offer and Nimbus's hurt feelings because of that eagerness, it is necessary to trace the perilous course of the Band's finances over the preceding decade. As we have seen, the Nimbus five-year recording contract of March 1982 was a lifeline to a drowning orchestra and one which the company extended for a further five years in 1987. The Band's principal revenue came from the Hanover Band Trust, £117,000 for the period 1983–86, of which

182

Nimbus, and Numa personally, supplied the greater part. Nimbus also made, in 1985, a four-year covenant for £26,000. Nevertheless by 1986 the Hanover Band had accumulated a modest deficit. In that year Adrian joined the Board of Hanover Band and the Hanover Band Trust in 1986 to keep an eye on Nimbus's substantial stake. From April to July 1988 Nimbus funded the Band again so that recordings – £226,000 worth – could continue and on 14 July Adrian noted that, 'In view of the Band's outstanding contribution to Nimbus's international reputation, £25K to be advanced against the covenant as a support pending the findings of the report. The Executive Board of Nimbus believes that the Hanover Band is an important long-term resource and all reasonable measures should be taken to facilitate their continued existence.'[20]

By 3 October 1988 Spicer and Pegler, Hanover Band's accountants, were expressing anxiety about the Band's financial status. Again Nimbus, which had already covenanted in April 1987 a further four years at £56,666 and despite its own financial difficulties, resolved the situation by its commitments to future recordings and loans and investments of £30,000.

On 26 June 1989 Gerald wrote to Neiman to confirm still further support,

> The Nimbus Foundation will make a grant to the Band of £50,000 [to help] appoint a Managing Director for the Band.
>
> [We will make a] further two year extension . . . contract between the Band and Nimbus.
>
> In view of the level of this further support we must have regular financial information.
>
> We are delighted that the Band and the recordings are achieving the recognition all our efforts so richly deserve. Many years of hard work and faith are set to bring a reward and we hope that the support and help outlined above will both enable the Band to sustain its current cash needs and more fully exploit the opportunities.[21]

On 14 October, after what had obviously been an uncomfortable visit to Wyastone Leys by Neiman, the Hanover Band Chairman of the time, Ken Aldred, wrote to him admonishing him for getting out of his depth and complaining of Nimbus's conduct of affairs.

There is a great lack of business procedures in our relationships with that company; and a lack of respect by Nimbus for the Board of this company.

The Hanover Band has improved its musical capability and its reputation tremendously over the past few years. But the management has remained static. The financial position has been a constant cause of concern with no real action taken to rectify it.

The Board of the Company [i.e. Hanover] is run on an amateur basis.

I resent, therefore, the implication of criticisms which you say have been made by Nimbus about our performance. In my view, many of the problems of the company have come about from a lack of professionalism in the Nimbus financial arrangements which may be their fault or the Band's, but are certainly not conducted in a way which is conducive to good financial management of the Hanover Band Limited.

I think the recording agreement with Nimbus is an excellent one and I was very impressed with their American operation.

I do not believe that you should put yourself in a position of going into Nimbus's premises and getting embroiled in talks which are obviously impossible for one person to be able to cope with against several executives from another company on their home ground. Under no circumstances do I think you should allow yourself to get into a position where you return to your own Board having been apparently browbeaten in the way that you were earlier this week.[22]

Nimbus now took over Numa's loans to the Band and Numa resigned, a step the managers regretted.

I did however, want to record the personal gratitude of both Caroline and myself for the immense amount of time, energy and financial support that you have given to the orchestra over its many years relationship with Nimbus.

I believe that Nimbus and the Hanover Band are synonymous and will remain so in the eyes of the record-buying public and it would be a great shame if, despite all these years of working and 'playing together', the more recent events that have caused us to be estranged at this time get in the way of achieving our joint artistic aims.[23]

Neiman was at that time seriously considering winding up the affairs of the Band and going into liquidation, but resolved instead to sort out the difficulties with loans and underwriting himself and he also agreed to pay back Numa's equity personally. On the same day the Band's new Chairman, Mr Simon Caradoc Evans, also wrote to Numa.

The financial situation the company found itself in and that you were informed about by Stephen was one of cash flow, and not profit. Within a few days we were able to sort it out.

It was for reasons of profit and *profit only* that we had to press for acceptance of the Hyperion contract. The company is so very appreciative of all that you and your colleagues at Nimbus have done over the years for the Band and we realise how uncomfortable the consideration of the Hyperion option has been for you.

By 2 November an obviously agitated Neiman was faxing Gerald. 'I will not speak to anybody else at Nimbus except you or Adrian. I remain flabbergasted at the problems that have occurred between us and wish to sort them out, however uncomfortable that may be.'[24]

Communication had broken down so far that Nimbus felt it necessary to get their lawyers, McFarlanes, to write a formal and slightly sniffy letter to the Band on 22 November.

> In the circumstances, it is not open to you to record for other record companies without written consent of Nimbus. We should make it quite plain that any attempts by you to avoid the terms of your contract will be the subject of appropriate action by our client.
>
> Our clients have, however, asked us to express their hope that normal working relationships between you and them can be restored, and (that you will give) your undertaking that you will not seek to record for other companies repertoire which you should record for Nimbus.[25]

However, by the following January both parties seem to have recognised the realities of the situation – that the Hanover Band desperately needed cash generating work and that Nimbus could not provide it in sufficient quantity.

The Chairman of the Band, Caradoc Evans, confirmed what had been agreed in a letter to Gerald.

> We agreed that,
> a. Nimbus Records wanted to continue recording with the Hanover, but
> b. you did not want to give advances and that from the Band's point of view advances are a very great consideration to us at the present time, and may decide the issue.
>
> We therefore have to consider very carefully other offers being presented to us, especially in view of our debt reduction programme.
>
> I take this opportunity to acknowledge your company's fax to us of 14 January, confirming in clause 3 that no recording can proceed.[26]

Adrian responded immediately in conciliatory tone: 'Should it be that Nimbus and the Hanover Band decide to go separate ways temporarily, I feel that we have sufficient in common to continue a dialogue which may bring us back together at an appropriate moment.'[27] Gerald followed this up on 11 February: 'It is certainly not our intention to enter into litigation that would create ill-will, be time-consuming and costly. Therefore we are happy to confirm that the Band is free to enter into discussions with other record companies for repertoire not already recorded by us.'[28] Neiman confirmed the armistice on 20 February: 'We will not be seeking to record repertoire already recorded by Nimbus within the terms of the contract. I am sure that the right decision has been made for neither the Hanover Band nor Nimbus to pursue the contract as we also agree that litigation will only create ill-will.'[29]

During 1991 Hanover Band switched its main recording contract to RCA – BMG Classics and an exchange of letters between Adrian and Roy Goodman in May and from Caroline Brown to Numa in June marked the end of the relationship.

> Dear Adrian,
>
> Well, we appear to have parted company.
>
> Nimbus, as a company, have not been noted for their communications to me, so I suppose it is nothing unusual for none to be made at the end! In fact, were it not for the CDs on the shelf, the Delius I happen to be listening to at the moment could persuade me that in fact it was all a dream.
>
> Thank you for that dream – I certainly matured with the experience – I think you and I had some good times.
>
> Good luck for the future,
> Best wishes.[30]

To which Adrian replied, 'I too wish you every success for the future. On the matter of communication and parting, I believe it was your decision and not one actually communicated to us prior to announcement. However, I trust your dream will not fade in your new surroundings.'[31]

Caroline Brown expressed the feelings of the Band.

> It is with much sadness that I feel now that you possibly consider that there will be no more future collaboration.
>
> Speaking for the members of the Band, they have asked me to express to you about their dismay and disappointment at the way

Roy so abruptly stopped the Mendelssohn cycle which was going extremely well last December.*

Keep the Hyperion project in perspective – as only one aspect of the Band's work.[32]

There the two parties tacitly agreed to leave the matter, apart from a slightly sour postscript in November in which Goodman faxed Adrian a copy of an article in Burrelles Newsletter. The article, while acknowledging the Hanover Band's debt to Nimbus, set out Goodman's dissatisfaction.

We are very grateful to Nimbus for giving us so many opportunities to record a vast repertoire, including a lot of things we really wanted very much to do. But in the end, I felt that we didn't have enough artistic control in what was happening with the recordings after we played.

I had no control over what arrived on the recording, and their ideas about what they liked in sound etc., often were rather different from mine. They determined exactly 100 percent of what went on the disc – I had no say in the matter. It always had been a running battle during the five years we worked with them. They would never send me a copy of the tape, and I was never in on the editing process.[33]

Adrian replied a little waspishly with a message via his assistant, Sylvia Strange. 'His only comment is, "Quite right, you never did have artistic control, did you?" '

In retrospect Adrian summed up the ten-year relationship with the Hanover Band as, 'an example of artistic commitment prevailing over experience and wisdom, we've lost hundreds of thousands on that project.'

During its decade of association with Nimbus the Hanover Band made its American Tour debut in 1985, its Prom debut in 1990 and, very largely thanks to Nimbus securing its financial survival, had become a landmark on the British musical scene. If ever the Nimbus policy of willingly losing money on the record label needed justification, this relationship surely provided it.

Looking back on all these achievements after the parting of their ways the Hanover Band's manager, Stephen Neiman, told Nimbus that it 'was the only record company to support them with advertising in all programmes and the only company to get discs on sale at every

*Literally downing fiddle in mid-recording and refusing to do more.

The Hanover Band conducted by Roy Goodman in a dinner concert at the Banqueting Hall in Whitehall.

concert.' Can one detect here the regretful tones of someone finding the grass on the other side of the fence a lot browner than he hoped?

Hard on the heels of the Hanover Band came the English Symphony Orchestra under its charismatic conductor William Boughton. When the BBC closed down its Midland Radio Orchestra in 1980, Boughton had taken the nucleus of the players and founded the Vivaldi Ensemble. They had made a recording for Meridian of Vivaldi's Music for Strings of which Nimbus's cutting skill had more than fully captured the quality of the original tape. Thus, when Meridian's conduct drove Boughton to bring the Ensemble's relationship with it to 'an abrupt conclusion', he thought of Nimbus as an alternative. Boughton recounted to me how the new relationship with Nimbus which was to prove a long, fruitful and unusually harmonious one, began.

> About ten o'clock one night I thought, 'Nimbus is a small company, there may be somebody there so I'll give them a ring on the off-chance.' Numa himself answered the 'phone and after a longish conversation, invited me down to see him.
>
> We hit it off at once because I think we're rather alike. We're both obsessed with a particular thing; me with creating a really good orchestra, Numa with creating and running a quality record company. There was a rapport between us and we embarked on a recording relationship which has been going for more than ten years now. We had expanded the Ensemble to be the Vivaldi String Orchestra but Numa had the brilliant idea that we should re-christen ourselves the English String Orchestra which was not only a much more marketable name but was particularly apt in view of the large amount of twentieth-century English repertoire that we played.

The first recordings were largely made possible by the existence of an £110,000 sponsorship of the orchestra from Mitsubishi as well as from the porcelain millionairess Mrs Helen Boehm who also ordered 4,000 copies of the LP that really established the ESO's recording reputation – all Elgar's Music for Strings – as Christmas cards! The CD version was one of the first half dozen to be issued by Nimbus and appeared in December 1983. By Boughton's own admission the ESO's very first recording session with Nimbus, Ravel's Introduction and Allegro for Strings and Harp, 'was not a success, but Numa and Adrian persisted with us and our second recording, the Elgar, was both musically and commercially a success. We went on then to have similar successes with English music which went down particularly well in the United States.'

Subsequently, the Orchestral Favourites and the Vaughan Williams recordings soon established themselves as Nimbus best-sellers in America with Orchestral Favourites ranking in Nimbus's all-time top ten. Adrian had no doubt as to the reasons for Nimbus's successful partnership with the ESO. 'William is one of the very, very few artists that we record who really is prepared to go for a performance on a recording. William's performances actually live up more to our declared ambition of total performance than those of anybody else. In the beginning he did it because it was our wish and then gradually he came to recognise that it was not just a quirk, that it really does work. Numa says he's going to be the next Boult.'

The recordings certainly helped the orchestra to spread its fame and extend its concert schedule from four concerts in its first year, 1983, to forty in 1985 and eighty in 1989. However, despite its success the orchestra made a loss of £8,000 in the 1984–85 season, in alleviation of which Nimbus offered to give ESO a royalty on recordings already made for which such was not yet due. By February 1986 Hugh Padley, the orchestra's Chairman wrote to 'confirm that we hope to develop a longstanding association with Nimbus' but also to chide gently with the perennial Nimbus artist's complaint. 'I believe you acknowledged that we had some concern with regard to the marketing of the recordings, upon which we are of course dependent for income.'[34]

Clearly Nimbus had not entirely achieved the aim declared in a letter to the orchestra in November 1982 when the partnership was being established. 'At the present time Nimbus Records have a reputation second to none for musical and technical excellence and we are now forming plans to see that our marketing skills become equally respected.'[35]

In 1986 the orchestra and Nimbus did establish an ingenious sponsorship scheme which gained the ESO another £10,000 from the ABSA (Association of Business Sponsorship in the Arts) Scheme. Just as the orchestra was getting financially secure, it was rocked by a serious piece of ill-luck in appointing David Hepworth as General Manager in 1988. Behind much grandiose talk of fancy schemes which did not materialise, he was embezzling the orchestra's funds. Hepworth was sent to prison for two-and-a-half years for this crime but that did nothing to compensate the orchestra for the £140,000 debt with which he had saddled it. Fortunately for the ESO, its principal creditors were those who had an interest in its survival so would not 'pull the plug' – the musicians themselves. Once again the ESO had to grasp its own boot straps and pull and did so with such determination that it continued to flourish first from a new headquarters in Worcester, and more recently a new base (and, it is hoped concert hall) in Malvern.

William Boughton conducting the English Symphony Orchestra in the Symphony Hall, Birmingham, in the first recording made there, prior to its official opening.

The control room of the Birmingham University Great Hall, whose remarkable acoustic qualities made it one of the Nimbus's most used recording venues.
Left to right: Adrian Farmer, Michael Bochman, leader, and William Boughton, founder and principal conductor of the English Symphony Orchestra.

Although the repertoire recorded has included Stavinsky, Tippett, Mendelssohn, Haydn, Boccherini, Tchaikovsky, Sibelius, Schoenberg and Strauss, the pinnacle of the Nimbus/ESO/Boughton achievement is undoubtedly its comprehensive coverage of English music of the twentieth century from an ambitious plan to record all the symphonies of Parry to many minor gems, as well as major compositions from Bridge, Britten, Butterworth, Elgar, Delius, Finzi, Holst, Vaughan Williams and Warlock. This it wisely packaged as a four-box set, 'The Spirit of England', of which the American Record Guide wrote, 'this set offers a true treasury of English string music in all its multi-faceted beauty. *All* are excellent (a tribute to the artistry of William Boughton) and the collection is a delight all round.'

Perhaps the most enterprising orchestral venture of the period sprang from Adrian Farmer's idea that 'an orchestra made up of half Viennese and half Hungarians playing Haydn in Eisenstadt has to be interesting.' Adrian invited the founder and conductor of the Austro-Hungarian Haydn Orchestra, Adam Fischer, and his much venerated musical associate Professor Hubner to visit Nimbus.* They all got on so well that Adrian decided to go ahead with the project and visited Eisenstadt to check out the location and, more particularly, the Haydnsaal, the very room in the Palace where so much of Haydn's music was first performed during his thirty years under the patronage of the Esterhazys. Adrian 'just walked into the hall, clapped his hands to test the acoustics, and realised that it was a wonderful environment for making the music that was written to be played there.' When the first recordings were made, the Nimbus project to record all the Haydn symphonies was a novel one, though it has since had a number of imitators. The project had been expensive and politically fraught, for it was conceived and launched before the collapse of communism that made such cross border ventures much easier. The series, when completed in the year 2000 will be a valuable 'document' as well as an enjoyable experience and is well on its way with Symphones 1-20 (not 11), 22, 24, 25, 40 and 45; 82–7 and all the London Symphonies, 93–104 already issued. When the London Symphonies were issued as a five CD set the *Guardian* wrote: 'In these grand surroundings the freely reverberant Nimbus recording gives the loud *tuttis* a breadth of scale to rival in sound at least . . . that of Karajan and the Berlin Philharmonic or Bernstein and the Vienna Philharmonic.'

Out of this grand venture sprang a no less exacting if smaller scale one in the same mould. Hungarian musicians of the Hungarian State Orchestra, some of whom had performed in the Haydn, playing Hungarian music, recorded for Nimbus probably the most exciting available version of Kodály's *Háry János*, the making of which Adrian happily recalls:

*A serendipitous by-product of these recordings has been the acclaimed discs Nimbus has since issued from the Brandis Quartet. Thomas Brandis happened to be 'in town' judging a competition on whose jury Adrian was also serving when the leader of the Austro-Hungarian Haydn Orchestra was suddenly taken ill. Brandis stepped in at very short notice and he and Adrian got on so well that they promptly struck a recording deal.

Gerhard Hetzel, konzert-meister of the Vienna Philharmonic, who died in a tragic mountaineering accident some months after his only concerto recording (both Bartok violin concertos), with Adam Fischer.

> The Hungarian project which grew out of it is another one. When we made the *Háry János* record, which was quite stunning, it was a complete performance; that's the way it came out. You can't beat it. They were excited to be in the Haydnsaal, to be out of Hungary, because this was still before the breakdown of communist regimes. When I turned up to do the recording they were expecting to be spread out all over the floor as they had been before, but I said, 'not on your life'. We built the stage out, sat them up there, got it looking right, and they played and it just poured out of them. After the recording I said to them 'you've given me, without any doubt at all, the best two days of orchestral experience I've ever had.'

This overview of Nimbus's astonishing output of orchestral recordings from 1982 to 1992, which would have been a credit to one of the giant record companies let alone to this smaller one, cannot conclude without reference to the recordings made with two of Britain's regional orchestras, the Scottish Chamber Orchestra and the BBC National Orchestra of Wales.

The Scottish Chamber Orchestra's 1986 *Midsummer Night's Dream*, described by the *San Francisco Chronicle* as 'a sensational recording ... a jewel among current listings', we have already referred to, and under its conductor Jamie Laredo the orchestra concentrated on Mendelssohn for Nimbus with recordings of the Scottish and Italian Symphonies and the two Piano Concertos, (with Joseph Kalichstein at the piano). The orchestra, in lighter hearted mood and under various conductors, tackled Rossini overtures, Sullivan overtures and *The Soldier's Tale* with Christopher Lee as narrator. (Nimbus has always had a soft spot for the spoken word from the early Birmingham recordings of Ann Todd and making books for the blind, to Sir John Gielgud's more recent and enchanting recordings of *Alice in Wonderland* and *Through the Looking Glass* and *The Happy Prince*.)

British actress Ann Todd who recorded
poetry and prose readings for Nimbus.

Sir John Gielgud who recorded Oscar Wilde's *The Happy Prince*, with Adrian Farmer.

With an orchestra on its own doorstep, the BBC Welsh Symphony Orchestra, the Nimbus partnership is of relatively recent origin stemming from the appointment in June 1988 of Geraint Lewis, now Assistant Director of Music. As a bilingual Welshman, Lewis has encouraged Nimbus to record contemporary music, by contemporary Welsh composers in particular, with felicitous results. The late William Mathias was particularly well-served by the orchestra, conducting or supporting Grant Llewellyn as conductor. CDs were made of Symphonies 1, 2 and 3, *Helios*, the Oboe Concerto and *Requiescat*. Of these recordings, the British Music Society wrote, 'these Nimbus CDs are very carefully produced, superbly recorded, have highly informative notes by Geraint Lewis and are adorned with beautiful paintings by John Piper.' A view which the American magazine *Fanfare* readily endorsed. 'As in other Nimbus releases, performances and recording qualities are peerless with Llewellyn, Cowley, the orchestra, engineers achieving that kind of resplendent and crystalline transparency of ambience that is so perfectly suited to the magically enraptured world Mathias, the sonic conjuror, brings into being . . . *Not to be missed by anybody!!!*'[36]

Christ Church Cathedral Choir, Oxford, surround director Stephen Darlington.

With John Scott's Organ Recital and Stephen Darlington and the Christ Church Cathedral Choir's recording of much of Mathias's church and choral music, the Nimbus collection provides a marvellous pool of reference for this joyously Welsh composer's work.

Alun Hoddinott is the best-known contemporary Welsh composer and four of his works: *The Heaven Tree of Stars*; *Star Children*; *Doubles* and *Passaggio*, are the first of what Nimbus hopes will be many recordings. As *Gramophone* observed, 'when given such fine and committed performances as those on this disc by an orchestra and its principal conductor, both currently in startling form, many composers will envy Hoddinott his good fortune.'[37]

197

Principal conductor of the BBC National Orchestra of Wales Tadaki Otaka who recorded the Rachmaninov symphonies and piano concertos with John Lill for Nimbus.

The eighty-eight strong orchestra, which faced the prospect of being closed down during a BBC economy drive in the early 1970s, flourishes under its principal conductor, Tadaaki Otaka, who has, according to Adrian Farmer, an unusual knack of knowing 'exactly the right moment to do a recording take – when the orchestra is rehearsed enough without being tired.' Evidently in the opinion of the *Daily Telegraph*, Otaka got it just right in the Nimbus recording of Rachmaninov's Second Symphony: 'Otaka finds those glorious moments where the brass, either buried or brash in so many performances, lend a subtle sharpening sheen to the colouring; and the strings are immaculate not just in lush melody but equally in their athletic articulation. Such technical questions pose no problems for the BBC Welsh, but the particular delight of this recording is its thorough evocation of that complex Rachmaninov mood of melancholy, energetic exhilaration and melody which touches the heart.'[38]

British pianist John Lill.

In an effective piece of marketing Nimbus rushed out the orchestra's recording of the Third Rachmaninov piano concerto with John Lill in time to coincide with the pianist's fiftieth birthday, prompting him to remark to Antony, 'I have never been so well looked after and never felt as though a record company was working so hard just for me.'

What produces such gems in general is hard to pinpoint but is largely abstract; a matter of mood, inspiration if you like, arising from the interaction of all the participants from the newest violinist to the conductor, the teaboy to the producer, the engineer to the agent. The 'big orchestras', except on the very 'big' occasions are less likely to have that subconscious interaction than the smaller ones aiming for the big time while still struggling simply to survive. Of this Adrian has no doubt.

> The out and out mistakes that were made did reinforce the fact that they had nothing to do with whether you were working with the most famous or less well known orchestras.
>
> We get the best out of it when the sense of commitment or family, or whatever you like to call it, is very strong. This can produce extraordinary results from something like the ESO which on paper, in those early days, looked as though it ought to be an absolute mess. There was something that they had which meshed with our approach which simply never worked with the London orchestras. Mark you, we also started off very well with a chopped down Philharmonia to do things with John Wallace but John put those together, he asked the players to do it and that worked very well. By contrast, sometimes I think some of the big and famous orchestras are too blasé. The full symphony orchestras themselves on many occasions didn't even know what they were playing until they turned up on the morning and saw the music on the stands. This was almost inevitable with the extent of their workload.

Following Nimbus's re-organisation and the consequent demands on financial resources, there has had to be a severe cutback in orchestral recording and a reappraisal of strategy. Adrian's view is that 'the record industry is in a diabolical state. There's just too much, it's become a commodity like Mars Bars – worse, it's down at the Smarties end of the market now. It doesn't matter how good the record is it gets swamped. People who pursue quality can simply go out of business.' And he is taking the appropriate steps to see that does not happen to Nimbus. 'For the first time we have a burden of commercial thinking on the record label, maybe it's a good thing rather than a burden, we had a much smaller budget for 1993 and it is the same again in 1994.'

Gerald very much endorsed that view. 'The label is getting near break-even now that we've taken decisions to do our own distribution in the UK and have developed a successful distribution and marketing operation in the USA. Unless you do that, going through an intermediary you don't get accurate feedback on what's going on on the retail side. The advantage with chamber music and solo is that you have an individual performance that is not going to be immediately superseded whereas with orchestral you have so many versions that however special a performance your conductor and orchestra have done it's so dependent on fashion, so you can't achieve what we have done with some of the chamber music where the performances are the reference versions.'

CHAPTER ELEVEN

Towards the end of Nimbus's decade of CD music-making it embarked on what was unchallengeably the most daring and successful journey of space and time travel ever undertaken by any record company, large or small. In March 1988 it launched its World Music Series which now encompasses the music of three continents and many cultures. In September 1989 *Prima Voce* was launched, a series which has travelled back almost a century to bring to life again for today's listeners the great singers of the past and particularly of the first two decades of the twentieth century.

Prima Voce had its seed sown in the visit by a fifteen-year-old boy to the cinema to see, and more importantly hear, Mario Lanza in *The Great Caruso* forty years ago. Norman White emerged into the street with two things kindled in his heart; curiosity about what Caruso himself had really sounded like, and a desire to sing. Here is not the place to recount the tale of how a combination of fine voice, dogged persistence and a little luck eventually established Norman as a successful singer with the Scottish Opera, but that he was himself an accomplished vocalist is an important element in the success of *Prima Voce*. It was through his running of the Friends of Scottish Opera also that he made the network of connections that led him to Peter Laister, who introduced him, in turn, to Nimbus.

However, the connections were only the pipeline. What flowed through it was a lifetime's passionate, obsessive, collecting of old recordings of great singers of the past which had grown out of the Caruso record given to him by an uncle who sympathised with his curiosity. On this collection he had spent every spare penny of his earnings as an electrician, TV engineer and eventually singer, until, by the time he met Nimbus, he had amassed some 20,000 records. He now has 40,000. No less importantly he had acquired an EM Ginn (EMG) mechanical gramophone on which to play them and he experimented with re-recording on tape by the simple expedient of placing a

Numa, Adrian and Norman White with the 78s that started the *Prima Voce* series.

microphone in front of the gramophone horn.

It was these tapes which he played on his first visit to Wyastone Leys where his listeners realised that here was the potential at least to prove Numa's lifelong contention that the art of singing had died and that few, if any, of today's singers could compare with their counterparts of the late nineteenth and the early part of the twentieth century. The issue of the first *Prima Voce* recordings certainly provoked the same thoughts among a number of reviewers. As *Classic CD* wrote: 'These recordings pose serious questions about the quality and commitment of much contemporary operatic singing and set a new benchmark against which modern exponents will have to be measured. If the first releases from Nimbus are anything to go by these will have some strong opposition from the voices of the past. The best of the historic recordings offer a sound, a technique, that simply is not there, even in world-class modern performers.'[1]

The first recordings were primitive affairs: the artist, invariably a singer, stood in front of a funnel-like horn and 'performed'. This he did straight through, as if to an audience, and indeed, as if for an audience, he or she would come to a recording session attired in full evening dress. Not only had the artist to sing straight through, but because the volume at which the recording apparatus recorded could not be varied, the singer had to vary his distance from the microphone as necessary. This gave real meaning to the title 'floor manager', for that functionary literally propelled the singer backwards and forwards to predesignated chalk marks on the floor at various distances from the microphone as the score dictated. One article described this process as one in which 'the singer and engineer did a kind of tango backwards and forwards in front of the microphone.'[2]

The soundwaves thus created travelled down the horn to impinge on a diaphragm whose reciprocal vibrations varied the undulation of a stylus cutting a track on a waxed disc. From the wax a metal master was made from which, in turn, shellac pressings for the consumer were moulded. When we complain of the cost of CDs today, we should perhaps remember that those early records cost a guinea for their seven or eight minutes, about two weeks' wages for an average industrial worker of the time.

The records thus manufactured were played back in the middle-class drawing-rooms of Europe, its colonial outposts and in America, on the

EMG Gramophone in which a thorn (later fibre) needle moving from side to side in the record grooves, vibrated a diaphragm to reproduce with great accuracy an analogue of most of the sound that had entered the replay horn's counterpart in the recording studio. The caveat 'most of' is necessary because in order to accommodate this monster in even the grandest of drawing rooms – it reached eight feet off the ground – the horn had to be curved round and this caused the loss of some lower frequency sounds. In the opinion of Sir Thomas Beecham, who first made a record in 1910, nothing more accurately captured the inner quality of the voice than this acoustic method, which was only superseded by electrical recording in the mid-1920s but continued to dominate vocal recording at least until the mid-1930s.

It was this process that Norman White, who now works in a cottage at the back of Nimbus's Wyastone Leys headquarters before driving back to Scotland for the weekends, and Gerald set out to recreate and translate to CD. Gerald's mechanical genius came up with one of those simple solutions that seem obvious only once accomplished and leave everyone saying 'why didn't I think of that?' If the curving of the replay horn and the limits to its size imposed by domestic architecture caused the loss of some of the sounds, and particularly the atmosphere-creating bass sounds, then what happens if you straighten it out and make it larger? Posing himself this question, Gerald then used a computer model to create a larger straight horn in glass fibre. It worked, and Gerald pushed the idea further to create the Mark III horn, nearly six metres long and over two metres across the mouth of the bell.

The family have affectionately christened Mark III, Saddam; the mother of all horns. This model, with a frequency response of down to fifty hertz, could reproduce sounds not far off the lowest octave on the piano. The first CD to be recorded off Saddam, Operatic Arias sung by the tenor Jussi Björling, was a sensational success.

The other technical innovation was the replacement of the original wind-up turntable by a Technics Transcription Table, with the ability to vary the speed of the turntable by computer control. This was needed because some old so-called 78rpm recordings were not made at 78rpm at all, but at anything from 62 to 85rpm, so that when the record was replayed at 78 the sound was raised or lowered as much as four semi-tones, thus extending the artist's tessitura. To hear what these long dead singers actually sounded like it is necessary to replay the performance at the speed at which it was originally recorded before transferring it to CD. Otherwise, high-tech plays little part in the *Prima Voce* process and as the *Independent* said, 'The recording cubicle at one end of the hall is spartan, with none of the paraphernalia of most recording companies – no bank of faders and equalisers, just one control knob and two Sony digital cassette recorders. Tucked away under a table is the Ambisonic encoder, and that's that.'[3]

The knack lies in getting the microphone position in front of the mouth of the horn so as to reproduce the original spatial acoustic relationship between the voice and the recording horn.

Like so many otherwise peaceful valleys of South Wales, the Wye Valley at Monmouth is tormented by the banshee shriek of jet fighters practising the destruction of the civilisation those below are so painfully trying to build. For this reason much of the *Prima Voce* recording is done at night when these abominable intruders are tucked up in their beds. To illustrate how sensitive a supposedly primitive acoustic recording method is, Norman tells the story of how on one such night, as they listened to the playback of a tape they had just recorded off disc, they heard a dog barking. Assuming it to be lurking outside in the bushes they scoured the immediate vicinity of the studio, but finding nothing returned somewhat irritably and recorded another take. When the same dog barked in exactly the same place they realised that it must have done so not in the present, but more than seventy years ago outside the windows of the original recording studio.

The records themselves are played with a Burmese thorn needle, whose resonant pliability clings to the groove as tightly as a car on a roller-coaster, whereas a diamond stylus bounces up and down and loses contact some of the time.

Unless the right records are under the needle, however, all this technical ingenuity is a waste of musical time and it is here that Norman's lifetime's experience and accumulated knowledge is invaluable. He has a world-wide network of dealers and friends, fellow enthusiasts, whom he visits, telephones, and corresponds with regularly in his search for not just the best performance of a particular artist's rendering of a particular piece – was Caruso's 'Questa O Quella' better in Camden on 16 March 1908 than it was in Milan on 11 April 1902? – but for the physically most perfect record. The companies which have original metal masters stored in their vaults have an advantage over those, such as Nimbus, which have to search out the most pristine shellac versions. British pressings are rarely of any use because the British companies, more interested in durability than audibility, mixed slate dust with their shellac to make the records last longer. As a result there is a terrible continuous crackle on most British records. American, French, German and best of all, surprisingly perhaps, Indian pressed records are more likely to meet the bill. Ideally they should never have been played, and therein lies the problem. As one old German lady said when Norman visited her in New York and sadly had to explain that her marvellous collection was too worn by playing to be of use, 'records that have not been played! Who has records that have not been played?' The answer is that among the literally thousands of records in garages and attics and dealers' back rooms through which Norman sifts in America and Europe each year, he sometimes finds the one that he has long searched for. Through Philip Moss, Nimbus's Public Relations Manager, Norman made a useful contact in 1992 with the archivists of the former Soviet regime's State Broadcasting System who have an enormous collection of early recordings from pre-revolutionary Russia. The best of these will soon be appearing through *Prima Voce* to give us an echo of another pantheon of great voices – Chaliapin (issued of course in *Prima Voce*) was not the only great Russian bass of the period!

There is no shortage of good raw material, and Nimbus approaches it with the reverence which is its due. Editing, as always, is minimal. Nimbus may eliminate a few of the worst clicks which can be heard on even the most perfectly preserved old record, but does not ever try to remove the hiss of the needle as it cut into the original wax master. As Adrian says, 'if you eliminate that, you lose some of the music, too.' Adrian's role in *Prima Voce* was to stand in the middle between Norman's unrestrained enthusiasm and his collector's occasional natural wish to produce something because of its rarity value alone, and Numa's very strong views about singing. Though, as Norman observed,

One of the reasons why the series works so well here and perhaps wouldn't have worked so well elsewhere is the influence of the Count in his passion about singing and his belief that contemporary singers have lost direction.

As far as technique is concerned he's totally right. You listen to his earliest recordings, his early singles, and they had a technique and ability that nobody has today. This series works because it is fulfilling the ambition here to let today's public hear what great singing really was like and the belief that it should come back.

Norman and Adrian have had some fierce arguments about which records should be or should not be a *Prima Voce* release, but as Adrian declared, 'His passion and dedication are undeniable and although we argue we are very close . . . Norman in his way is about as close a member of the family as people have got.'

Commercial judgement has also had to come into the process of choosing because, 'if you look at the lists, some of the best records haven't sold particularly well. All the tenors will always sell more than any other voice irrespective of how good they are. Caruso, Gigli, Björling *were* wonderful but some of the most ravishing records are of people like Norena, Battistini, wonderful voices but they won't sell.'

Commercially, however, *Prima Voce* has been a runaway success. Of the first batch of six issued, 35,000 had sold in eight weeks and today the series accounts for about a quarter of all Nimbus sales. Moreover, it is very profitable, for there are no fees or royalties to be paid to the performers. No wonder Nimbus is trying to spin off other similar projects from the basic *Prima Voce* idea and the Hermes series which it launched at that time to do the same for early jazz recordings. The company is working with another enthusiastic time-traveller on developing an electrical pick-up to recreate the early electrical recordings of the 1930s and 1940s for which their own contemporary pick-ups are insufficiently reliable. However, the backbone of the *Prima Voce* series remains the early vocal recordings and Nimbus's unique method of replicating them, a method widely but not universally praised. Nimbus's most hostile critic was Keith Hardwick of EMI who had been much involved in developing and applying the £6,000 an hour CEDAR (Computer Enhanced Digital Audio Restoration) electronic system of reproducing old recordings to CD. When the first of the *Prima Voce* series were released he wrote a savage attack on them on 5 December 1989 in a letter to *The Record Collector*.

> In my view . . . the Nimbus 'breakthrough' in archive sound reproduction is not so much a breakthrough, rather a breakdown . . .
>
> Now, to the Nimbus CDs. Let me say at the outset that they seek to put the technique of 78 transfers back by 30–40 years . . .
>
> What do we find with the Nimbus transfers? A complete absence of

The combined old and new team.
left to right: Nicholas Watson, Gary Helfrecht, Gerald, Michael, Colin Dix and Adrian.

Gary Helfrecht, Vice President of Nimbus Technology and Engineering America.

Jonathan with Roger Nute, NTE's General Manager.

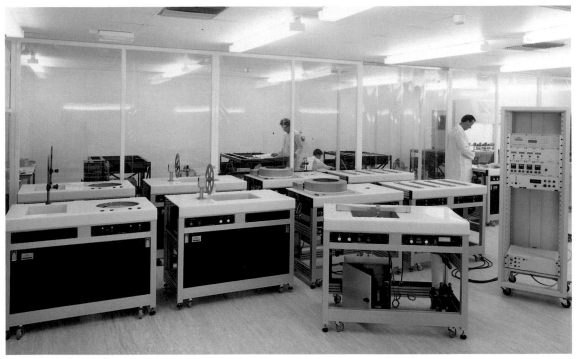

New mastering equipment being constructed.

Final assembly of a Laser Beam Recorder.

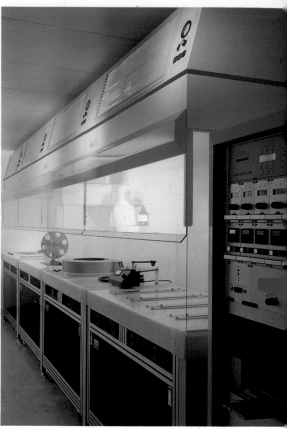

Installed master preparation line.

The new automated master preparation line

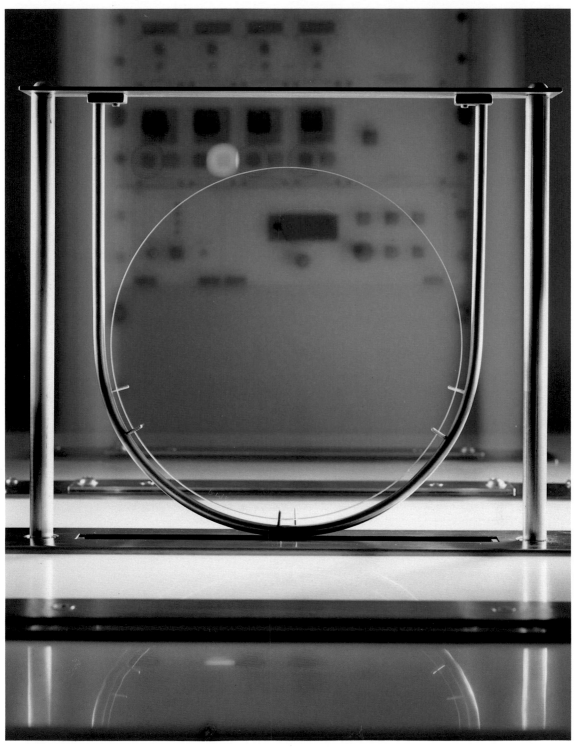

Glass master disc before baking.

The auto spin developer.

The Nimbus Halliday Laser Beam Recorder in action.

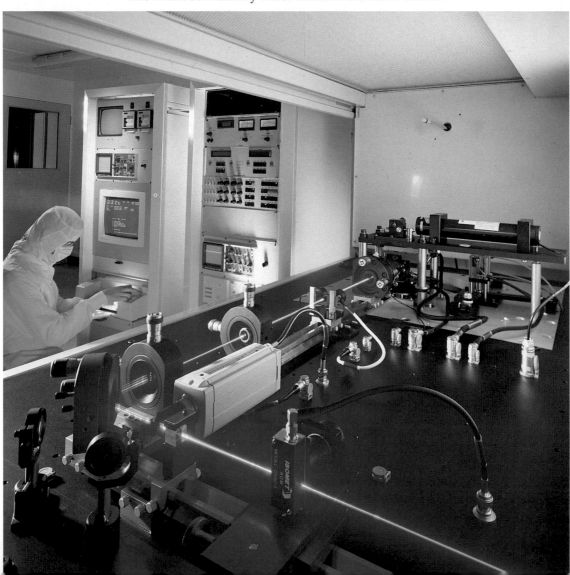

Numa contemplating his paintings.

Numa's last painting.

any sound above 4 KHz – and swathes of echo (described as Ambisonic technology) . . .

. . . to play an electrical record through an acoustic machine will have two effects:

No frequencies above 4 KHz will be reproduced – the sheen on violins, the brilliance of the upper woodwind *and* the upper partials (harmonics) of the human voice will be absent.
The arbitrary bumps of the acoustic machine *and the horn resonance* will colour the reproduction.

So, how does this affect the Nimbus transfers, as compared with the same 78s transferred by more conventional, logical and scientific means? . . . Nimbus recordings have a superficially 'open' air, due entirely to the spurious echo added . . .

In addition to subjecting my ears to these travesties, I have also put a couple of them into our EMI-Cedar computer, so as visually to compare 'ours' to 'theirs'. The evidence of the eyes totally validates what science and ears alike knew; the Nimbus frequency response collapses at about 3.8 KHz; there is a 'bump', common to all of them, at about 5.5 KHz – this is due to the resonance of the EMG horn inside which they quaintly hang the microphone. The echo is, of course, nothing else but room resonance.

Why then have some critics (but not all, by any means) gone overboard to praise these 'cottage-industry' efforts? A very good question.[4]

Numa was furious, as a note and draft letter of reply to the company's lawyer, Nick Thomas, indicates:

Numa has asked me to request a sharp response to the enclosed from Keith Hardwick . . . make it quite clear to Mr Hardwick that comments like 'cottage-industry efforts' will not go unnoticed by us . . .

. . . We do, however, take great exception to a number of your vitriolic comments and regard them as libellous. Should your letter be published to a wider audience, we will have no hesitation in taking such steps to ensure that the poisonous nature of those comments are repudiated. Your vituperative statements are regarded by us as insulting to the company, other members of the industry and the Crown.[5]

Perhaps recognising a mirror image of their own occasional bias in one passionately advocating a dear cause, Nimbus's final letter for publication in response to Hardwick was a much more balanced, and therefore effective riposte.

We all owe Keith Hardwick a great debt for bringing to the record-buying public so many treasures of our recorded heritage.
. . . to our ears Mr Hardwick's transfers represent the best that

is being achieved using electric transfers from 78s.

That does not make electric transfers the only valid way to hear the great voices of the past.

... the recording engineers of the early decades of this century ... judged their work using acoustic horn gramophones.

You can quote numbers as long as you wish but we have to rely on our own subjective aural judgement, just as the engineers of that past age did when they made the recordings which allow us this extraordinary time-travel.

Really Mr Hardwick, you do yourself a disservice to descend to comments about 'cottage-industry' efforts. Nimbus is a leader in optical disc and recording technology.

... We advise anyone interested in great performances by great artists to compare for themselves the different ways of transferring these recordings to CD. We are confident that most people will agree that our *Prima Voce* series gives more enduring satisfaction than the electric transfers available.[6]

Hardwick appears to have been in a fairly small minority, for honour and praise were heaped on the early *Prima Voce* releases. No less than five of the first nine were awarded recognition by the influential French music magazine, *Diapason D'Or* in 1990 in the historic Music Category in its annual awards. (In the same year, incidentally, that Martin Jones won the Solo Category, the first time one company had ever carried off two awards.) The critics too, were full of praise,

To stand, as I did, in front of this horn was an astonishing experience: the volume of sound coming directly from the soundbox is startling and the quality quite unlike anything from loudspeakers. I had the uncanny and curiously moving sensation of being in the presence (at last I know the meaning of the word) of a singer, a voice, long gone but still living on.[7]

Nimbus Records is to recorded music what a real ale brewery is to beer.[8]

Evening in a Mediterranean courtyard: Tetrazzini singing the mad scene from *Lucia di Lammermoor*. The purity and immediacy of the sound is astonishing; even on a personal CD player, the richness and warmth of this recording from the very infancy of recorded sound (she died in 1940) seems disconcertingly intimate.

The Prima Voce series upsets our cosy view of the nostalgia market . . .[9]

Thomas Beecham's recording of *The Magic Flute* was the first full recording of the work ever, ... Produced in 1937 [by] ... His

Master's Voice . . . Now that its copyright has expired, Nimbus has released it . . .

The value of the new Nimbus release lies in particular in this latter point. An orchestra has hardly ever been experienced so vividly from a historic recording; it is as if the musicians and the soloists too stood directly before you in your living room . . .[12]

It is responses such as these that have encouraged Norman to persist through some fairly strained times with Nimbus. 'Sometimes in the middle of the night I wake up with the screaming horrors. Why am I doing it?'

Whatever strains and arguments there are bound to be between dedicated musicians of very strong convictions, between Norman White and the Nimbus team, there is a mutual recognition of their common desire to give people the very best musically and technically of what all of them regard as the Golden Age of singing. As Norman says, 'It's so important to me to get these voices heard as they've never been heard before that I'll put up with almost anything to be given the opportunity to do this. That's what I'll always be grateful to Count Labinsky for and for realising that there was something special to be done. To my dying day I'll be grateful for that.'

Classic CD summed up Norman's considerable achievement with *Prima Voce*, which now runs to fifty titles. 'The revelation that his work has generated is akin to the furore in the nineteenth century when new techniques in cleaning revealed the full colour range used by Renaissance masters.'[13]

Norman White is a classic example of the Nimbus philosophy of finding an enthusiastic expert and, more or less, giving him his head. Robin Broadbank is another. Robin was originally recruited as a recording engineer and then a producer in Adrian's team. Where Norman is a wonderfully exuberant enthusiast Robin is in much quieter mould, but no less passionate or determined about his own particular Nimbus project – the World Music Series of which Adrian admiringly recalls the birth.

The World Music Series exists only because Robin wanted to do them. The World Music Series doesn't exist because I wanted to or Numa wanted to and if Robin left it would stop instantly. Robin was the first person to come in when we started to build up the recording team and he worked on the classical music with me. Then one day he

211

came to me and said, 'there's something else I'm interested in. Would you mind if we recorded a little bit of Indian music?' I said 'no, do you know anything about it?' He replied 'Well, yes, I do actually and it won't cost very much.' So it started just like that.'

As it turned out the series began with a flamenco recording with Paco Peña in 1987 followed by two Andalucian flamenco recordings and, later, Paco Peña's Misa Flamenco – all of which are in Nimbus's top ten best-seller list. The Indian Classical Masters series was launched in 1988 with one CD in March, one in April, two in June, five in 1989 and another six in 1990. By the time the first ten were out *Musical Opinion* was commenting, 'It goes without saying that the performances are exemplary. It need hardly be added that with each issue Indian Classical Masters is becoming indispensable for devotees of both traditions of Indian classical music.'[14]

By early 1991 the scale of the series prompted *Fanfare*'s first issue of that year to observe:

> Nimbus seems bent upon capturing the CD market for classical Indian music, for the total they have issued, including these four discs, is fifteen. All are superbly recorded, probably the best-sounding series of Indian music which we have had thus far. Performances also seem to be uniformly good.
>
> All four discs, like the others in this series, were recorded in the Nimbus studios in Wyastone Leys and have the typical sense of depth and direction of other Nimbus issues. The spatial effects are uncanny. Very detailed and informative notes are provided.[15]

Encouraged by these successes Robin began to pursue the music of other cultures, from the familiar fiddling of Donegal recorded at the Fiddlesticks Festival in Cork in 1991, to the very unfamiliar music of South East Asia and, due out in 1994, Chinese traditional music. Robin has just returned, like some eccentric hunter of exotic musical butterflies, from Latin America, with another cultural catch, (Choro music from Salvador, Polcas from Paraguay and music from Pernambuco in North East Brazil) which will be issued shortly.

A continual stream of fine soloists and chamber groups, magnificent orchestral and choral recordings, the spoken word, jazz in the Hermes Series, *Prima Voce*, World Music – a musical cornucopia poured out by a handful of people from a remote country house in South East Wales, was suddenly threatened with extinction when, on 5 November 1991, Robert Maxwell plunged to his mysterious death.

212

Paco Peña (*right*) from Andalucia and Eduardo Falú from Argentina, discussing Flamenco from the old world and the new.

Fong Naam, Thai classical musicians.

Wu Man, a virtuoso of the Chinese Pipa.

Indian musician Ram Narayan and his daughter Aruna Narayan playing sarangis.

The Trebunia family of musicians from Zakopane in the Tatra mountains, Poland.

The Familia Valera Miranda from Cuba.

Indian musicians.
Left to right: Subhen Chatterjee (tabla), Sudha Datta (tambura), Giriji Devi (vocalist), Ramesh Misra (sarangi).

Indian musicians, Shruti Sadolikar with Anand Kunte (sarangi) and M Kothare (tabla).

CHAPTER TWELVE

Maxwell's demise did not have any immediate effect on Nimbus which was by now in good shape and running profitably, but by 5 December 1991, when Kevin and Ian Maxwell resigned from all MCC subsidiaries, the danger signals were flying. While the significance of those signals was not lost on the Nimbus management they were unable to act and when MCC went into receivership under Price Waterhouse on 20 December the company was so badly caught on the hop that it was nearly put out of business. In the first place the bank promptly appropriated just under £1 million in the Nimbus account under the MCC set-off banking arrangements to which Nimbus had reluctantly agreed only two months earlier. Secondly, the banks immediately froze all Nimbus accounts and overdraft facilities so that they could not draw cheques for even the most pressing day-to-day bills, let alone almost £1 million for the wages bill for December. Fortunately Gerald had the private home telephone number of the local Director of Lloyds Bank and cajoled and persuaded him to allow sufficient overdraft facilities there and then so as not to spoil everyone's Christmas and the company's prospect of survival.

If the immediate crisis was over, the longer term had yet to be resolved because from early 1992 the administrators were trying to dispose of MCC's shares in Nimbus. Ironically, it was the troubled and troublesome American connection which provided the eventual solution.

Although the decision to build a plant in America was clearly rightly made in terms of the long-term profitability of the manufacturing side, it had been problematic from the outset. Initially it overstretched the resources of the original shareholders and drove them into Maxwell's arms; then its constant demands for cash and delays in generating revenue caused a great deal of friction with Maxwell, although by the time of his death it was generating a positive cash flow; finally it produced a series of debilitating personnel and management problems which required the personal on-the-spot intervention of the Founders to rectify.

The logic of the move to the USA was inescapable, for it was clearly nonsensical to go on supplying that market from the UK at a loss and equally nonsensical simply to ignore the largest and fastest growing CD market in the world. The first step had been to open a New York office in February 1987 to promote both sales of Nimbus's own records and of its UK manufacturing facility in the first instance, and then to front the sales and PR drive for the new American plant in Charlottesville. The New York office got off on the wrong foot and never recovered its balance until it was finally closed in May 1991, as Stuart Garman recalls.

> I was very nervous about New York because they always seemed to be asking for funds and there was never any explanation of how they were spent. When I eventually got a set of management accounts I could see that money had been going out recklessly and without authorisation. I was asked on a Friday night if I could go to America on Saturday morning because by then we realised that we had to do something. I went over with Adrian and we went into the office, looked into the books, examined some of the vouchers and saw the things that had been going on. Unfortunately, the Vice President had neglected to control the financial situation and committed the company to expenditure over and above its agreed limit, so on the Monday I fired him. He went quite berserk and threatened me at my hotel. He then went to the office and caused pandemonium, so that same day we had to get a court injunction to prevent him pestering us or turning up at the office again. He had an enormous ego; we even found in the drawers a set of posters for talks he was giving in which he called himself President of Nimbus, but he was wonderful at getting great publicity for the label.

Indeed, through his efforts, two Nimbus CDs, the ESO recordings of Vaughan Williams and of Orchestral Favourites, had been in the US Classical top ten for the previous four months.

Nor were these the only successes of the label in the first couple of years of the American operation, for public and Press alike had welcomed both the quality of the recordings and their greater availability through US manufacture and distribution. The files are full of letters like the following:

> The quality is superb – when compared to other CDs – you really do have them ranked . . .[1]

218

From the first notes of music, I said *'This is the sound I've always wanted'* and from the conductor's point of view!! With a huge hall, and your microphone placement it's as though an entire orchestra and hall is being rented just for *my* pleasure . . .[2]

The newspapers were equally kind:

The newest blockbuster on the American classical recording scene is Nimbus . . . If you've never heard of the company, you shall. Everything points to it being a major force in the field, both for its original approach to sound, its individual, highly inventive concepts of artists and repertory.

. . . What I've heard so far has been tremendously impressive on all counts.

And rather than merely dive into esoteric repertory, the pattern at Nimbus has been to find holes in the catalogue, and then fill them. . . .[3]

Recordings by these phenomenal artists, still-vital voices of an earlier time, cap the first wave of compact discs to hit America's shores from the British label Nimbus.

. . . the Nimbus label itself, an imaginative and thrilling series of new productions and vintage re-masterings, seems likely to catch the fancy of classical collectors across the board. Both Cherkassky and Perlemuter enjoy warm, spacious sound recording – a quality that distinguishes most of the Nimbus CDs sampled in this survey.[4]

. . . its sensationally good sound, that can only be good news for America, as is the news that Nimbus CDs are now plentiful on these shores at competitive prices.[5]

Public estimation of the Nimbus records as shown in their purchases was high. In 1988 Nimbus had six records in the Billboard Classical (top twenty equivalent) chart and two in the crossover chart and was rated the seventh classical label in the United States, ahead of several of the 'big names'. So why was Nimbus in the USA not even cash positive until April 1990 and not into profit until 1992. Why did CD-ROM, of which so much was hoped, incur losses at the rate of half a million dollars a year?

A major factor was that the decision to set up in America was probably a year or so too late to catch the main CD growth cycle as it had in the UK. By the time Nimbus USA was open for business, there were a number of well-established competing CD plants and less than 30 per cent of the American market was 'free', i.e. not pressed in-house for itself by one of the big labels. As a result, Nimbus finished up in the early days with 200 small customers, each of which required much administrative attention but yielded little profit.

The Maxwell connection did Nimbus far more harm than good in the United States, losing the CD-ROM side valuable business from rival publishers such as McGraw Hill, without bringing in a single order from MCC group companies or their contacts. When Maxwell publicly announced that he wanted to sell his controlling stake in Nimbus, confidence in its viability, in the USA in particular, was undermined. Nimbus suffered the disadvantages both of the Maxwell connection *and* of the threatened severance of that connection.

The Maxwell management practice of holding back money from its subsidiaries for expenditure which had long been agreed, cost the American operation dear. New plant, approved on 22 February 1988, was not delivered until the autumn for this reason, nor operating until early 1989. The delays in commissioning also arose from Nimbus's dislike of putting things on paper and just as in the early days of the CD there are various jottings to the effect that only Jonathan knew how the mastering lathe worked, so there are similar notes at this period that if Lyndon Faulkner, the Cwmbran plant manager who was helping to get the US plant up and running, were to leave, things would grind to a halt. It is noteworthy now that, for the first time, Nimbus Technology & Engineering Ltd. is systematically drawing up parts lists and drawings from which to build, maintain and operate the lathes it now makes for sale.

The consequence of these delays was that although sales for pressings were on target for July 1988, by August they were falling behind because of lack of planned capacity. All this endorsed the general poor opinion Americans often have of British technology and confirmed the view that Nimbus was 'just a music label'.

Even as a music label it was not as successful as it might have been commercially, not just because of the problems at the New York office but because, after an initial burst, the label's US distributor, A & M, fell short of Nimbus sales targets and, in addition, was then purchased by Polygram, a major Nimbus competitor so, in April 1990, the connection was broken. Nimbus gradually set up, with more success, a piecemeal, state by state approach involving ten different firms of sale representatives under the direct control of the label's Virginia office.

The real problem on the manufacturing side, however, was that this time the Nimbus policy of appointing senior managers on the basis of personal liking and of expertise in something quite different misfired. Mark Galloway had done an excellent job in getting the US factory built on time but, as Gerald now admits, 'Mark Galloway was the Contracts Manager for the building company we employed and then we invited him to come and join us to run the place once it was built which was a mistake because he was better at starting things than the day-to-day running of them.'

Howard Nash was even more unequivocal. 'It was appallingly managed which was a matter of great frustration to the rest of us. He was always producing new budgets when he was challenged with not achieving the old and they'd always have credence, which rather puzzled us.'

That Mark remained in the post so long was not just a matter of the family's liking for him, although that must account in part for the tolerance of his shortcomings. He did give every appearance of being in control through streams of memos about actions he had taken and demands for or complaints about action in the UK, at least to sufficient extent to persuade one management consultant to write: 'Mark Galloway, the USA director, is perhaps the most important Nimbus strength ... However, [he] has no service contract [and] should he leave at a moment's notice Nimbus, in its current state of infancy, would then be operationally paralysed.'[6]

In March 1988, recognising that blood was required and that the US organisation was getting very top-heavy, Mark initiated a purge. '[We have made a] complete restructure of our management. In February we released our Vice President/General Manager, the Production Manager, the Buyer, one Shift Manager and completely re-organised our Customer Service Department. This radical change was largely due to several managers having been hired by previous management more on a 'friendship' basis than on a basis of experience ... I request that lines 5 and 6 be purchased immediately for July delivery ...'[7]

But, as Gerald realised, the restructuring had been misconceived. 'One of the things we found in America was that, by tradition, they created management structure with lots of layers and very little communication and endless opportunities for passing the buck downwards without much loyalty in either direction. That was why we had a union trying to get in there. Numa, Michael and I had to go round and talk to everyone in the plant, on the shop floor, and just give them someone to talk to, which they'd been missing and they voted against unionising. We got rid of several layers of management and promoted people from the shop floor which did an enormous amount to put the situation right. And then we got in a very good new manager, Gary Helfrecht, who was very good with people, to take the plant over.'

In August 1989 Peter Laister persuaded the Founders and then Maxwell of the advantage of operating the UK and US plants under a single management, with Howard Nash in charge of the manufacturing side. Adrian was to control the music label on both sides of the Atlantic and Mark Galloway was effectively demoted to CD-ROM Manager.

We have already seen why CD-ROM failed in America. As its UK guru, Emil Dudek, said, 'We always felt the American division should be autonomous; the market's very different and it should be run by Americans for Americans, but perhaps we left it alone too much, so it never had the advantage of Gerald popping his nose in frequently.'

Sadly, in CD-ROM too, Mark lost money and the final stage of the purge is noted in a cryptic fax from Gerald to Patrick J Call, a consultant called in to assist with the restructuring. 'Howard Nash will be over on Thursday late afternoon/early evening . . . to effect a proper hand-over from Mark Galloway who we have asked to cease his duties for Nimbus by end of business on Friday . . .'[8]

After leaving Nimbus Mark later became a Minister of religion.

The early problems in America had their repercussions in Britain, for having despatched Lyndon Faulkner to the US to get things going there, Nimbus, following the failure of professional plant managers at Cwmbran, appointed Martin Thorne, the architect who had designed and supervised the building of the factory, but had no qualification other than general intelligence to run a high-technology-based plant. This was a bold move on both sides which, sadly, did not come off, but this time the mistake was quickly recognised, Lyndon was recalled from the US and Martin and Nimbus parted amicably and remain good friends.

Today the American factory has thirteen presses at work and turns out thirty-five million CDs a year. It now makes a good profit and looks set for a much larger one, thus vindicating the original decision by Nimbus to set up in America. Perhaps this is little comfort to the Founders now that they no longer own it. Yet fate did again play its part in so much as the Chicago lawyer, Bill McGrath, who represented a group of investors interested in CD-ROM spotted the opportunity when Maxwell died to acquire that business in Charlottesville and was thus alerted to the possibilities of the group as a whole.

In order to protect the position of the Founders, family and management on 28 November 1991 Gerald wrote to Laister, not only Chairman of Nimbus but Deputy Chairman and now acting Chairman of MCC. 'I feel it is very important that I confirm to you that the management team have the most serious resolve to effect a management buy-out of MCC's holding on suitable terms to be agreed. Can you please confirm that MCC would be open to an offer from the management team.'[9]

The management buy-out team consisted of Gerald, who was to be Managing Director, Lyndon Faulkner, Howard Nash, John Denton, Stuart Garman and Gary Helfrecht, the US Manager, and it began to try to negotiate a deal with various merchant banks. Numa and Michael were quite content with these approaches as they intended to withdraw from active involvement. Peter Laister, as acting Chairman of MCC, was precluded initially, until MCC was finally in administration, from doing anything more than advise at arm's length. By Christmas he was relatively free to turn his attention back to Nimbus and in his own words, 'what I found was chaos. The management running to a series of London institutions for money, Numa, Michael and Gerald quite happy about it. I had to say to them "Your ideas will not work out the way you think they will. The terms you will achieve will allow neither management nor Founders to fulfil their hopes or plans. First we must very clearly define a structure you can all endorse." '

What Peter proposed was that the label would have to stand on its own feet, that the technology business and its patents be separated out and that the main business to be sold would be the CD pressing operation. At this early stage this suited neither Founders nor management. The Founders have never regarded the label as a separate business and wanted to keep the company as it was. The management were not particularly interested in the label which they regarded as inescapably loss-making. They wanted to buy out the manufacturing and technology businesses, but were only prepared to keep the label if that was necessary to get a deal. Their idea was simply to buy the MCC 75.1 per cent and then break the operation up.

By early January 1992 the predators were descending on Wyastone

Leys. Lloyds were interested but were anathema to Numa and in any case refused to contemplate Gerald as Managing Director or to have anything to do with the label. Alan Sugar of Amstrad made an offer which was by his own admission derisory.

> I feel at this stage that the administrator will not be happy with my offer, but given that we are a straightforward organisation and we tend to come to the point much quicker than others, and indeed have the cash available, then it may be possible for them to recognise that our offer is indeed the best at their disposal considering the founder shareholders and existing management may be the real catalysts in any sale of Nimbus.
>
> I will indeed be putting an offer forward to the administrator and I guess in the short-term it will be treated as derisory until they have examined all other avenues.
>
> A M Sugar[10]

There was a management buy-in proposal led by a Mr Glyn Williams which basically did no more than offer to buy 100 per cent of the equity from the current shareholders for just under £8 million, all of which would have gone to the administrator to pay the company's debts. Nor would there have been any working capital for Nimbus nor any involvement for the Founders. Jonathan and most of the managers were offered jobs but not directorships. A number of other interested parties such as Candover did not get to the stage of making a serious offer and it soon became apparent that there were only three choices; winding up the company, a deal with the merchant banking group Granvilles, or a deal with Chicago-based CD group introduced by the lawyer Bill McGrath. The American group was the first to get its act together and make a concrete offer but there were two initial problems. The first was that it was simply too small to produce the necessary finance. This it resolved by embracing as principals in its proposed deal the American investment bank Donaldson, Lufkin and Jenrette (DLJ).

The second set of objections was set out in a facsimile to Bill McGrath from Gerald on 27 February.

> Two things [give] cause for concern, [the] proposed composition of the board and the degree of key top management involvement has moved a fair distance from our understanding.
>
> The funding would be in the form of true equity of between £7.5m and £10m and bank debt of £15m.

224

The minority shareholders will receive . . . cash and a donation to the Nimbus Foundation (for their 25 per cent). They will purchase 10 per cent of CD manufacture and CD-ROM, at a cost of up to £1m.

The Nimbus Classical Label will be spun off to the minority founder shareholders who will take on all its assets and liabilities and ongoing costs. We would ensure that all label product is manufactured by the new pressing company at most favoured nation terms.

The New Technology Company [would grant an] interest of 20 per cent in this new company.

George Marton [is] giving clear signals that he expects to be chief operating executive.[11]

By now the MCC Administrator was keen to get any deal sewn up and obviously felt that the Founders were using their powers of pre-emption to prevaricate and procrastinate and so wrote to them on 5 March a letter intended to put pressure on them to conclude a deal quickly. 'I have been concerned about the differing interests of the various parties involved in the disposal process of MCC's shareholding in Nimbus. I now believe that the management team have a direct conflict [of interest].'[12]

This was always a fatal approach with the Nimbus family and in any case the Founders were more interested at this stage in a deal with DLJ, who Peter and Adrian had just been to see in the United States.

All the Administrator's letter did was to provoke an indignant reply from Peter on behalf of the Nimbus Board.

All Board members are very aware of the responsibilities that they have to ensure that the interests of all 'Stake Holders' are properly served and that their own, or indeed any other interests must be regarded as entirely secondary. We held a special Board Meeting on 21 January, to emphasise and record this duty.

I do have an equal concern that you and Chris may be taking a view at times that Nimbus and its Directors should be acting as though they were in Administration. This is of course not the case and the duties of the Nimbus Board must take into account the well-being and interests of ALL Stakeholders.

We do not agree that you have 'jurisdiction' over the Management. You have ultimate sanction of being able, as majority shareholder, to replace the Board, but this is an entirely different matter.

You state that the Directors may, as members of the MBO, have a direct conflict of interests. I would like this comment to be withdrawn in writing.

225

It is entirely proper that they should look beyond a sale, instead of only seeking maximum short-term value.

The Founders have a final pre-emption right.

[It is] strongly in the interests of the Company that the sale should be completed as soon as possible.

Examples are that Dunn & Bradstreet will not credit rate Nimbus under the present situation; many suppliers are now requesting payment up front with resultant additional cost, and so on.[13]

The Founders were in a strong negotiating position in so far as they had the ability to block for a considerable time any alternative deal which they did not like and with Nimbus running on a cash positive basis at the time could afford to wait a little. The pre-emption clause in the shareholders' agreement with MCC, by which the Founders had the right to match any outside offer, enabled Nimbus, through the skilful footwork of its lawyers, to buy sufficient time for a rescue package to be put together.

A hiccup occurred in the DLJ negotiations over the rate to be paid for the final £1 million of the deal, but it was clearly an easily removable one, so Tom Dean of DLJ and Bill McGrath returned to the United States leaving a representative in London to complete and sign on his behalf. However, the newly appointed UK lawyers, Paisners, who had already caused complications by re-negotiation of points which had already been agreed, refused to allow the signing to proceed. As McGrath wrote to Gerald on 6 May: 'I have heard from Tom Dean that negotiations with DLJ have been suspended. When I left London on the morning of 16 April, I mistakenly thought that I had succeeded to everyone's satisfaction. [There were] so many parties involved [it led to] confusion, delay and misunderstandings.'[14]

Peter was furious, but felt the problem could be resolved. Numa, however, went completely off the deep end, flatly refused to have anything more to do with 'untrustworthy Americans' and promptly switched his allegiance to Granvilles. Inevitably, the other members of the family followed his lead.

Before any deal could be concluded, with anyone, a considerable amount of tidying up had to be done through the spring and summer of 1992. Nimbus had three major pieces of litigation pending over various claims against it in connection with the rights to CD technology. Provision simply for the cost of fighting the cases was in excess of £1 million and the possible costs of losing them introduced an element of uncertainty which was a deterrent to any would-be purchaser. Nimbus had declined to take a licence from Discovision Associates, a Californian company owned by Pioneer, and the case was due for hearing in March 1992. A Canadian company, Optical Recording Corporation, was also suing for a licence Nimbus denied that it required and Nimbus was applying to have the case transferred to the High Court and a Summary Declaration that it did not infringe any parts of the ORC patent which might be valid. Defence costs had been budgeted at almost half a million for this case alone. In the case of Thomson, who alone had a strong patent, Nimbus agreed to a retrospective royalty per disc. The third case was part of Nimbus's long-running battle with Philips over the royalty rate (not being paid at all by some of Nimbus's competitors) whose UK licence to the company had expired in March 1992 but whose US licence at 3 cents a disc plus annual escalation, granted in 1986, still had several years to run. Stuart Garman was largely responsible for dealing with these matters and described the relationship with Philips, as 'professional rather than cordial . . . we have not toed the party line.' Nimbus had not been paying royalties in the US since June 1991 owing to its dispute with Philips about who was liable for subordinate claims arising out of the CD licence Eindhoven had granted. To maintain goodwill and get the potential embarrassment off the books, Nimbus offered to resume payment with effect from June 1992.

Another element of uncertainty facing any would-be purchaser was the takeover by EMI of Virgin Records. Virgin was one of Nimbus's largest clients. Its new parent had not currently the capacity to handle the pressing, so there was unlikely to be any adverse impact in 1992, but was in the process of expanding its plant. The loss of this turnover would have to be made up from elsewhere by 1993.

If these difficulties on Nimbus's side were making negotiation slow they were not the only ones. Whether from greed or the necessity of keeping its own equity partners on board, Granvilles kept altering the conditions of the supposedly agreed deal to the detriment of Nimbus so that an already financially unattractive proposition became even less acceptable. As Howard Nash explained. 'Laister felt the American approach would give us more secured finance though we didn't like the management implications, indeed, so much so that several of us would have reconsidered our positions if it had gone that way at the time. At the end of the day we thought we had the debt and the equity in place for Granvilles. Then their preference shares which played a large part suddenly had to have a cumulative running yield. The goal posts were being moved and we felt increasingly nervous about it as a series of little amendments kept being fitted in so the deal was not very attractive.'

These negotiations continued throughout the late summer, with Peter shunted to the sidelines by both Granvilles and the Administrator from whom Granvilles had obtained an option. Only when signature of the Granville deal was barely a week away did Peter push himself back into the picture.

I got so angry with myself, I said, I can't allow this, this is going to be a disaster, it will break apart within a year. I can't allow this, I've given five or six years of my life to it, so I engineered the Americans into making another bid and it was the best balanced bit of negotiation and arrangement I've ever done. I had one week to do it with only the very tacit consent of the Founders. They thought we would fall between two stools and I was saying they were going to fall off their chosen one anyway. I was afraid the Founders would either fall out or be pushed out by Granvilles within months and that in any case the proposed deal provided too little new money to resolve the company's problems. I asked them to allow me to follow up DLJ if it did not prejudice the Granville deal. They were now beginning to realise what the Granville deal meant but it was still a deal and Numa was in a very worried state again and felt they could not risk losing the bird in hand. It was a disaster. Adrian realised that it was a disaster and gave me some support. The Administrators didn't want the American deal, fought it vigorously, said they wouldn't contemplate it under any circumstances. They had a deal and that was that. The management wanted to go with Granvilles because Granvilles had promised them everything on the Christmas tree. DLJ weren't all that keen because they'd been thrown out once and been told not to come back, so they didn't want to come back again because they felt the Founders might turn against them once more.

The family willingly gives credit now to Peter for his perception and persistence at this critical time as Adrian acknowledged.

It was always Peter who said, every day, this is not a good option because there's no actual money coming into the business, it's all paper money, it's all debt. Coming back again with DLJ was only because Peter stuck to his guns. Peter and I went to New York and when we came back we had to say to Numa, Gerald and Michael, 'well we know we think we've done the deal with Granville but there's a better deal still to be done.' But it wasn't actually Peter's money or his neck on the line and it was the Founders who had to make the decision to renege on the Granville deal and go back into the grey area of having no deal in the hope of getting a better one. Granville was furious. The management were furious, they'd had stars in their eyes about the deal. Everybody was furious.

Howard described what followed:

> Really this marked the division into two camps. Already we'd had Board meetings where in-put from the various directors round the table hadn't been welcomed. We were very depressed with the Granville situation and felt we had nowhere to go, when it turns out that DLJ were already down in Cardiff talking to the administrators basically negotiating a new deal which was just dropped on us. The blow was that it had been happening without our knowledge, but it wasn't such a great disappointment as it would have been had the Granville deal not gone sour. Granvilles behaved with such indecent haste in opting out, and demanding their fees, etc. when the DLJ deal came through that relations between us became pretty cool.

Stuart Garman, who had taken the view that Jonathan and Adrian should not be shareholders in the new company and that Peter was not essential to the deal, had seen things much the same way from an even earlier stage. 'Effectively there were two camps then. The Founders found all this very difficult to accept and accused me of double dealing. The principle of it was they really didn't want management to own it. After that they spent all their time in the cottage and when they did come back to the office it was invariably to shout at me and continue to accuse me of collusion. It was then, I believe, that they decided to find an alternative solution to the management's buy-out proposal.'

At the same time, it transpired that Granvilles (the management's pre-ferred choice) had been to see the Administrator without the Founders knowledge.

Peter, with Adrian's support, stuck to his guns. 'I gradually worked through this chess game. I flew over to America at my own cost and got an American lawyer to come over here, and the key man from DLJ, Tom Dean, to fly from Los Angeles to London instead of going back to New York. DLJ was exceptional and behaved in a way that I can't conceive of any British investor behaving and at the end of it all, we did it, and started a new era.'

The deal, on which hands were shaken in principle on 27 August, was an extraordinarily complex one, of which the documentation alone ran to over 1,000 pages, but had to be completed by 1 October. Because of the Administration a series of intricate interlocking steps had to be taken before a cryptic memo from Gerald, which members of the management buy-out team and other senior managers found on their desks when they arrived for work on 27 August, could be turned into reality.

Interim Conduct of Nimbus Business

The Founders have, in the early hours of this morning, signed an unconditional contract for the sale of their shares in Nimbus Records Limited to DLJ.

[You] will not . . . do any action or permit anything to be done outside the normal course of the company's business. [This is] an express instruction to observe this requirement.[15]

Howard Nash, John Denton and Lyndon Faulkner were present at the Board Meeting, to which the DLJ offer was put and voted with the other directors to accept it and to inform Granvilles that their deal would not go ahead.

The research and development and technical aspects of the business, including all the technical patents, and the music label were then sold to one of the Founders' old companies, Amber Records, an extant shell that had never traded, for £1 each. Prudently, two days before the DLJ deal, the Nimbus Board had agreed to write off the intangible assets on the balance sheet of nearly £1.5 million which represented the 'value' of the recordings made by the music label. In effect Nimbus was making a gift of all future earnings from the 'back catalogue' to whoever acquired the label business. In order to give the label a breathing space to build up sales volume, its profit and loss account had been sheltered from the full impact of the cost of new recordings by spreading them over three years. Such growth was not achieved so it was decided to revert to the previous practice of charging the full cost of a recording in the month of its issue. This would have happened even without the DLJ bid. Correspondingly, however, the new company inherited the recording contract liabilities of the old record company and forfeited the benefit of its tax losses. The residue of the company which DLJ had bought changed its name to Nimbus USA which in turn briefly owned the name Nimbus Records Ltd. This was immediately changed to Nimbus Manufacturing Ltd., thus freeing the name Nimbus Records for Amber, which then translated itself into the new Nimbus Records Limited, thus completing the circle.

Numa with Peter Elliott, Vice President of the Nimbus label in the United States.

Numa with Thompson Dean of DLJ, Merchanting Banking New York, celebrating another successful step towards the sale of CD plants, Autumn 1992.

So although the Founders and family received only a modest sum in cash (they had already acquired Wyastone Leys and its estate in 1987) they now owned, with more or less 'clean' balance sheets, businesses with the potential to make and sell the Nimbus/Halliday CD mastering lathe and associated hardware and know-how for CD production lines, the development of new technology (at which we shall look in the next chapter) and the record label. They then divided these into separate businesses; Nimbus Records Limited for the label, and Nimbus Technology & Engineering Limited for the technical and R&D Activities, all under a holding company, Nimbus Communications International Limited. The family thus now found itself in control of a much more 'family-sized' business, employing some sixty people rather than the 600-plus of the old company which better suited their style and inclination. The new American owners retained the old CD pressing business and the CD-ROM business in both Britain and the United States. They also retained the entire management team, except Company Secretary, Stuart Garman, for whom there was no role, and to the relief of all the senior managers, left Lyndon Faulkner as overall Chief Executive.

The board of the new Nimbus company relaxing after their escape from Captain Maxwell's jaws.

As part of the deal each company had retained a small stake in the other company's business, but whether or not this made sound commercial sense it was not psychologically acceptable for very long, and by the end of 1993 neither had any part of the other's equity.

Howard Nash summed up the situation when he spoke to me in November 1993. 'In the end, we cannot argue with the fact that this DLJ deal has been the best for everybody and though, in our opinion, the Founders probably secured a less advantageous initial deal financially, psychologically they got what they wanted. We felt we had delivered what we originally said, the label and the technology company. It has all been very difficult and very emotional and none of us want to go through that nightmare again.'

A wish heartily endorsed by the Nimbus family.

In the event, although the Founders demonstrated their practical resilience by rapidly turning the new group into a profitable enterprise, awakening from the bad dream was a slow and emotionally painful process.

CHAPTER THIRTEEN

It was only natural that the Nimbus parents, and the three Founders in particular, should find it very hard to cope with their child, now re-named Nimbus Manufacturing, going off to lead an entirely independent life. As Adrian said, 'The emotional attachment to the idea of the manufacturing business was a hard one to give up but I think we are better off without it if not the profit that it generated in its hey day.'

The 'child' saw the problem the same way. 'In retrospect I think the Founders felt they were going to have the same amount of in-put into the new company as they had before. While that might have worked with Maxwell it wasn't going to work with a New York bank and the operational management really went along with the view that it would have to be run differently as they recognised the commercial realities.'

As so often when the younger members of a family grow up and go their own way, it took a couple of monumental rows over relatively trivial issues to clear the air and re-establish the relationship as one of affectionate respect between independent adults.

The first of these rows was over the logo of Nimbus Manufacturing. It had been a condition of the DLJ deal that the Founders would retain the famous Nimbus logo (which adorns the jacket of this book). This caused no difficulties to anyone, but it left the manufacturing company without a logo. Various modernistic designs had been produced, before the parting of the ways, for use in the CD-ROM and pressing business, to give them a more high-tech image, but these had been set aside for more urgent matters. The managers of manufacturing say that they were under the impression that the Founders had seen and approved the logo which had in any case been set out on one side at the signing and exchange of documents ceremony for the DLJ deal. The Founders say they approved no such designs and were entirely unaware it had been adopted until they saw it 'scruffily reproduced' on the top of a photocopy at the signing ceremony. A perfectly understandable misunderstanding, but when Numa later saw the chosen design on the new company's letterhead he was furious and raged savagely at the executives of Nimbus Manufacturing, forgetting in his anger that they were no longer his subordinates. They, for their part, had spent £40,000 on the new corporate identity and were not going to abandon it for what they saw as an irrational outburst and went ahead. Even in the calmer atmosphere of today each side sticks firmly to its version of events, but aesthetically, it has to be said, it is hard not to sympathise with Numa's reaction.

There were practical difficulties, too, because the physical transfer of papers and information to the new manufacturing company took place so quickly that Chandos Ellis had only a few days, instead of the three months he had expected, to set up an independent accounting system for Nimbus Records, which still suffers from the resulting information deficiencies, and had to rely on Cwmbran for paperwork for some time.

The other major row between the Founders and the new manufacturing company's management arose in connection with the mastering of CDs for the Cwmbran plant. Manufacturing wanted the Nimbus/Halliday lathes on which their masters were made moved to Cwmbran but the family resisted the move because they felt it imprudent and unplanned and said so. However, their advice was ignored with, later, technically embarrassing consequences for Manufacturing.

Howard Nash gave me his version of why Manufacturing insisted on the move. 'After ignoring Manufacturing for a while Numa started to go round our plant at Monmouth making a number of rather unhelpful statements [he was complaining about its dirty state in his usual vehement manner] and Lyndon rather bluntly told him to stop. Numa said, "I've never been spoken to by anybody in my life like that." He rang me for comfort but didn't get it.'

Peter Laister recollects another incident. 'Numa was reacting very strongly, like a child having his most precious possession taken away. I was then still Chairman of both companies, so in the middle of the two camps, and had several fierce disagreements with him. There were several great confrontations with the management. Numa decided Manufacturing was going bust and that the Founders wanted to withdraw totally. I advised them this was silly and they said, "no, we want the money now, and anyway it's going to go bankrupt." I was regarded as disloyal for even trying to dissuade them. Unhappily this started to destroy our relationship.'

The Founders saw it very differently. They thought that the business and reputation they had spent fifteen years building up was running on to the rocks of ruin without their hands on the tiller. It took them time to accept that rocks or no rocks the manufacturing company was now steering its own course and there was nothing they could or should do about it. As Michael acknowledges: 'It was very difficult for us all to see the business we had developed taken over and run by people who had been our subordinates, who we'd brought up in the business, like Lyndon Faulkner who'd been promoted from the shop floor where he'd been an electrical engineer to becoming factory manager.'

Although Peter may have been right in financial terms about the Founders disposing of their shares in Manufacturing, psychologically he was wrong and, subconsciously or otherwise, the Founders must have recognised that a harmonious and constructive relationship would only be possible when all links between the two companies had been severed. New mastering lathes for the CD plant were later supplied to Cwmbran and Peter eventually resigned as Chairman of Nimbus Communications International in December 1993, while remaining Chairman of Nimbus Manufacturing. No sooner had he done so than he and Numa started to make up their quarrel.

As soon as this process of separation was under way, feeling between the 'two camps' became friendlier again as both went successfully on their separate ways but with, as Howard admits, more than a nostalgic glance over the shoulder.

> Manufacturing has been on target for its first twelve months as an independent company.* The operational management would have preferred to retain the old links out of a degree of affection and loyalty to the original Founders and the antagonism that there has been between us has been a source of sadness for us.
>
> Then one day Numa, Gerald and Michael came round the factory unexpectedly and there was a little bit more of the old warmth and feeling restored. We've all been through tough times individually and we've all been supported by them. Numa especially would stand up for individuals whom MCC had taken unfairly against.
>
> They built a manufacturing business employing 800 people in two continents. How many people do that? An incredible technological achievement as well but anyway these achievements were incidental, secondary to their main objective – producing musically and technically outstanding records.

*It currently produces 70 million compact discs a year.

Emil Dudek, one of the very few senior people to remain on friendly terms with both camps throughout the painful transition, analyses what has happened. 'The Founders are now admitting to themselves that Nimbus Manufacturing has gone off on its own and they can't hang on to it and they're concentrating on the new things which are more exciting.'

Exciting things certainly lie ahead for Nimbus Records though their realisation will increasingly depend upon the three younger members of the inner family. The tragedy for Nimbus of Numa's sudden and unexpected death from a stroke on 28 January 1994 was that right up to that day he seldom showed any sign of declining vigour. Particularly once he had thrown away the pethidine crutch, he was bursting with new ideas for Video-CD, for an international magazine of the Arts and new ideas from artificial intelligence to changing social patterns in a world to be dominated by the growth of China. He himself was painting and writing prolifically and had just made an emotionally highly charged recording of Duparc and Fauré songs. Nor was the spark of mischief

Numa singing in the small recital room at Carnegie Hall, New York.

Numa and Adrian
rehearsing for the
recording of Arie
Antiche in the music
room of Numa's house.

dead. He had been recording at the age of almost seventy, with quite astonishing effectiveness, in his original high voice and although the disc will probably be released under his usual singing name of Shura Gehrman, as a Nimbus record, he toyed for some time with the notion of teasing the musical establishment by releasing it under the *Prima Voce* label and the name Alexander Zobinoff, pretending that it was a discovery of the last castrato from the Russian archives. But as Numa said, 'If you are wicked they never forgive you, you know, but it's the nearest thing to bel canto anybody is going to hear whether they like it or not.' Prudence prevailed and Alexander Zobinoff was not added to the long list of Numa's alter egos.

Immediately post-Maxwell, Numa starts expanding again.

There was still plenty, too, of the old dynamic belligerence as he contemplated the future. 'Now we're starting a new business and using our own money instead of fucking retiring and going out to grow an herbaceous border', and then a typical Numa tangential thought – 'I like roses, the proper ones that have a smell.'

240

It was significant, however, that Numa's attention seemed to be as much, or even more, focused on his personal artistic expression in various media than on the hurly-burly of the business world in which Nimbus is re-establishing itself. Symptomatic of this trend is the major role now played by the Nimbus Foundation. This was created by the Founders in 1987 and they transferred to it a substantial part of their shareholding in Nimbus before both the Maxwell and the DLJ deals. The Nimbus Foundation is a charity whose first and most spectacular step has been to build probably the finest concert hall in Wales – acoustically perhaps, in the whole of Britain – which was opened by His Royal Highness, The Prince of Wales on 5 May 1993.

HRH The Prince of Wales with the Directors, having just opened the Performing Arts Centre on 5 May 1993.

The purpose of the Foundation is to support the Arts and especially to encourage the appreciation of serious music. It will promote live events in music and related arts, make audio and video recordings and provide a venue for broadcast co-productions.

The concert hall was the Foundation's first priority, providing a building where the best conditions for live performance, sound recording and filming could co-exist. The physical and acoustic design of the building was undertaken by Gerald and is modelled on the finest traditional concert venues to be found in Europe. The main auditorium has 550 seats and a stage area that can comfortably accommodate a classical symphony orchestra. It is fully equipped with permanent and separate facilities for sound and vision, and has a spectacular location on land adjacent to Nimbus Records' Wyastone Leys headquarters overlooking the Wye Valley.

The unique feature of the Wyastone Leys Concert Hall is that it was designed from the acoustics outwards not the architecture inwards. Sound quality was paramount at every stage, and although from the outside the building itself looks a little like Battersea Power Station without the chimneys, once inside the listener is treated to an auditory experience which this frequent concert-goer for one has not heard surpassed elsewhere. But now, with Numa gone and Michael gradually moving towards a well-deserved retirement into private life, what next for Nimbus?

As Adrian said:

> It was as if Numa had anticipated the question, challenging other people to find out how much of the business they were prepared to take on.
>
> Nimbus had become an overgrown family business and although that was becoming a little better in balance, the rules of the business were definitely those of a family. It had one head and he was deferred to.
>
> The problem of that change is going to come in the next four or five years: will Nimbus stay a family business and if so who will become the head of it? It also has the hurdle to cross of how does a first generation business become a second generation business. Anyway, if Maxwell's strategy had worked we'd be a public company by now and I'm very glad we're not. There is a natural progression one can see but whether that's the one that will happen, I'm not sure.

Michael saw the situation quite clearly even when Numa was alive. 'Numa's beyond retiring age and I'm just approaching it and although a lot of energetic people don't retire we have to think about where Nimbus will be a decade from now when we're not directly involved and may not even be around. We have to make sure that the team that is taking it on is a strong team. The main difficulty is finding someone who has Numa's ability to take the leaps into the future.'

With the hiving off of the pressing business, the nature of Nimbus has changed dramatically yet again. From the 'stack 'em high and sell 'em cheap' of CD pressings, of tens of millions of low cost items with tiny and vulnerable profit margins, it has become a high-technology precision engineering business selling a few Nimbus/Halliday mastering lathes at a high cost – over £1 million each – and high profit margins. As a percentage of turnover, gross profits have never been higher, and greater financial discipline on the label side means that, for the time being at least, these profits are not being poured into a bottomless pit. An alliance was formed in December 1992 with Leybold AG which sells the Nimbus/Halliday mastering lathe outside Nimbus for the first time since it was invented a decade ago. Already fifteen lathes, and a number of automated CD production lines, have been sold, including two to China* – another example of Nimbus's far-sightedness, for the first Board minute of the potential importance of the Chinese market appears in May 1985. The company took this process a major step further by appointing Public Relations Director, Philip Moss, in the summer of 1994 to the new post of Head of Asia and Pacific Operations, with a dual brief to develop the ultra-high technology markets of Australasia and the low technology mass markets of China and South East Asia. As well as buying CD lathes, China has already taken out Nimbus Video-CD Compression Licences (as has Poland). These sales are based on the Nimbus reputation for reliability and the fact that the lathe is virtually maintenance-free, qualities attested to by John Town, Mastering and R&D manager of the now quite independent Nimbus Manufacturing Inc. in the USA. 'We have never required an emergency visit throughout our five-year history to maintain production or quality. This would only be possible with a system with no major inherent design flaws . . . We run the equipment twenty-four hours a day, seven days a week. The inherent reliability of the system allows us to have only daytime technician coverage . . . I would say the Nimbus/Halliday mastering lathe is the most reliable piece of major equipment in the plant.'

---

* Others include: Sonopress in Germany and Brazil; Woongjin in Korea; Summit in Singapore; Tryptich, Astral; Nimbus, Donelly, Capitol/EMI and J/V in the USA; Mayking, Nimbus and Distronic in Britain.

The signing of Nimbus's first sale of mastering equipment to China.

But Adrian, perhaps because he is the youngest member of the family, put his finger on a long term danger. 'A more difficult problem is if we are going to be a technology-based company for our growth, how do we ensure that we stay in front. We'll have to build up a better technology team as all we have at present is Jonathan but he's a one-off; doesn't like to be part of a team.'

At present Nimbus remains well in front of the industry because of a development of which note first appears on 29 September 1987 – Video-CD and the high density disc of which prototypes were being produced by June 1988.

Right from the outset Jonathan had designed large performance margins into the electronics of the mastering lathe so that it could run at four to six times the anticipated required speed, thus enabling mastering to be carried out much more quickly and productively. It was also possible to lay down four channels of sound as a potential advancement of Nimbus's Ambisonic recording method.

Thus it was that, when Numa asked one of those penetratingly fundamental questions that were his forte, the Nimbus/Halliday lathe was already well on its way to providing the answer. Numa, on looking at a magnified picture of the 'pits' in a standard CD, noticed how relatively widely spaced they were and asked if all the space was really necessary. The answer, of course, was 'no, if the process of making them could be more finely controlled than anyone had previously managed.'

Whereas a laser spot mastering in real time will take eighty minutes to travel the 35mm information area of a normal density CD, a four times density spiral will take five hours twenty minutes. Therefore control of smoothness and precision are essential, particularly if you then also want to master at two or three times 'real time'.

The speed and control of the mechanical movement is not the only technical problem to be solved if the density of information on a CD is to be increased significantly – something Gerald regards as essential to its second decade of development regardless of advances in digital data compression. Coating systems have to produce an extremely consistent thickness across layers twice as thin as the already infinitesimal 0.13 microns of a standard CD and surface testing equipment has to be capable of detecting much smaller, but now equally significant, defects in coatings and the master. The economics of CD pressing demand that masters be recycled, a process susceptible to minute flaws that might have been acceptable at normal density but not at times two or times four. All this Nimbus had achieved by late 1988.

But what commercial application could this high density potential have? Sound CDs were already long enough for virtually all applications and longer playing time was of little interest to the industry. Initial interest came in the CD-ROM field. For example, geological surveys for the oil industry in the United States literally took warehouses of nine-track computer tapes to store their information on, all of which had to be copied at great cost, every three years, to guard against deterioration. Double, let alone quadruple, density CD-ROM storage would obviously be a boon in such applications.

On 12 September 1988 an event occurred which was to show Gerald and Jonathan the direction in which perhaps the most profitable use of their developments might lie. Mr Kosuda, JVC's Corporate Planning Chief, came on a visit to Wyastone Leys to demonstrate a CD graphics machine showing the kind of crude cartoons which feature in computer games. Gerald remembers:

> We were talking about higher densities and Jonathan produced the
> disc and showed it to them and they said well why don't we stick
> it in the player and see what happens, so we did. As soon as it was
> played there was much bowing and nodding and we said 'very, very
> good player' and they said 'very, very good disc', but this gave us the
> clue that standard players were not far off being able to play these
> discs and some could just do it. At that time there simply wasn't the
> consumer application for it because video hadn't reached the point
> where it could be compressed onto a CD, apart, perhaps, from RCA,
> with their Digital Video Interactive, which was way ahead of its time.
> Had they not concentrated exclusively on putting it in computers as
> a universal system they might not have missed the Video-CD boat.

Mr Kosuda expressed the opinion that, 'only companies who have
developed mastering systems will be able to join this race and as far
as we can discover neither Sony nor Philips can do it yet.'

Even in September 1988, with many problems still unresolved, it
was clear that 12cm Video-CD would be of superior quality to tape.
Moreover, progress in digital compression for the medium suggested
breakthroughs could not be far off. One of the most important of them
was made at Nimbus. Under Numa's probing insistence that the double density capacity of the Nimbus/Halliday lathe be demonstrated at
MIDEM, the major European shop window for the music industry, in
France in January 1993 by means of a Nimbus Video-CD demonstration,
Jonathan came up with another of his brilliant pieces of lateral thinking.
C-Cube had developed a very powerful chip that needed to be fed with a
constant stream of data. The major companies were pursuing Video-CD
via a computer using discrete packages of data in bursts, and not getting
very far. Jonathan, recognising that a CD audio player produces the
constant stream of data the C-Cube chip requires, simply decided to
cut out the intermediary steps that were proving such an obstacle to
firms like Sony and Philips. Like many creative people, Jonathan works
best when the adrenalin is set flowing by impossible deadlines and he
managed to get the prototype running on the night before the Nimbus
team were due to leave for MIDEM.

With commendable scientific detachment Nimbus's record of the
event merely states that 'using a stand-alone decoder it was demonstrated that a standard CD audio player with a digital output can

246

deliver MPEG 1 compressed digital audio and video. ... In the Nimbus demonstration of a 135 minute Video-CD we have used a standard mid-price CD audio player, without modification, to play 2 × density.'

The Nimbus demonstration caused a great stir at MIDEM and no little unease among the giants. Here was a CD video system which could be used straightaway on about a third of the world's 120 million installed CD audio players – those with a digital output socket – and the majority of new ones, by the simple addition of a small 'black box' between player and domestic TV set which would cost no more than £150 as against the £6–700 for the new CDI and Video-CD equipment of firms such as Philips. Know-how licences have already been sold to two Far Eastern manufacturers for the video decoder, but there is a new air of realism at Nimbus these days and a clearer recognition that commercial success is rarely about technical excellence but more a matter of international politics and corporate financial muscle. The big electronics firms are in the business of creating huge markets for expensive new hardware, not of satisfying consumer needs by cheap solutions using existing equipment. The Japanese now seem to dominate international standards in electronics and already there is a new MPEG II standard designed to ensure that all 'electronic vision', satellite signals, Video-CD etc., are compatible and conform to the marketing requirements of the larger electronic firms. Companies like Philips in Holland seem to go along with these moves quite willingly. Jonathan's black box Video-CD converter, ingenious enough though it is, is not patentable, so Nimbus will be concentrating on areas where its know-how and lead times are dominant – compression and mastering.

Michael expressed today's more judicious approach to expansion.

> Our main concern is to get video onto compact discs. We are only putting forward an alternative to one that has been suggested which we will do as a licensing operation. It would be too colossal for us to do ourselves. There are certain niche markets that can make use of the technology we have developed which will suit us very well.
>
> We will continue to expand compact disc technology, but we wouldn't want to get into the production of recordable disc which will be dependent on where the cheapest place in the world to make things is. We will make the mastering equipment, though!

Gerald looks forward confidently to that situation. 'We have the best mastering equipment and compression equipment for compressing MPEG video and it doesn't really matter which system is finally adopted because our equipment will still be able to do it.'

By 1989 the mastering system could already achieve four times density on a CD, but this could not in any way be played on a domestic CD player. Jonathan has now built a laboratory prototype which can play four times density using a blue gas laser. At present this method of reading is far too expensive for a domestic player, but because greater detail or greater storage require a shorter wavelength, the semi-conductor manufacturers are working hard on solving the problem at an economical price.

Developing the blue light laser system will probably take another couple of years when half the quadrupling will be used to put a full-length feature film on one disc and the other half will be used to get improved quality so the next generation of Video-CD will be better than existing broadcast standard.

The old MPEG 1 single density disc will be the spearhead of massive production in China, but elsewhere the battle to meet the newer MPEG 2 standard is on between the Phillips/Sony consortium, working to three times density, and other Japanese/American consortia working on four times density. One of these latter groups, working in the closest secrecy with Nimbus, is expected, at the time of writing, to announce a major breakthrough in mid-1995. Single density, with only seventy minutes playing time, needs two discs to accommodate the standard length Cinema film which will be the software backbone of Video-CD. This will significantly increase the cost, particularly where 'blockbusters' are involved which will probably need three discs. Triple density (a little over one hundred minutes) can put some seventy-five per cent of backlog films onto one disc, but four times (about one hundred and thirty-five minutes) can accommodate well over ninety per cent in this way. Most new films are much more longwinded than their predecessors and the majority will require quadruple density production to get them on a single disc and therefore competitively priced marketplace.

Whatever the outcome of the battle between the various electronic giants, Nimbus is in the enviable position of being the leader in the development of in-house compression technology, in-house compression services, and the design and manufacture of the mastering lathes needed to produce Video-CDs to the new standard. Independent of CD manufacturers, film-makers and retailers alike, Nimbus is already looked up to as the best objective source of both advice and technology.

Nor are the latest developments at Nimbus confined to compression technology. Jonathan and Colin Dix have been developing more sophisticated fully automated complete CD production lines. The Nimbus automated system can be added onto existing equipment and has already been installed in Brazil and at Sonopress in Germany. The new approach uses six baking ovens producing ten to twelve coated glass masters an hour which serve six Laser Recorders working at double speed on a three-shift day or four in a two-shift day. A new Surface Analyzer has replaced the old Surface Tester and checks both the surface for defects and the coating for thickness. Unusable masters, five to ten per cent, are now automatically rejected and ejected from the system. If the rejection rate rises above ten per cent an audible alarm alerts the operator and the Analyzer tells him precisely what the problem is. A single operator can work the whole down line process because he needs to attend the glass-coated mastering stage only every seventy minutes. No less importantly, the system is fixed, thus pre-empting the deleterious short cuts sometimes taken by operators, but it can be bypassed and the entire system be worked manually, if necessary.

Nimbus joined forces with C-Cube Micro Systems of California in October 1993 to develop a real time video compression system which will enable film and video producers to produce their own tapes ready for Video-CD mastering. When all this happens Nimbus will be there. Meanwhile, its technology and engineering subsidiary will be generating profits both by the selling abroad of standard Nimbus/Halliday lathes – perhaps Nimbus will earn a Queen's Award for Exports to add to its one for technology – and by offering a high density mastering and digital compression service for companies wishing to produce Video-CD discs – undoubtedly the new format for vision by the end of the millennium.

It looks as though Nimbus will soon find itself again where it was in the late 1970s (when Numa first realised that the future lay predominantly with vision), with a solid core business generating profits to be spent, not on high-living for the shareholders and directors, but on new technical developments thought up by Gerald and Jonathan and, as always, on music. Adrian has several options open to him. 'It's less of a concern to me which way the artistic side of the business will go because there are so many different routes, it's more a matter of having to choose.'

One option that he recently aired was that Nimbus might get out of pure sound altogether and concentrate on the visual and audio-visual arts, but this was not an option that the family, which had created a catalogue they had 'been through hell for' to use Numa's words, could seriously consider. Not that Numa was optimistic about the prospects for quality sound recording. 'Sound is in the ditch and is going to stay in the ditch; it's way down in the mud now and is not going to get out again. What we have to do is to make sure that we keep our ditch clean. That's the best we can hope for.'

Adrian's strategy for doing this will be to use the marvellous new concert hall for recording first-class chamber music but record less in the way of orchestral works. This is not just a matter of cost, though current financial restraints have imposed a budget on the label which is only a small fraction of what it spent in its profligate heyday. As Adrian pointed out, the decision is more because the orchestral catalogue is overcrowded. 'There are sixty-one CD versions of the Mendelssohn violin concerto and many of them re-issues of the great performances like Kreisler and Menuhin and so on. There's just no point.'

The fruits of this approach are already gratifyingly apparent. Quite apart from the Medici Quartet recordings already described, other quartets, such as the Alberni, Brandis and Franz Schubert Quartets have all been producing excellent work. Then there are the Christ Church Cathedral Choir recordings, John Lill recording the Rachmaninov piano concerti with the BBC National Orchestra of Wales and Rachmaninov solo piano works, Kevin Bowyer's complete Bach organ works, and Ben Hudson and Mary Verney recording all the Beethoven violin sonatas on original instruments.

Modern composers continue to be supported – there is a new work from George Benjamin in production – but even more remarkable, perhaps, is the plan to resurrect the work of the late Romanian composer Nikolai Bretan. When his daughter married one of President Kennedy's leading economic advisers, Harry LeBovit, Ceausescu promptly suppressed all performance of his delightfully lyrical music. Now his daughter Judit has nearly completed her crusade to republish and record every note and Nimbus will be issuing three one-act operas and a full-length opera in the next eighteen months as the start of this process.

The list of innovative recordings is impressive. Exciting new developments are reaching fruition on the *Prima Voce* side and in America. The manufacture of special new pick-ups for transferring the electrical recordings for the 1920s and 1930s will open up access to a new range of great past instrumental performances as will the transfer of all the Duo-Art piano roles of the Aeolian Company. A series of forty to fifty CDs of the greatest pianists of the period 1905–1930 will enable us to hear Prokofiev playing Prokofiev, Cortot playing Ravel, performances by Liszt's pupil Friedheim, complete sonatas from the romantic Friedman heard hitherto only in popular snippets and de Pachman in his pre-electric recording prime, among many other notable performances. These may well be coupled with great contemporary performances of the same works so that the old hypothetical comparisons of the giants of yesterday and today can now be put to practical test.

In the summer of 1994 Nimbus broke new ground with its first recording in America in which the Kansas City Chorale made a recording of American choral music which has already reached third place in the Chicago regional billboard and is demonstrating to the American classical music-lover that Nimbus is a US label not just an import.

As Nimbus continues to innovate in what it records so it does in the means of reproducing its recordings. In 1994 a deal was struck with Meridian Audio for the inclusion of the ambisonics system in its home theatre decoder. This multi-choice system allows the listener to decide in what mode he wishes to listen and of course match it to the mode in which the recording was originally made. The system has everything needed to give the listener the complete surround sound experience. Although it costs just under £2,000, the steady flow of sales demonstrates the popularity of this particular form of extra high fidelity reproduction for the serious music listener.

Nevertheless, there are still some dangers and potential weaknesses for Nimbus Records as there are for Nimbus Technology & Engineering. William Boughton's observations are shrewd on this score. 'Until fairly recently Nimbus was administratively chaotic but the marketing has improved since they took over their own distribution. One appreciates that a small company, of course, can't devote very much in the way

251

of resources to the promotion of each individual CD, but it's a pity the directors have adopted an increasingly ivory tower attitude and don't go out into the market-place to promote Nimbus itself. Adrian used to do this most effectively, but now seems much too tied up with other things and I think the projection of the Nimbus label suffers as a result.'

Antony Smith feels this is a typical and natural artist's attitude and a little unfair. 'Success breeds success and soon our hard work and direct approach to retailers was gaining more magazine reviews, bigger royalties for artists and awards such as Diapason D'Or. But, of course, people soon forget about the past and take the present as the norm. As soon as this happens they always want more and more.'

Adrian seems well aware of the problems.

> In the past we haven't applied sufficient energy and resources to the marketing side of our activities, but now we have created a completely new marketing team.
>
> We ourselves are weak in marketing and publicity because I don't think any of us are temperamentally good at going out and telling people about what we've done and how good the records are. And telling them without browbeating them. We have all of us, when we've tried to be our own marketeers, taken an extremely aggressive approach to it. Sleeve notes and editorials for catalogues sometimes have a very aggressive way of putting things.
>
> Music-making is very restricted in this country, therefore things that try to be bold and step outside that tend to be misunderstood.

While it is true that Adrian can spare less time for the label now, the marketing team under his lieutenant, Antony Smith, is increasingly active. Without the financial resources of the giants to achieve volume sales by blanket promotional campaigns Nimbus knows that it must target its potential customers very closely, so, as well as its own sales and information service to retailers it has been building up a large direct mail data base. The Nimbus marketing team believes that a major change is about to take place in the way records are sold, with the smaller retail outlets rapidly disappearing in the way that small bookshops have largely disappeared over the past two decades. They see the megastores and direct selling as the two principal outlets for CDs. To anticipate this change Nimbus has built up a direct mailing list of 25,000 names in Britain and 30,000 in the USA, growing at 1,000 a month, as well as collaborating with the major direct mail record

Antony Smith (*left*), currently Sales and Marketing Manager, with his predecessor Roger Bateson at the start of Numbus's UK distribution.

clubs in Britain, Continental Europe and America. 'Ultimately,' says Antony Smith, 'this will be the only way you can buy our kind of classical recordings. Retail is not interested in quality, only in quantity and margin.'

But, if John Wallace's complaint is typical, has Nimbus entirely shed some of its old faults? 'I don't know if this marvellous Sousa festival concert is going to be recorded because it's very difficult to get answers out of Nimbus. I wrote to them about a year ago saying we're going to do this concert and did they want a Sousa sequel, but I've never heard back and I'm not sure what to do about it.'

Or, as another 'old faithful', Martin Jones put it in a letter to the Founders: 'We do understand that things have been very difficult for you for many months, but please, please, could you spare just a couple of minutes to let me know what is going on. My practising schedule is becoming impossible to organise.'[1]

Sentiments again echoed by Peter Laister. 'They're becoming too internal again. They don't go into the world except through Adrian and occasionally Jonathan. Technically this doesn't matter too much but commercially it gives too narrow a view.'

The Nimbus team not unreasonably counters such accusations by pointing out that the division of labour whereby Michael and Gerald generally mind the shop while Adrian and Jonathan go out on the road not only suits them but works. In the first five months of 1993, for example, Adrian and Jonathan visited China, Hong Kong, Korea, Germany and the USA. Adrian also made trips with Peter Laister to China, Hong Kong, Japan – where they visited seven major electronics companies including JVC, Sony and Toshiba – and to Dallas and Hollywood where they negotiated with Disney, MCA, Columbia and Warner Brothers. On many of these trips, senior executives Philip Moss and Anthony Smith accompanied them and there were whole 'team' delegations to MIDEM. Just as these encounters were usually at Board or top management level so were the forty-three visits to Wyastone Leys in that period (only 100 working days) usually hosted by Michael and Gerald, from firms as diverse and important as the BBC, Sony Broadcasting, Polygram, Warner Home Video, Texas Instruments, Mitsui, W.H. Smith, Hong Kong and Singapore government representatives, Microsoft, Kingfisher, Rediffusion and BT to name but a quarter of them. It is largely because these marketing activities are usually low-key that they can be missed by the outside observer.

Now that Numa is dead and Michael contemplates retirement, the family is taking in a new generation again, as it did when CD was developing. There are to be some technical children for Jonathan to develop and there are already several marketing and management cousins or uncles to help Gerald and Adrian make sure that the high quality Nimbus products in both its fields are cost-effectively produced and, particularly in the case of the label, shouted about loudly from the rooftops. When competing with firms such as EMI, who will regularly buy up the shop windows of all the leading retailers to promote a new record, an equally high profile is essential, and Nimbus is determined to have one.

Whatever new Nimbus does musically, it will be awaited eagerly by the many music-lovers who look to it to set standards and apprehensively by the opposition. The Proprietor and Chief Executive of a leading music magazine generously summed up the significance of Nimbus in the world of recorded music. 'We live in an age of mediocrity where there is a degree of sameness about so many things, both products and people, and whatever you may say about Nimbus, and our relationship has not always been of the easiest, it is a company with character. It's different. It's a company that's made you sit up and think about what it's doing and why it's doing it. To me that is important. It helps to keep interest alive. It helps in the long-term to encourage the other major companies to reconsider what they are doing and how their activities measure up to what Nimbus is doing. Rivals ignore what is going on at Wyastone Leys at their peril.'

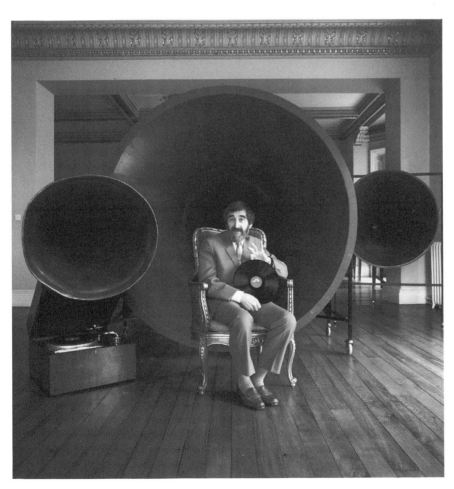

Numa with the three horns used in recording the *Prima Voce* discs.

EPILOGUE

When Count Numa Labinsky died on 28 January 1994, a few days after this book was finished I prepared to redraft the text, alter perspectives, only to realise as I reappraised what I had written that Numa had yet another achievement to add to his long list and one of which even the closest members of the family, I suspect, had only the occasional inkling. I needed to change very little because this astonishing man had already imparted such impetus and direction to Nimbus that it was as if he had anticipated that it might soon have to do without him. However sadly he will be missed on a personal level and however much Nimbus had depended on his vision of the future, he had deliberately made himself dispensable.

This book was commissioned so that publication would coincide with the tenth anniversary of Nimbus producing Britain's first commercial CD and the twenty-fifth anniversary of the start of serious music recording by Nimbus at 6 Butler's Road, Birmingham, the true birthday of Nimbus Records although the company was not formally registered until 1971.

For me, as author, the most striking and praiseworthy element of this commission has been the spirit in which it was made. It is relatively easy to say 'we want no eulogy, we want the statue, warts and all.' It is much harder actually to allow the warts to be seen, inspected, and described in detail. The openness of the Nimbus 'family' has made my task both easier and more interesting. Moreover, since no one believes great achievements can only stem from perfect beings – though many would have us believe that their great achievements indicate their own perfection – it seems to me that accomplishments shown to be the work of men not gods, men with vices as well as virtues, defects as well as talents, are enhanced in stature thereby. The Nimbus family has had the moral courage to allow what it has achieved to be seen in such perspective. They lose nothing by having done so.

The achievements of Nimbus have indeed been memorable.

In science it has pioneered developments in acoustic, digital and Ambisonic recording and, above all, in the information-carrying capacity of the compact disc, which have significantly influenced the course of audio and data recording and could yet be the basis also of video entertainment and information retrieval into the twenty-first century. In Jonathan Halliday Nimbus has an electronic engineer of genius.

In technology Nimbus has shown itself capable again and again of realising the most sophisticated and demanding concepts in practical terms. It has devised and built and now sells to the world CD and Video-CD manufacturing equipment of unsurpassed quality and ingenuity. In Gerald Reynolds it has a mechanical engineer of outstanding originality and a shrewd businessman.

In music many of its recordings have become the bench mark by which all subsequent recordings of a work are judged. Soloists, ensembles, orchestras that the world might, to its loss, have passed by or never heard, now enjoy worldwide reputations thanks to their recordings with Nimbus. In Norman White's *Prima Voce* series and in Robin Broadbank's World Music series Nimbus has created archive material which scholars and music-lovers alike will still be giving thanks for a century hence. The relentlessly high musical standards imposed by the Founders have been rigorously sustained under Adrian's direction for the past ten years.

In the business world Nimbus's growth was phenomenal by any standards. On the solid base of hard graft for twenty years from 1957 to 1977, built out of sheer determination to the point of obstinacy, a business was constructed whose turnover grew 7,600 per cent in the ten years 1982 to 1992, from less than half a million pounds to thirty eight million pounds, whose number of employees rose over ten thousand per cent in the same decade from a bare half dozen to almost 700. A business once known only to a handful of aficionados in Britain is now a much respected name to both music-lovers and to specialists in audio and video engineering in five continents.

Behind these astonishing achievements in business, technology and the arts, has lain the dynamic obsessiveness, the visionary perception and the implacable pursuit of quality of Numa Labinsky, while quietly moving in the interstices between every element of this human matrix, anticipating problems and turning rivalry to synergy, has been the gentle wisdom of Numa's lifelong partner, Michael Reynolds.

In the course of writing this book I have discovered that the Nimbus family's greatest achievement is not any of the astounding things it has done, but the way it has done them. The Founders, the inner family and the extended family have demonstrated that it *is* possible to integrate commerce and culture; to harmonise purpose within a community of people and not just to recognise, but to exemplify the belief that whether in science, the arts or the world of commerce the element of paramount importance is the element of the participants' common humanity.

APPENDICES

APPENDIX A
World Sales in the audio media in millions   260

APPENDIX B
Encoding in the Nimbus/Halliday lathe   261

APPENDIX C
Discography   263

APPENDIX A
World Sales in the audio media in millions

	CDs	LPs	Cassette	Value $m
1984	20	800	800	12,000
1985	61	730	950	12,250
1986	140	690	970	14,000
1987	260	590	1150	17,000
1988	400	510	1390	20,300
1989	600	450	1540	21,600
1990	770	339	1446	24,090
1991	976	175	1240	26,360
1992	1163	116	1603	28,980

APPENDIX B
Encoding in the Nimbus/Halliday lathe

During the laser mastering, the signal on the tape is played back, decoded in the processor, and then re-encoded into CD format by the specialised electronics of the CD encoder. Simultaneously, a stream of subsidiary (subcode) data carrying continuous track-timing information derived from the customer's 'PQ' data is fed via the encoder to the laser beam recorder, where it takes its place amongst the audio signals recorded on the disc.

The properties of the CD encoding format are remarkable. The audio data, taken in units ('blocks') of 24 eight-bit bytes representing six samples of (two-channel) information, is first expanded to 32 bytes by the addition of eight error protection bytes, derived from and related to the audio data, in two stages, separated by an extensive interleaving or dispersing of the data in time. The added error protection bytes ensure that, when the disc is eventually played, the decoder can to a large extent detect and correct erroneously read information by deducing what it should have been. The interleaving, and the reciprocal de-interleaving in the player, has the virtue that erroneous information due to localised faults on the disc is dispersed in time before it reaches the decoding stage, so that the job of correcting it is made easier. The error correction is such that faults up to a certain magnitude are completely corrected and are totally inaudible. Only when this threshold is exceeded is anything untoward heard.

In a later stage of the encoding process, these 32 eight-bit bytes, together with one byte of subcode data, are transformed into the same number of 14-bit words separated by three-bit 'merging' patterns. These words are then fed serially (bit by bit, 4.3 million bits per second) to the laser beam recorder, where they are used to turn the laser light on and off while it is focused on the rotating master disc.

Superficially, the effect of replacing the eight-bit bytes by fourteen-bit words appears to have been one of increasing the amount of information to be recorded. In actual fact the 4.3 MB/sec data rate is a misleading fiction, because the fourteen-bit patterns which are used are carefully selected according to certain criteria, one of which is that there are never less than three identical bits in a row. The 'merging' bits are likewise chosen such that this remains true wherever one pattern joins up to the next one. So the highest modulation frequency which is ever actually present on the disc is only about 700 kHz, which is less than it would have been if the eight-bit bytes had been recorded directly. Meanwhile, certain other virtues have been gained, notably that the average mark/space ratio of the recorded signal remains close to unity. This means that the line of pits on the disc presents, in aggregate, a uniform appearance to the optical pickup in the player – hence the performance of the servo which is used to follow this track when playing the disc is more constant than it would otherwise be.

APPENDIX C

Discography

The details enclosed in this listing are correct at the time of going to press. Nimbus no longer manufactures or distributes LP records and all Compact Discs marked * have been deleted. For an up-to-date listing and full catalogue please write to: Nimbus Records Limited, Wyastone Leys, Monmouth, England, NP5 3SR.

LP Listings

2101	Ravel Piano Works, Vol 1, **Vlado Perlemuter**		Sonata, **Vlado Perlemuter**
2102	Ravel Piano Works, Vol 2, **Vlado Perlemuter**	2126	Schumann Fantasie/Schubert Wanderer Fantasy, **Ilan Rogoff**
2103	Ravel Piano Works, Vol 3, **Vlado Perlemuter**	2127	French Songs Vol 3, Debussy, **Hugues Cuenod/Martin Isepp**
2104	Satie Socrate, **Hugues Cuenod/Geoffrey Parsons**	2128	Soler Harpsichord Sonatas, Vol 2, **Gilbert Rowland**
2105	Rakhmaninov Corelli Variations, **Martin Jones**	2129	Schubert Sonatas, D. 537, 571, 664, **Luc Devos**
2106	The Art of **Youra Guller**	2130	Schubert Winterreise, **Shura Gehrman/Nina Walker**
2107	Beethoven Sonata Op.10 No. 3/Schubert Sonata D.784, **Imogen Cooper**	2131	Schubert Winter Journey, **Shura Gehrman/Nina Walker**
2108	Weber Grand Duo/Brahms Sonata No 1, **Jack Brymer/David Lloyd**	2133	Chopin Etudes, Opp 10 & 25, **Ronald Smith**
2109	Chopin Sonatas Nos 2 & 3, **Vlado Perlemuter**	2134	French Wind Quintets, **Pro Arte Wind Quintet**
2110	Chopin Ballades, 1-4, **Vlado Perlemuter**	2135	Schubert Fair Maid of the Mill, **Shura Gehrman/Nina Walker**
2111	Brahms Cello Sonata No. 1/Schubert Arpeggione, **Amaryllis Fleming/Geoffrey Parsons**	2136	Chopin Etudes, Opp 10 & 25, **Ken Sasaki**
		2137	Ysaye Six Sonatas, Op. 27, **Oscar Shumsky**
2112	French Songs, Vol 1, **Hugues Cuenod/Geoffrey Parsons**	2138	Brahms Cello Sonatas, **Alexander Michejew/Geoffrey Parsons**
2114	Beethoven Sonatas Opp.110 & 111, **Willem Brons**	2139	Music for harp and strings, **Susan Drake/ESO/Boughton**
2115	Schubert Moments Musicaux/Impromptus, **Marta Deyanova**	2140	Mozart Violin Concertos 4 & 5, **Oscar Shumsky/SCO/Tortelier**
2116	Schumann Carnaval/Liszt La Leggierezza, **Marta Deyanova**	2141	Haydn Trumpet and Horn Concertos, **John Wallace/Michael Thompson/Philharmonia**
2117	Kodály & Bridge, Cello Sonatas, **Alexander Michejew/Martin Jones**	2142	Bach Violin Concertos, **Oscar Shumsky/John Tunnell/Robin Miller/SCO**
2118	French Songs Vol 2, **Hugues Cuenod/Geoffrey Parsons**	2143	Chopin Nocturnes, **Vlado Perlemuter**
2119	Rakhmaninov Preludes, **Marta Deyanova**	2144	Mozart Serenades, ECO/**José-Luis Garcia**
2120	Fauré Dolly Suite, **Cyril Smith & Phyllis Sellick**	2145	Gottschalk The Lady Fainted, **Alan Marks**
		2146	Dvorak & Tchaikovsky, String Serenades, ESO/Boughton
2121	Franck Sonata/Schumann Fantasiestücke, **Alexander Michejew/Geoffrey Parsons**	2147	Vaughan Williams Tallis Fantasia/Greensleeves, ESO/Boughton
2122	Debussy, Images for piano, **Roy Howat**	2148	The Amazing Mr Smith - Bach/Busoni & Beethoven/Liszt, **Ronald Smith**
2123	Soler Harpsichord Sonatas, Vol 1, **Gilbert Rowland**	2150	Beethoven Symphony No 1/Piano Concerto No 1, **Mary Verney/Hanover Band**
2124	Chopin Scherzi 1-4, **Marta Deyanova**		
2125	Beethoven Prometheus Variations/Liszt	2151/2	Beethoven Symphony No. 5/Piano

	Concerto No. 3, **Mary Verney/Hanover Band**
2153	**Shura Cherkassky** 'In Concert 1984', Volume 1
2154	**Shura Cherkassky** 'In Concert 1984', Volume 2
2301/3	The Last Three String Quartets, **Chilingirian String Quartet**
45001/4	German and French Songs - 4 LP set - Brahms/Schubert/Schumann/Fauré/Gounod, **Shura Gehrman/Nina Walker**
45005	Comparisons - Beethoven Hammerklavier, **Bernard Roberts**
45006	**Welsh Brass Consort** - Recital
45007	Mussorgsky, Pictures from an Exhibition, **Shura Cherkassky**
45008	The Last of the Troubadours, **Martin Best Ensemble**
45009	Benjamin Piano Sonata/Duo/Flight, **George Benjamin/Ross Pople/Kathryn Lucas**
45010	**Equale Brass Quintet** - Recital
45011	Chopin Preludes, **Vlado Perlemuter**
45012	English Songs, Vol 1, **Shura Gehrman/Adrian Farmer**
45014	'Cabaret', Berlin/Eisler/Gershwin/Joplin/Porter, **Equale Brass**
45015	Chopin Polonaises/Fantasie/Barcarolle/Berceuse/**Vlado Perlemuter**
45016	Balakirev Islamey/Tchaikovsky Sonata in G, **Shura Cherkassky**
45017	The Dante Troubadours, **Martin Best Ensemble**
45018	Stravinsky Petrouchka Dances, **Shura Cherkassky**
45019	Bellman Songs and Epistles, **Martin Best**
45020	Souster Sonata/Equalisation, **Nash Ensemble/Equale Brass**
45021	Chopin Ballades/Nocturnes/Scherzo No 4, **Shura Cherkassky**
45022	Elgar Works for string orchestra, **ESO/Boughton**
45023	Songs of Chivalry, **Martin Best Ensemble**
DC 905	Rakhmaninov Sonata No 2/Skriabin Sonata No 5, **Marta Deyanova**
DC 906	Beethoven Diabelli Variations, **Bernard Roberts**

Cassettes
| 4101/2 | Monkey - read by Kenneth Williams |

Box Sets
NI 1785	Beethoven Complete String Quartets, **Medici String Quartet**
NI 1786	Rakhmaninov Symphonies 3 CD Set, **BBC National Orchestra of Wales/Otaka**
NI 1787	Chopin Piano Music 6 CD Set, **Vlado Perlemuter**
NI 1788	Brahms Complete Piano Music 6 CD Set, **Martin Jones**
NI 1789	Haydn Selected Symphonies 3 CD Set, **Hanover Band/Goodman**
NI 1791	Mozart Special Anniversary Box, **Hanover Band/Goodman**
NI 1792	Beethoven Complete Piano Sonatas 11 CD Set, **Bernard Roberts**
NI 1793	The Complete Nimbus Recordings 8 CD Box Set, **Shura Cherkassky**
NI 1797	Oscar Wilde The Happy Prince, **Sir John Gielgud**

Full Price Releases
* NI 5001	Nimbus Natural Sound
NI 5002	The Dante Troubadours, **Martin Best Ensemble**
* NI 5003	Beethoven Symphony No.1 & Piano Concerto No.1, **Mary Verney/ Hanover Band/Monica Huggett**
* NI 5004	Bacchanales, **Equale Brass**
NI 5005	Ravel Piano Works Vol.1, **Vlado Perlemuter**
NI 5006	Songs of Chivalry, **Martin Best Ensemble**
* NI 5007	Beethoven Symphony No.5, Overtures, **Hanover Band/Huggett**
* NI 5008	Elgar Complete Works for Strings, **English String Orchestra/Boughton**
NI 5009	Mozart Violin Concertos Nos.4 & 5, **Oscar Shumsky/Scottish Chamber Orchestra**
NI 5010	Haydn Trumpet and Horn Concertos, **Michael Thompson/John Wallace/Philharmonia/Warren-Green**
NI 5011	Ravel Piano Works Vol.2, **Vlado Perlemuter**
NI 5012	Chopin Nocturnes, **Vlado Perlemuter**
NI 5013	Beethoven & Bach Piano Transcriptions, **Ronald Smith**
NI 5014	Gottschalk Piano Music, **Alan Marks**
* NI 5015	Nimbus Natural Sound Sampler
* NI 5016	Dvorak & Tchaikovsky Serenades, **English String Orchestra/Boughton**
NI 5017	Italian Trumpet Music, **John Wallace/Philharmonia**
NI 5018	The Golden Echo, **Michael Thompson/Philharmonia**
* NI 5019	Vaughan Williams Works for Strings, **English String Orchestra/Boughton**
NI 5020	**Shura Cherkassky** In Concert 1984 Vol.1
NI 5021	**Shura Cherkassky** In Concert 1984 Vol.2
NI 5022	Schubert Schwanengesang, **Shura Gehrman/Nina Walker**
NI 5023	Schubert Fair Maid of the Mill, **Shura Gehrman/Nina Walker**
NI 5024	Schumann Dichterliebe, **Shura Gehrman/Nina Walker**
* NI 5025	Britten Works for Strings, **English String Orchestra/Boughton**
NI 5026	Skriabin & Shostakovich Preludes, **Marta Deyanova**
NI 5027	Satie Socrate, **Hugues Cuenod/Geoffrey Parsons**
NI 5028	Schubert Die Winterreise, **Shura Gehrman/Nina Walker**
NI 5030	The Art of **Youra Guller**
* NI 5031	Beethoven Symphony No.2 & Piano Concerto No.3, **Mary Verney/Hanover Band/Huggett**
* NI 5032	Orchestral Favourites Vol.1 - Pachelbel Canon, **English String Orchestra/Boughton**
NI 5033	English Songs, **Shura Gehrman/Adrian Farmer**
NI 5034	Beethoven 3 Piano Sonatas, **Ronald Smith**
NI 5035	Haydn & Boccherini Cello Concertos,

NI 5036   Alexander Michejew/English String Orchestra/Boughton

NI 5036   Oscar Wilde The Happy Prince Part 1, **Sir John Gielgud**

NI 5037   Oscar Wilde The Happy Prince Part 2, **Sir John Gielgud**

NI 5038   Chopin Piano Sonatas 2 & 3, **Vlado Perlemuter**

NI 5039   Ysaye Violin Sonatas, **Oscar Shumsky**

NI 5040   Beethoven Eroica Variations, **Bernard Roberts**

NI 5041/2   Mendelssohn A Midsummer Night's Dream, **Scottish Chamber Orchestra/Laredo**

NI 5043   Chopin/Schubert/Schumann Piano Works, **Shura Cherkassky**

NI 5044   Chopin Piano Works, **Shura Cherkassky**

NI 5045   Liszt/Stravinsky Piano Works, **Shura Cherkassky**

NI 5046/7   Alice in Wonderland, **Sir John Gielgud**

NI 5048/9   Schubert Last 3 Quartets, **Chilingirian Quartet**

NI 5050   Beethoven The Complete Piano Sonatas Vol. 1, **Bernard Roberts**

NI 5051   Beethoven The Complete Piano Sonatas Vol. 2, **Bernard Roberts**

NI 5052   Beethoven The Complete Piano Sonatas Vol. 3, **Bernard Roberts**

NI 5053   Beethoven The Complete Piano Sonatas Vol. 4, **Bernard Roberts**

NI 5054   Beethoven The Complete Piano Sonatas Vol. 5, **Bernard Roberts**

NI 5055   Beethoven The Complete Piano Sonatas Vol. 6, **Bernard Roberts**

NI 5056   Beethoven The Complete Piano Sonatas Vol. 7, **Bernard Roberts**

NI 5057   Beethoven The Complete Piano Sonatas Vol. 8, **Bernard Roberts**

NI 5058   Beethoven The Complete Piano Sonatas Vol. 9, **Bernard Roberts**

NI 5059   Beethoven The Complete Piano Sonatas Vol. 10, **Bernard Roberts**

NI 5060   Beethoven The Complete Piano Sonatas Vol. 11, **Bernard Roberts**

NI 5061   Beethoven Piano Sonatas Opp. 110 & 111, **Youra Guller**

* NI 5062   Nimbus Digital Sampler 1986

NI 5063   Stravinsky The Soldier's Tale, **Christopher Lee/Scottish Chamber Orchestra**

NI 5064   Chopin Preludes, **Vlado Perlemuter**

* NI 5065   Trumpet Concertos & Fanfares, **The Wallace Collection/Philharmonia**

NI 5066   Sullivan Overtures, **Scottish Chamber Orchestra/Faris**

NI 5067   Mendelssohn Italian & Scottish Symphonies, **Scottish Chamber Orchestra/Laredo**

NI 5068   Butterworth/Parry/Bridge, **English String Orchestra/Boughton**

NI 5069   Mendelssohn Caprices & Scherzi, **Martin Jones**

NI 5070   Mendelssohn Sonatas, **Martin Jones**

NI 5071   Mendelssohn Preludes & Fugues, **Martin Jones**

NI 5072   Mendelssohn Variations/Fantasie, **Martin Jones**

NI 5073   Mendelssohn Songs Without Words Vol.1, **Martin Jones**

NI 5074   Mendelssohn Songs Without Words Vol.2, **Martin Jones**

NI 5075   At First Light, **George Benjamin/London Sinfonietta**

NI 5076   Ravel Quartet & Strauss Sextet, **Medici String Quartet**

NI 5077   Shostakovich & Debussy Quartets, **Medici String Quartet**

NI 5078   Rossini Overtures, **Scottish Chamber Orchestra/Laredo**

NI 5079   Trumpet Music from the Italian Baroque, **The Wallace Collection/Philharmonia/Warren-Green**

NI 5080   Bach/Debussy/Chopin Piano Works, **Vlado Perlemuter**

NI 5081   Cantigas de Santa Maria, **Martin Best Ensemble**

NI 5082   English Folk Songs, **Shura Gehrman/Adrian Farmer**

NI 5083   Vaughan Williams Mass in G Minor, **Christ Church Cathedral Choir/Stephen Darlington**

* NI 5084   Mahler Des Knaben Wunderhorn, **London Philharmonic Orchestra/Morris**

* NI 5085   Mahler Das Klagende Lied, **New Philharmonia/Morris**

NI 5086   Bartók Works for Strings, **English String Orchestra/Menuhin**

NI 5087   Stravinsky The Firebird Suite, **London Symphony Orchestra/Rozhdestvensky**

NI 5088   Stravinsky Petrouchka, **London Symphony Orchestra/Rozhdestvensky**

NI 5089   Alkan Music for Organ, **Kevin Bowyer**

NI 5090   Franck/Grieg/Messiaen/Rakhmaninov Piano Works, **Shura Cherkassky**

NI 5091   Bernstein/Chopin/Pabst/Schubert Piano Works, **Shura Cherkassky**

* NI 5092   Nimbus Digital Sampler

NI 5093   Flamenco Guitar, **Paco Peña**

NI 5094   Rakhmaninov 24 Preludes, **Marta Deyanova**

NI 5095   Chopin Etudes, **Vlado Perlemuter**

NI 5096   Haydn Symphonies Nos. 100 & 104, **Hanover Band/Goodman**

* NI 5097   Stravinsky Apollo, Tippett Double Concerto, **English String Orchestra/Boughton**

* NI 5098   'Make We Joy' Christmas Music by Holst & Walton, **Christ Church Cathedral Choir/Darlington**

* NI 5099   Beethoven Symphony No.6, **Hanover Band/Goodman**

NI 5100   Palestrina Mass for Pentecost, **Christ Church Cathedral Choir/Darlington**

NI 5101   Finzi Clarinet Concerto, **Alan Hacker/English Symphony Orchestra/Boughton**

NI 5102   Arie Antiche, **Alfredo Kraus**

NI 5103   Hindemith Music for Brass, **The Wallace Collection**

NI 5104   Mozart Horn Concertos, **Anthony Halstead/Hanover Band/Goodman**

* NI 5105   Haydn Symphonies Nos.101 & 103, **Austro-Hungarian Haydn Orchestra/Fischer**

NI 5106   Rossini Operatic Arias, **Raul Gimenez/**

	Scottish Chamber Orchestra		**English String Orchestra/Boughton**
NI 5107	Argentinian Songs, **Raul Gimenez/Nina Walker**	NI 5143	Mendelssohn String Symphonies Vol.3, **English String Orchestra/Boughton**
NI 5108	Schumann Etudes Symphoniques, Kreisleriana, **Vlado Perlemuter**	NI 5144/8	Beethoven Symphonies Nos. 1-9 (5 CD Set), **Hanover Band/Goodman/Huggett**
NI 5109	Beethoven Missa Solemnis, **Hanover Band/ Goodman**	* NI 5149	Beethoven Symphony No.7, **Hanover Band/ Goodman**
NI 5110	Indian Classical, **Shivkumar Sharma**	NI 5150	Lassus Choral Works, **Christ Church Cathedral Choir/Darlington**
NI 5111	Indian Classical, **Hariprasad Chaurasia**	NI 5151	Schoenberg Verklarte Nacht/Strauss Metamorphosen, **English String Orchestra/ Boughton**
NI 5112	Mendelssohn Piano Concertos Nos.1 & 2, **Joseph Kalichstein/Scottish Chamber Orchestra/Laredo**		
* NI 5113	Janacek String Quartets, **Medici String Quartet**	NI 5152	Indian Classical, **Hariprasad Chaurasia**
		NI 5153	Indian Classical, **Imrat Khan**
* NI 5114	Franck Piano Quintet & Fauré Quartet, **John Bingham/Medici String Quartet**	NI 5154	Weber Overtures, **Hanover Band/Goodman**
		NI 5155	Rule Britannia, **John Wallace/English String Orchestra/Boughton**
NI 5115	Liszt Operatic Paraphrases, **Alan Marks**		
NI 5116	Azahara, **Paco Peña**	NI 5156	Mendelssohn Quartet Op. 13/Shostakovich Piano Quintet, **John Bingham/Medici String Quartet**
NI 5117	Holst The Planets, The Perfect Fool, **Philharmonia/Boughton**		
NI 5118	Indian Classical, **Imrat Khan**	NI 5157	Mozart & Beethoven Quintets, **Vlado Perlemuter/Albion Wind Ensemble**
NI 5119	Indian Classical, **Ram Narayan**		
NI 5120	Popular Operatic Overtures, **Philharmonia/ Boughton**	NI 5158	Mendelssohn Symphony No.4/Piano Concerto No.1, **Christopher Kite/Hanover Band/Goodman**
NI 5121	Virtuoso Trumpet Concertos, **John Wallace/ Philharmonia/Wright**		
* NI 5122	Beethoven Symphony No.3, **Hanover Band/ Goodman**	* NI 5159	Haydn Symphony Nos.94 & 100, **Austro-Hungarian Haydn Orchestra/Fischer**
NI 5123	Bach/Handel/Scarlatti Arias for Soprano and Trumpet, **Helen Field/John Wallace/ Philharmonia**	NI 5160	Debussy Complete Piano Music Vol.1, **Martin Jones**
		NI 5161	Debussy Complete Piano Music Vol.2, **Martin Jones**
NI 5124	The Essential **Colin Wilson**	NI 5162	Debussy Complete Piano Music Vol.3, **Martin Jones**
NI 5125	Weelkes Choral Works, **Christ Church Cathedral Choir/Darlington**	NI 5163	Debussy Complete Piano Music Vol.4, **Martin Jones**
NI 5126	Haydn Symphonies Nos.94/95, **Hanover Band/Goodman**	NI 5164	Debussy Complete Piano Music Vol.5, **Martin Jones**
NI 5127	Saint-Saëns/Dvorak Cello Concertos, **Alexander Michejew/London Symphony Orchestra/Boughton**	NI 5165	Fauré Piano Music, **Vlado Perlemuter**
		NI 5166	Vaughan Williams Choral Works, **Christ Church Cathedral Choir/Darlington**
NI 5128	Rimsky-Korsakov Scheherazade, **Philharmonia/Boughton**	NI 5167	Benjamin/Boulez/Harvey, **London Sinfonietta/Benjamin**
NI 5129	Sousa Great Marches, **The Wallace Collection**	NI 5168	Gypsy Flamenco, **Cante Gitano**
* NI 5130	Beethoven Symphonies Nos.4 & 8, **Hanover Band/Goodman**	NI 5169	Sibelius Pelleas and Melisande, **English String Orchestra/Boughton**
NI 5131	Smetana String Quartets, **Medici String Quartet**	* NI 5170	Schumann Papillons/Carnaval, **Bernard D'Ascoli**
NI 5132	Rossini Soirees Musicales, **June Anderson/ Raul Gimenez**	NI 5171	Grieg/Mendelssohn Psalms, **Oslo Cathedral Choir/Kvam**
NI 5133	Beethoven Sonatas Opp. 57 & 81a, **Vlado Perlemuter**	* NI 5172	Schubert Symphonies Nos.3 & 5, **Hanover Band/Goodman**
* NI 5134	Beethoven Symphony No.9, **Hanover Band/ Goodman**	* NI 5173	Beethoven String Quartets Op.18 Nos. 1-3, **Medici String Quartet**
* NI 5135	Haydn Symphonies Nos.96 & 102, **Austro-Hungarian Haydn Orchestra/Fischer**	NI 5174	Bellman Songs, **Martin Best Ensemble**
		NI 5175	Berlioz Symphonie Funebre et Triomphale, **The Wallace Collection**
NI 5136	Elgar Pomp & Circumstance Marches, **English String Orchestra/Boughton**	NI 5176	Skriabin & Prokofiev, **Marta Deyanova**
NI 5137	Thys Yool - A Medieval Christmas, **Martin Best Ensemble**	NI 5177	Guitar Music, **Stepan Rak**
		NI 5178	Piano Music for 3 Hands, **Cyril Smith/ Phyllis Sellick**
* NI 5138/9	Beethoven and the Philharmonic, **Hanover Band/Goodman**	* NI 5179	Haydn Symphonies Nos.22/24/45, **Austro-Hungarian Haydn Orchestra/Fischer**
NI 5140	Mendelssohn & Shostakovich Octets, **Medici & Alberni String Quartets**		
NI 5141	Mendelssohn String Symphonies Vol.1, **English String Orchestra/Boughton**	NI 5180	Weber Symphonies/Horn Concerto, **Anthony Halstead/Hanover Band/ Goodman**
NI 5142	Mendelssohn String Symphonies Vol.2,	NI 5181	Schumann Piano Music, **Alan Marks**

NI 5182	Indian Classical, **Hariprasad Chaurasia**	* NI 5228	Mozart Clarinet Concerto/Symphony No. 40, Eine Kleine Nachtmusik, **Colin Lawson/ Hanover Band/Goodman**
NI 5183	Indian Classical, **Ram Narayan**		
NI 5184/5	Méhul 4 Symphonies, **The Gulbenkian Orchestra/Swierczewski**	NI 5229	Bartók Miraculous Mandarin, **Hungarian State Symphony Orchestra/Fischer**
* NI 5186	Beethoven String Quartets Op. 18 Nos. 4-6, **Medici String Quartet**	* NI 5230	Haydn Symphonies Nos. 99 & 104 **Austro-Hungarian Haydn Orchestra/Fischer**
NI 5187	Mussorgsky Pictures at an Exhibition, **Ronald Smith**	NI 5231	Debussy Selected Songs, **Hugues Cuenod/ Martin Isepp**
NI 5188	Italian Oboe Concertos, **John Anderson/ Philharmonia/Wright**	NI 5232	Grainger Piano Music Vol. 2, **Martin Jones**
NI 5189	Telemann Trumpet Concertos, **John Wallace/English Symphony Orchestra/ Boughton**	NI 5233	Indian Classical, **Nishat Khan/Irshad Khan**
		NI 5234	Britten Serenade for tenor, horn & strings / Nocturne, **Anthony Halstead/Jerry Hadley/ English Symphony Orchestra/Boughton/**
NI 5190	Haydn Horn Concertos, **Anthony Halstead/ Hanover Band/Goodman**		
NI 5191	Vaughan Williams String Quartets 1 & 2, **Medici String Quartet**	NI 5235	Strauss Tone Poems, **BBC National Orchestra of Wales/Otaka**
NI 5192	Prokofiev Peter and the Wolf, **English String Orchestra/Menuhin**	NI 5236	Gabrieli and his Contemporaries, **The Wallace Collection/Wright**
NI 5193	Beethoven Diabelli Variations, **Bernard Roberts**	NI 5237	Byrd Mass for 5 Voices, **Christ Church Cathedral Choir/Darlington**
NI 5194	Tchaikovsky Symphony No.5, **London Symphony Orchestra/Frühbeck de Burgos**	* NI 5238	Schumann Piano Music Vol. 3, **Daniel Levy**
		NI 5239	'Dedications', **Stepan Rak**
NI 5195	Indian Classical, **Imrat Khan/Vajahat Khan**	* NI 5240	Haydn Symphonies Nos.6-8, **Austro-Hungarian Haydn Orchestra/Fischer**
NI 5196	Encuentro, **Paco Peña/Eduardo Falu**		
NI 5197	Poulenc & Martin Masses, **Christ Church Cathedral Choir/Darlington**	* NI 5241	Mozart Requiem, **Hanover Band/Goodman**
		* NI 5242	Beethoven String Quartets Opp. 74 & 95, **Medici String Quartet**
* NI 5198	Schubert Symphonies Nos.1 & 4, **Hanover Band/Goodman**		
		NI 5243	Mathias Church & Choral Music, **Christ Church Cathedral Choir/Darlington**
* NI 5199	Haydn Symphonies Nos.97/98/27, **Austro-Hungarian Haydn Orchestra/Fischer**		
		NI 5244	Grainger Piano Music Vol. 3, **Martin Jones**
NI 5200/4	Haydn The London Symphonies, **Austro-Hungarian Haydn Orchestra/Fischer**	NI 5245	Indian Classical, **Ram Narayan**
		NI 5246	Copland Orchestral Works, **English Symphony Orchestra/Boughton**
* NI 5205	Beethoven Overtures, **Hanover Band/ Goodman**		
		NI 5247	Images & Impressions, **Judith Hall/Elinor Bennett**
NI 5206	Elgar Enigma Variations, Overtures, **English Symphony Orchestra/Boughton**		
		NI 5248	Soler 15 Harpsichord Sonatas, **Gilbert Rowland**
* NI 5207	Beethoven String Quintet in C, Quartet Op. 59 No. 1, **Medici String Quartet**		
		NI 5249	Chopin The Four Ballades, **Bernard D'Ascoli**
NI 5208	Vaughan Williams/Delius Florida Suite, **English Symphony Orchestra/Boughton**	* NI 5250	Schumann Piano Music Vol. 4, **Daniel Levy**
		NI 5251	Cante Flamenco Gypsy Flamenco
NI 5209	Chopin The Four Ballades, **Vlado Perlemuter**	* NI 5252	Schubert Symphonies Nos. 2 & 6, **Hanover Band/Goodman**
NI 5210/3	The Spirit of England, **English Symphony Orchestra/Boughton**		
		NI 5253	Schubert Die schöne Müllerin, **Shura Gehrman/Nina Walker**
NI 5214	Fauré/Gounod/Ravel Songs, **Shura Gehrman/Nina Walker**	* NI 5254	Beethoven String Quartets Opp. 130 & 133, **Medici String Quartet**
* NI 5215	Schumann Piano Music Vol. 1, **Daniel Levy**		
* NI 5216	Haydn Symphonies Nos. 93 & 95, **Austro-Hungarian Haydn Orchestra/Fischer**	NI 5255	Grainger Piano Music Vol. 4, **Martin Jones**
		* NI 5256	Schumann Piano Music Vol. 5, **Daniel Levy**
		NI 5257	Indian Classical, **Dr N Ramani**
NI 5217	Tippett Ritual Dances **English Northern Philharmonic/Tippett**	NI 5258	Haydn Violin Concertos & Symphony No. 25, **Austro-Hungarian Haydn Orchestra/ Fischer/Küchl**
NI 5218	Taverner Missa Mater Christi, **Christ Church Cathedral Choir/Darlington**		
* NI 5219	Schumann Piano Music Vol. 2, **Daniel Levy**	* NI 5259	Mozart Symphony No.41 & Piano Concerto No. 20, **Hanover Band/Goodman/ Christopher Kite**
NI 5220	Grainger Piano Music Vol. 1, **Martin Jones**		
NI 5221	Indian Classical, **Budhaditya Mukherjee**		
* NI 5222	Schubert Symphony No.9, **Hanover Band/ Goodman**	NI 5260	Mathias Symphonies Nos. 1 & 2, **BBC National Orchestra of Wales/Mathias**
		NI 5261	Riquier The Last of the Troubadours, **Martin Best Ensemble**
NI 5223	Chopin Etudes, **Ronald Smith**		
NI 5224	Donizetti and Bellini, Operatic Arias, **Raul Gimenez/Scottish Chamber Orchestra**	NI 5262	Brahms Complete Organ Music, **Kevin Bowyer**
		NI 5263	Indian Classical, **Brij Narayan**
* NI 5225	Beethoven String Quartets Op. 59 Nos. 2 & 3, **Medici String Quartet**	NI 5264	Waldteufel The Skaters' Waltz, **The Gulbenkian Orchestra/Swierczewski**
NI 5226	Liszt Piano Music, **Alan Marks**		
NI 5227	Indian Classical, **Dr L Subramaniam**	* NI 5265	Haydn Symphonies Nos. 1/2/4/5/10, **Austro-Hungarian Haydn Orchestra/**

	Fischer
NI 5266	Tippett Crown of the Year, **Christ Church Cathedral Choir/Darlington/ Medici String Quartet/Martin Jones**
NI 5267	Copland Piano Works, **Alan Marks**
NI 5268	Indian Classical, **Budhaditya Mukherjee**
* NI 5269	Haydn Symphonies Nos. 88/90/92, **Austro-Hungarian Haydn Orchestra/Fischer**
NI 5270/3	Schubert The Symphonies **Hanover Band/ Goodman**
* NI 5274	Schubert Symphony No.8 & Rosamunde, **Hanover Band/Goodman**
NI 5275	Kodály/Bridge Cello Sonatas, **Alexander Michejew/Martin Jones**
NI 5276	Indian Classical, **Zia Mohiuddin Dagar**
NI 5277	Sibelius/Khachaturian Violin Concertos, **Hu Kun/Royal Philharmonic Orchestra/ Menuhin**
NI 5278	Vivaldi Glorias,**Christ Church Cathedral Choir/Hanover Band/Darlington**
* NI 5279	Beethoven String Quartets Opp. 127 & 131, **Medici String Quartet**
NI 5280	Bach Organ Works Vol. 1, **Kevin Bowyer**
NI 5281	Songs from Argentina, **Eduardo Falu**
NI 5282	Schubert Winter Journey, **Shura Gehrman/ Nina Walker**
NI 5283	Weill Symphonies Nos. 1 & 2, **The Gulbenkian Orchestra/Swierczewski**
NI 5284	Kodály Háry János, **Hungarian State Symphony Orchestra/Fischer**
* NI 5285	Beethoven String Quartets Opp. 132 & 135, **Medici String Quartet**
NI 5286	Grainger Piano Music Vol. 5, **Martin Jones**
NI 5287	Byrd Mass for 4 Voices, **Christ Church Cathedral Choir/Darlington**
NI 5288	Misa Flamenca, **Paco Peña**
NI 5289	Bach Organ Works Vol. 2, **Kevin Bowyer**
NI 5290	Bach Organ Works Vol. 3, **Kevin Bowyer**
NI 5291	Chopin Piano Concerto No. 1/Weber Konzertstucke, **Hanover Band/Goodman/ Christopher Kite**
NI 5292	Rakhmaninov Corelli Variations, **Martin Jones**
NI 5293	Schubert Six Moments Musicaux, **Marta Deyanova**
NI 5294	Bliss A Colour Symphony, **BBC National Orchestra of Wales/Wordsworth**
NI 5295	Britten The Young Person's Guide to the Orchestra, **English Symphony Orchestra/ Boughton**
NI 5296	Parry Symphony No.1 & From Death to Life, **English Symphony Orchestra/ Boughton**
NI 5297	Chopin Complete Scherzi & Impromptus, **Marta Deyanova**
NI 5298	Indian Classical, **Hariprasad Chaurasia**
NI 5299	Liszt Phantasie, Schumann Sonata, **Vlado Perlemuter**
NI 5300	Mozart Operatic Arias, **Raul Gimenez**
NI 5301	Tippett Triple Concerto/Piano Concerto, **BBC Philharmonic/Tippett**
NI 5302	Byrd Mass for 3 Voices, **Christ Church Cathedral Choir/Darlington**
NI 5303	Offenbach Music from the Operettas, **The Gulbenkian Orchestra/Swierczewski**
* NI 5304	Brahms Piano Music Vol. 1, **Martin Jones**
NI 5305	Hindustani Classical Vocal, **Sulochana Brahaspati**
NI 5306	Prokofiev/Tchaikovksy Romeo & Juliet, **BBC National Orchestra of Wales/Otaka**
NI 5307	Hindustani Classical Vocal, **Salamat Ali Khan/Sharafat Ali Khan/Shafqat Ali Khan**
NI 5308	Shostakovich Piano Concertos, **Martin Jones/English Symphony Orchestra/ Boughton**
NI 5309	Bartók Dance Suite, **Hungarian State Symphony Orchestra/Fischer**
NI 5310	'Celebration' - Christmas Fanfares & Carols **BBC Welsh Chorus** with readings by Aled Jones
NI 5311	Rakhmaninov Symphony No.1, **BBC National Orchestra of Wales/Otaka**
NI 5312	Haydn Quartets Opp.77 & 103, **Franz Schubert Quartett**
NI 5313	Schubert String Quintet in C, **Brandis Quartett/Wen-Sinn Yang**
NI 5314	Indian Classical, **Buddhadev Das Gupta**
NI 5315	Hindustani Classical Vocal, **Girija Devi**
NI 5316	Ives Central Park in the Dark, **The Gulbenkian Orchestra/Swierczewski**
NI 5317	Souster Sonata/Equalisation, **Equale Brass/ The Nash Ensemble/Friend**
NI 5318	Mendelssohn Scottish Symphony, **Hanover Band/Goodman**
NI 5319	The Sleeping Angel, **Fong Naam**
NI 5320	Fiddle Sticks, Irish Traditional Music from Donegal
* NI 5321	Haydn Symphonies Nos. 9/12/13/40, **Austro-Hungarian Haydn Orchestra/ Fischer**
NI 5322	Rakhmaninov Symphony No.2, **BBC National Orchestra of Wales/Otaka**
NI 5323	Indian Classical, **Dr L Subramaniam**
NI 5324	Gottschalk Piano Music for 4 Hands, **Alan Marks/Nerine Barrett**
NI 5325	Bach Violin Concertos, **Oscar Shumsky/ Scottish Chamber Orchestra**
NI 5326	Virtuoso Piano Showpieces, **Martin Jones**
NI 5327	French Wind Music, **Pro Arte Wind Quintet**
NI 5328	Taverner to Tavener, **Christ Church Cathedral Choir/Darlington**
NI 5329	Barber Violin Concerto/Bernstein Serenade, **English Symphony Orchestra/Boughton/ Hu Kun**
NI 5330	Strauss/Martinu/Françaix Oboe Concertos, **John Anderson/Philharmonia/Wright**
* NI 5331	Haydn Symphonies Nos. 14-17, **Austro-Hungarian Haydn Orchestra/Fischer**
NI 5332	Siamese Funeral Music, **Fong Naam**
NI 5333	Bartók Violin Concertos Nos. 1 & 2, **Gerhart Hetzel/Hungarian State Symphony Orchestra/Fischer**
NI 5334	Tippett/Berkeley/Berkeley, **English String Orchestra/Boughton**
NI 5335	The Sound of St. John's, **Choir of St. John's College, Cambridge/Guest**
NI 5337	Le Maître de la Mélodie, **Hugues Cuenod**
NI 5338	Choros from Brazil, **Os Ingênuos**
NI 5339	Howards End Soundtrack featuring **Martin Jones**
NI 5340	Ravel/Chopin/Beethoven/Mendelssohn Piano Works, **Vlado Perlemuter/Adrian**

Farmer

* NI 5341	Haydn Symphonies Nos. 89 & 91, **Austro-Hungarian Haydn Orchestra/Fischer**
NI 5342	Amiscellany, **John Amis and Friends**
NI 5343	Mathias Symphony No.3/Oboe Concerto, **David Cowley/BBC National Orchestra of Wales/Llewellyn**
NI 5344	Rakhmaninov Symphony No.3, **BBC National Orchestra of Wales/Otaka**
NI 5345	Boyce The Eight Symphonies, **English Symphony Orchestra/Boughton**
* NI 5347	Respighi Ancient Airs & Dances, **English Symphony Orchestra/Boughton**
NI 5346	Hindustani Classical Vocal, **Shruti Sadolikar**
NI 5348	Rakhmaninov Piano Concerto No.3/Piano Sonata No. 2, **BBC National Orchestra of Wales/Otaka**
NI 5349	Brahms Piano Concerto No. 1/Dohnányi Nursery Variations, **Mark Anderson/Hungarian State Symphony Orchestra/Fischer**
NI 5350	Dear old Erin's Isle, Irish Traditional Music from America
* NI 5351	Mozart String Quartets K.575 & K.589, **Franz Schubert Quartett**
NI 5352	Flamenco de la Frontera, **Paco Del Gastor**
NI 5353	Beethoven String Quartets Op.18 Nos. 4-6, **Brandis Quartett**
NI 5354	Birds, Beasts & Flowers A programme of poetry, prose & music narrated by **Princess Grace of Monaco/Richard Pasco**
NI 5356	Indian Classical, **Imrat Khan**
NI 5357	Hoddinott The Heaventree of Stars, **Hu Kun/BBC National Orchestra of Wales/Otaka**
NI 5358	The Virtuoso Violin, **Daeshik Kang**
NI 5359	Persian Classical Music, **Hossein Omoumi**
NI 5360	Taverner Music for Our Lady & Divine Office, **Christ Church Cathedral Choir/Darlington**
NI 5361	Schumann 6 Fugues on B-A-C-H/Reubke 94th Psalm, **Kevin Bowyer**
NI 5362/3	Bartók The Wooden Price Suite, **Hungarian State Symphony Orchestra/Fischer**
NI 5364	Walton Choral Works, **Christ Church Cathedral Choir/Darlington**
NI 5365	Indian Classical, **Hariprasad Chaurasia**
NI 5366	Finzi/Parry/Bridge, **English Symphony Orchestra/Boughton/Martin Jones**
NI 5367	Mathias Organ Music, **John Scott**
NI 5368	Chinese Music for the Pipa, **Wu Man**
NI 5369	Hoddinott Piano Sonatas Nos. 1-5, **Martin Jones**
NI 5377	Bach Organ Works Vol. 4, **Kevin Bowyer**
NI 5378	Sundanese Classical Songs, **Imas Permas/Asep Kosasih**
NI 5379	Janacek & Fauré String Quartets, **Medici String Quartet**
NI 5380	Tchaikovsky String Quartets Nos.1 & 3, **Franz Schubert Quartett**
* NI 5381	Mozart String Quartets K.465 & K.590, **Franz Schubert Quartett**
NI 5382	Beethoven String Quartets Op.59 Nos. 1 & 3, **Brandis Quartett**
NI 5383	Traditional Music from Cape Breton Island
NI 5384/5	Alice Through the Looking Glass, **Sir John**

Gielgud

NI 5386	**Henry Kelly**'s Classic Challenge Vol. 1
NI 5387	**Henry Kelly**'s Classic Challenge Vol. 2
NI 5388	**Henry Kelly**'s Classic Challenge Vol. 3
NI 5392	Michael Haydn Flute Concertos, Joseph Haydn Symphony No. 22 **István-Zsolt Nagy/Austro-Hungarian Haydn Orchestra/Fischer**
NI 5393	Chopin Scherzo No. 3/Mazurkas, **Vlado Perlemuter**
NI 5394	Palestrina Missa O Sacrum Convivium, **Christ Church Cathedral Choir/Darlington**
NI 5395	Arie Antiche, **Shura Gehrman/Adrian Farmer**
NI 5396	Fauré & Duparc Songs, **Shura Gehrman Nina Walker/Adrian Farmer**
NI 5397	The Music of Lorestan, Iran
NI 5398	Pernambuco's music from Brazil
NI 5399	Tchaikovsky Souvenir de Florence, String Quartet No. 2, **Franz Schubert Quartett**
NI 5400	Bach Organ Works Vol. 5, **Kevin Bowyer**
NI 5401	Music from Southern Laos
NI 5402	Indian Classical, **Z M Dagar,** Volume 2
NI 5403	J C Bach Six Grand Overtures, **English Symphony Orchestra/Boughton**
NI 5404	Choros from Bahia
NI 5405/6	Szymanowski Complete Piano Music Vol. 1, **Martin Jones**
* NI 5407	Haydn Symphonies Nos. 3/11/18/19/20, **Austro-Hungarian Haydn Orchestra/Fischer**
NI 5408	Langlais Organ Music, **Kevin Bowyer**
NI 5409	Hindustani Classical Vocal, **Ghulam Mustafa Khan**
NI 5410	Hindemith/Weill/Schulhoff String Quartets, **Brandis Quartett**
NI 5411	Hindemith/Schoenberg/Pepping Organ Works, **Kevin Bowyer**
NI 5412	Thai Classical Music, **Prasit Thawon Ensemble**
NI 5414	Advent Carols from St. John's, **Choir of St. John's College, Cambridge/Robinson**
NI 5415	Across the Waters, Irish Traditional Music from England
NI 5416	Buddhist Ensemble from China
NI 5417/8	Haydn Symphonies Nos. 88-92 & Sinfonia Concertante, **Austro-Hungarian Haydn Orchestra/Fischer**
NI 5419/20	Haydn The Paris Symphonies, **Austro-Hungarian Haydn Orchestra/Fischer**
NI 5421	Cuba: The Son, **Familia Valera Miranda**
* NI 1403	Albinoni/Pachelbel/Elgar/Vaughan Williams String Classics, **English String Orchestra/Boughton**
* NI 1404	Beethoven The Authentic Overtures, **Hanover Band/Huggett/Goodman**
* NI 1405	Italian Trumpet Spectacular, **John Wallace/The Wallace Collection/Philharmonia**
* NI 1407	Vaughan Williams/Butterworth English Masterworks, **English String Orchestra/Boughton**
* NI 1408	Mendelssohn Symphony No. 4, **Scottish Chamber Orchestra/Laredo**
* NI 1409	Favourite Chopin, Vlado Perlemuter
NI 1414	Mussorgsky Songs & Dances of Death, **Shura Gehrman**

| NI 1415 | George Benjamin Piano Sonata, **George Benjamin** |
| NI 1432 | George Benjamin Sudden Time, **London Philharmonic/Benjamin** |

Mid-price Vintage Jazz
HRM 6001 Duke Ellington
HRM 6002 Louis Armstrong
HRM 6003 Bessie Smith
HRM 6004 Hot Jazz
HRM 6005 From Broadway to Hollywood, **Lawrence Tibbett**

Mid-price Classical Releases
NI 7007	Meditations for a Quiet Night
* NI 7008	World Music Sampler Vol. 1
NI 7009	Meditations for a Quiet Dawn
NI 7010	Meditations at Sunset
NI 7011	The Art of Paco Peña
NI 7012	Vivaldi Concerti & Baroque Trumpet Music, **John Wallace/Philharmonia/Warren-Green/Wright**
NI 7013	Vaughan Williams Orchestral Favourites Vol. 3, **English Symphony Orchestra/Boughton**
NI 7014	World Music Sampler Vol. 2
NI 7015	Elgar Orchestral Favourites Vol. 4, **English Symphony Orchestra/Boughton**
NI 7016	Haydn Trumpet Concerto & Other Classical Concerti, **John Wallace/Philharmonia/Warren-Green**
NI 7017	Britten Orchestral Favourites Vol. 5, **English Symphony Orchestra/Boughton**
NI 7018	Beethoven Symphonies Nos. 3 & 4, **Hanover Band/Goodman**
NI 7019	Orchestral Favourites Vol.1 - Pachelbel Canon, **English String Orchestra/Boughton**
NI 7020	Respighi Ancient Airs & Dances, **English Symphony Orchestra/Boughton**
NI 7021	Make We Joy Christmas Music by Holst & Walton, **Christ Church Cathedral Choir/Darlington**
NI 7701	Chopin & Liszt Piano Works, **Shura Cherkassky**
NI 7702	Debussy Piano Favourites, **Martin Jones**
NI 7703	Grainger Piano Favourites, **Martin Jones**
NI 7704	Mendelssohn Piano Favourites, **Martin Jones**
NI 7705	Schumann/Franck Piano Works, **Shura Cherkassky**
NI 7706	Mussorgsky/Rakhmaninov/Brahms Piano Works, **Shura Cherkassky**

PRIMA VOCE
NI 7801	Great Singers Volume 1 1909-1938
NI 7802	Divas Volume 1 1906-1935
NI 7803	Enrico Caruso
NI 7804	Giovanni Martinelli Volume 1 1915-1928
NI 7805	Rosa Ponselle Volume 1 1923-1939
NI 7806	Amelita Galli-Curci
NI 7807	Beniamino Gigli Volume 1 1918-1924
NI 7808	Luisa Tetrazzini
NI 7809	Enrico Caruso in Song
NI 7810	Titta Ruffo

NI 7811	Ernestine Schumann-Heink
NI 7812	Great Singers Volume 2 1903-1939
NI 7813	Tito Schipa
NI 7814	Claudia Muzio
NI 7815	Giuseppe de Luca
NI 7816	Lauritz Melchior
NI 7817	Beniamino Gigli Volume 2 1925-1940
NI 7818	Divas Volume 2 1909-1940
NI 7819	Royal Opera House Covent Garden
NI 7820	John McCormack in Opera
NI 7821	Eidé Norena
NI 7822	Great Singers in Mozart
NI 7823/4	Feodor Chaliapin (2 CD Set)
NI 7825	Lawrence Tibbett in Opera
NI 7826	Giovanni Martinelli Volume 2 1913-1923
NI 7827/8	*Die Zauberflöte* (2 CD Set)
NI 7829	*Louise*
NI 7830	Richard Tauber in Opera
NI 7831	Mattia Battistini
NI 7832	Maria Ivogün
NI 7833	Tauber & Schöne in Operetta
NI 7834	Caruso in Ensemble
NI 7835	Jussi Björling - The First Ten Years
NI 7836/7	Conchita Supervia (2 CD Set)
NI 7838	John Charles Thomas
NI 7839	Prima Voce Party
NI 7840/1	The Era of Adelina Patti (2 CD Set)
NI 7842	Jussi Björling Volume 2 1936-1941
NI 7843/4	*Cavalleria Rusticana & Pagliacci* (2 CD Set)
NI 7845	Giacomo Lauri-Volpi Volume 1 1922-1942
NI 7846	Rosa Ponselle Volume 2 1918-1939
NI 7847	Kirsten Flagstad
NI 7848	Great Singers at the Berlin State Opera
NI 7849	Frieda Hempel
NI 7850	Antonio Cortis
NI 7851	Legendary Voices
NI 7852	Amelita Galli-Curci Volume 2 1917-1930
NI 7853	Giacomo Lauri-Volpi Sings Verdi
NI 7854	John McCormack in Song
NI 7855	Great Singers at the Metropolitan Opera New York
NI 7856	Legendary Tenors
NI 7857	Geraldine Farrar in Italian Opera
NI 7858	Great Singers at La Scala, Milan
NI 7859	Excerpts from Faust and French Opera
NI 7860	Plançon and Eames
NI 7861	The Spirit of Christmas Past
NI 7862/3	*La Bohème* (2 CD Set)
NI 7864	More Legendary Voices
NI 7865	Great Singers at the Mariinsky
NI 7866	Caruso in Opera Volume 2
* NI 1430	Prima Voce Sampler

3 CD Box Sets
NI 1783	Opera House slipcase (La Scala/Berlin/Covent Garden)
NI 1790	Caruso (Arias/Ensembles/Songs)
NI 1794	Tenors box (Caruso/Schipa/McCormack)
NI 1795	Divas box (Ponselle/Galli-Curci/Norena)

Cassettes
NC 1791	Mozart Special Anniversary Box, **Hanover Band/Goodman**
NC 1797	The Happy Prince, **John Gielgud**
NC 1799	The Soldier's Tale/Peter & the Wolf,

Christopher Lee

NC 5005/11 Ravel Piano Works, **Vlado Perlemuter**

NC 5006 Songs of Chivalry, **Martin Best Ensemble**

NC 5019 Vaughan Williams Works for Strings, **English String Orchestra/Boughton**

NC 5025 Britten Works for Strings, **English String Orchestra/Boughton**

NC 5032 Pachelbel's Canon, **English Symphony Orchestra/Boughton**

NC 5041/2 Mendelssohn A Midsummer Night's Dream, **Scottish Chamber Orchestra/Laredo**

NC 5044 Chopin Piano Works, **Shura Cherkassky**

NC 5046/7 Alice in Wonderland, **Sir John Gielgud**

NC 5065 Trumpet Concertos & Fanfares, **The Wallace Collection/Philharmonia**

NC 5066 Sullivan Overtures, **Scottish Chamber Orchestra/Faris**

NC 5068 Butterworth/Parry/Bridge, **English String Orchestra/Boughton**

NC 5073 Mendelssohn Songs Without Words Vol. 1, **Martin Jones**

NC 5087 Stravinsky The Firebird Suite, **London Symphony Orchestra/Rozhdestvensky**

NC 5088 Stravinsky Petrouchka, **London Symphony Orchestra/Rozhdestvensky**

NC 5093 Flamenco guitar, **Paco Peña**

NC 5096 Haydn Symphonies Nos. 100 & 104, **Hanover Band/Goodman**

NC 5098 Make We Joy, Christmas Music, **Christ Church Cathedral Choir/Darlington**

NC 5099 Beethoven Symphony No. 6, **Hanover Band/Goodman**

NC 5101 Finzi Clarinet Concerto, **Alan Hacker/ English Symphony Orchestra/Boughton**

NC 5104 Mozart Horn Concertos, **Anthony Halstead/Hanover Band/Goodman**

NC 5106 Rossini Operatic Arias, **Raul Gimenez/ Scottish Chamber Orchestra**

NC 5109 Beethoven Missa Solemnis, **Hanover Band/ Goodman**

NC 5116 Azahara, **Paco Peña**

NC 5117 Holst The Planets, The Perfect Fool, **Philharmonia Orchestra/Boughton**

NC 5120 Popular Operatic Overtures, **Philharmonia/ Boughton**

NC 5129 Sousa Great Marches, **The Wallace Collection**

NC 5137 Thys Yool - A Medieval Christmas, **Martin Best Ensemble**

NC 5141 Mendelssohn String Symphonies Vol. 1, **English String Orchestra/Boughton**

NC 5142 Mendelssohn String Symphonies Vol. 2, **English String Orchestra/Boughton**

NC 5144/7 Beethoven Symphonies (4 Cassette set), **Hanover Band/Goodman/Huggett**

NC 5154 Weber Overtures, **Hanover Band/Goodman**

NC 5155 Rule Britannia, **John Wallace/English String Orchestra/Boughton**

NC 5167 Benjamin/Boulez/Harvey Orchestral Works, **London Sinfonietta**

NC 5172 Schubert Symphonies Nos. 3 & 5, **Hanover Band/Goodman**

NC 5190 Haydn Horn Concertos, **Anthony Halstead/ Hanover Band/Goodman**

NC 5196 Encuentro, **Paco Peña/Eduardo Falu**

NC 5200/3 Haydn The London Symphonies, **Austro-**

Hungarian Haydn Orchestra/Fischer

NC 5210/3 The Spirit of England, **English Symphony Orchestra/Boughton**

NC 5217 Tippett Ritual Dances, **English Northern Philharmonic/Tippett**

NC 5220 Grainger Piano Music Vol. 1, **Martin Jones**

NC 5222 Schubert Symphony No. 9, **Hanover Band/ Goodman**

NC 5224 Donizetti and Bellini Operatic Arias, **Raul Gimenez**

NC 5228 Mozart Symphony No. 40, Eine Kleine Nachtmusik, **Hanover Band/Goodman/ Colin Lawson**

NC 5229 Bartók Miraculous Mandarin, **Hungarian State Symphony Orchestra/Fischer**

NC 5232 Grainger Piano Music Vol. 2, **Martin Jones**

NC 5235 Strauss Der Rosenkavalier - Waltzes, **BBC National Orchestra of Wales/Otaka**

NC 5241 Mozart Requiem, **Hanover Band/Goodman**

NC 5243 Mathias Church & Choral Music, **Christ Church Cathedral Choir/Darlington**

NC 5244 Grainger Piano Music Vol. 3, **Martin Jones**

NC 5246 Copland Orchestral Works, **English Symphony Orchestra/Boughton/John Wallace**

NC 5251 Cante Flamenco Gypsy Flamenco

NC 5252 Schubert Symphonies Nos. 2 & 6, **Hanover Band/Goodman**

NC 5255 Grainger Piano Music Vol. 4, **Martin Jones**

NC 5259 Mozart Symphony No. 41/Piano Concerto No. 2, **Christopher Kite/Hanover Band/ Goodman**

NC 5260 Mathias Symphonies Nos. 1 & 2, **BBC National Orchestra of Wales/Mathias**

NC 5264 Waldteufel The Skaters' Waltz, **The Gulbenkian Orchestra/ Swierczewski**

NC 5270/3 Schubert The Symphonies, **Hanover Band/ Goodman**

NC 5274 Schubert Symphony No. 8/Rosamunde, **Hanover Band/Goodman**

NC 5277 Sibelius/Khachaturian Violin Concertos, **Royal Philharmonic Orchestra/Menuhin/ Hu Kun**

NC 5278 Vivaldi Glorias, **Hanover Band/Christ Church Cathedral Choir/Darlington**

NC 5283 Weill Symphonies Nos. 1 & 2, **The Gulbenkian Orchestra/Swierczewski**

NC 5284 Kodály Háry János, **Hungarian State Symphony Orchestra/Fischer**

NC 5286 Grainger Piano Music Vol. 5, **Martin Jones**

NC 5288 Misa Flamenca, **Paco Peña**

NC 5294 Bliss A Colour Symphony, **BBC National Orchestra of Wales/Wordsworth**

NC 5295 Britten The Young Person's Guide to the Orchestra, **English Symphony Orchestra/ Boughton**

NC 5302 Byrd Mass for 3 Voices, **Christ Church Cathedral Choir/Darlington**

NC 5303 Offenbach Music from the Operettas, **The Gulbenkian Orchestra/Swierczewski**

NC 5310 Celebration Christmas Fanfares & Carols, **BBC Welsh Chorus with readings by Aled Jones**

NC 5319 The Sleeping Angel, **Fong Naam**

NC 5320 Fiddle Sticks

NC 5322 Rakhmaninov Symphony No. 2, **BBC**

National Orchestra of Wales/Otaka

NC 5335 The Sound of St. John's, **Choir of St. John's College, Cambridge/Guest**

NC 5338 Chorus from Brazil, **Os Ingênuos**

NC 5339 Howards End Soundtrack featuring **Martin Jones**

NC 5342 Amiscellany, **John Amis & Friends**

NC 5344 Rakhmaninov Symphony No. 3, **BBC National Orchestra of Wales/ Otaka**

NC 5350 Dear old Erin's Isle, Irish Traditional Music from America

NC 5354/5 Birds, Beasts & Flowers A programme of poetry, prose & music narrated by **Princess Grace of Monaco & Richard Pasco**

NC 5384/5 Alice Through the Looking Glass, **Sir John Gielgud**

NC 5386 **Henry Kelly's** In-Car Challenge 1

ENDNOTES

CHAPTER ONE
1. Francis Baumli PhD, Philosopher, Musicologist, Illinois.
2. Sir William Glock, September 1993.
3. *Los Angeles Herald Examiner*, 21 June 1987.
4. *Practical Hi-Fi* (Classical), undated.
5. *Kettering Evening Telegraph*, 25 February 1981.
6. Keith Grant in *For The Record*, November–December 1987.
7. *Milwaukee Sentinel*, 31 July 1987.
8. Frank Granville Barker, Nimbus Catalogue.
9. Andrew Keener, *Hi-Fi News*, Autumn 1980.
10. Nimbus CD Catalogue 1986.

CHAPTER THREE
1. *San Francisco Chronicle*, 2 June 1987.
2. *Los Angeles Herald Examiner*, 21 June 1987.
3. Ian Webb, *The Quest for Quality*, Industrial Society Press, 1991.

CHAPTER FOUR
1. *Le Matin*, 19 January 1986.
2. *Le Monde de la Musique*, June 1989.
3. *Le Matin*, 30 January 1986.
4. The *Guardian*, 7 August 1987.

CHAPTER FIVE
1. Letter from Bernard Roberts to Michael Holloway, 9 November 1979.
2. Stephen Walsh, *Sunday Observer*, 31 October 1992.
3. *Gramophone*, March 1978.
4. *Kettering Evening Telegraph*, 25 February 1981.
5. Letter from John Wallace to Adrian Farmer, 3 March 1990.
6. Letter from Adrian Farmer to John Wallace, 19 March 1990.
7. Letter from Christian Hocks to Numa Labinsky, September 1978.
8. Letter from Numa Labinsky to Christian Hocks, 20 September 1978.
9. Letter from Adrian Farmer to Alexander Michejew, 1 December 1988.
10. Letter from Numa Labinsky to Alexander Michejew, 25 January 1989.
11. Letter from Adrian Farmer to Alexander Michejew, 27 January 1989.

CHAPTER SEVEN
1. Ian Webb, *The Quest for Quality*, Industrial Society Press, 1991.
2. Letter from Sir John Harvey Jones to John Griffiths, 2 July 1993.

CHAPTER EIGHT
1. *Ham & High*, 13 May 1983.
2. Letter from Adrian Farmer to Oscar Shumsky's agent, September 1981.
3. Letter from Oscar Shumsky to Adrian Farmer, 30 April 1983.
4. Letter from Oscar Shumsky to Adrian Farmer, 17 September 1983.
5. Letter from Oscar Shumsky to Numa Labinsky, 31 October 1983.
6. Letter from Oscar Shumsky to Numa Labinsky, 10 November 1983.
7. Letter from Numa Labinsky to Oscar Shumsky, 23 November 1983.
8. Letter from Oscar Shumsky to Numa Labinsky, 6 January 1984.
9. Letter from Oscar Shumsky to Adrian Farmer, undated.

10. Letter from Oscar Shumsky to Numa Labinsky, 22 March 1984.
11. Letter from Oscar Shumsky to Adrian Farmer, 5 April 1984.
12. Letter from Adrian Farmer to Oscar Shumsky, 5 April 1984.
13. Letter from Oscar Shumsky to Adrian Farmer, 18 April 1984.
14. Letter from Adrian Farmer to Oscar Shumsky, 1 May 1984.
15. Letter from Richard Apley (Ibbs & Tillet) to Adrian Farmer, 6 June 1989.
16. Nimbus Records document, 26 June 1990.
17. *Baltimore Sun*, date unknown.
18. Letter from Andrew Green (Ibbs & Tillet) to Nimbus, 20 May 1982.
19. Letter from Andrew Green (Ibbs & Tillet) to Nimbus, 21 February 1983.
20. Letter from Andrew Green (Ibbs & Tillet) to Nimbus, 16 May 1983.
21. Letter from Christa Phelps-Barnard to Adrian Farmer, 18 May 1988.
22. Letter from Leonard Bernstein to Shura Cherkassky, 22 April 1988.
23. Letter from Adrian Farmer to Shura Cherkassky, 20 June 1988.
24. Letter from Adrian Farmer to Shura Cherkassky, 13 October 1988.
25. Letter from Adrian Farmer to Christa Phelps-Barnard (Ibbs & Tillet), 13 October 1988.
26. Letter from Christa Phelps-Barnard to Adrian Farmer, 14 October 1988.
27. Telex from Christa Phelps-Barnard to Adrian Farmer, 3 November 1989.
28. Telex from Christa Phelps-Barnard to Sylvia Strange, 14 November 1989.
29. Facsimile from Don Trend to Christa Phelps-Barnard, Artists Management International, 4 October 1991.
30. Letter from Gerald Reynolds to Ibbs & Tillet, October 1991.

CHAPTER NINE
1. Letter from Robert Maxwell to Nimbus Records Ltd., 30 September 1987.
2. Press Release, 2 November 1987.
3. Letter from Robert Maxwell to Numa Labinsky, 11 November 1987.
4. Memorandum from Richard Cockton to Howard Nash, 15 August 1991.
5. *News Digest* re. Pergamon, October 1988.
6. Memorandum from SHG to EHF, 20 September 1988.
7. Memorandum from Numa Labinsky to Nimbus managers, 27 October 1988.
8. File note of conversation between Gerald Reynolds and Richard Ainsworth-Morris, 4 November 1988.
9. 'Nimbus in the UK' (Peat Marwick for MCC), November 1988.
10. Transcription of telephone conversation between Numa Labinsky and Robert Maxwell, 14 November 1988.
11. Nimbus Press Release, January 1989.
12. Nimbus Bulletin, January 1989.
13. Letter from Numa Labinsky, Michael and Gerald Reynolds to Robert Maxwell, January 1989.
14. Letter from Nimbus to Robert Maxwell, 27 August 1988.
15. Memorandum from Peter Laister to Robert Maxwell, 8 May 1989.
16. Inter-company memorandum from Michael Reynolds to E Graham (MCC), 9 May 1989.
17. Memorandum from Peter Laister to Robert Maxwell, copies to J P Ansalmini, Ian Maxwell, 12 June 1989.
18. Memorandum from Peter Laister to Robert Maxwell, copy to Ian Maxwell, 23 June 1989.
19. Letter from N A Thomas (MacFarlanes) to Numa Labinsky, undated.

CHAPTER TEN
1. Letter from Nimbus Records Ltd. to Nicholas Curry, 24 November 1986.
2. Letter from Paul Robertson to Numa Labinsky, undated.
3. *Hartford Courant*, 6 August 1987.
4. Letter from Nicholas Curry to Nina Walker, 18 November 1987.
5. *Classical Music*, 22 December 1990.
6. Letter from Adrian Farmer to Paul Robertson, 14 November 1990.
7. Letter from Paul Robertson to Nimbus Records Ltd., 16 May 1991.
8. Letter from Paul Robertson to Adrian Farmer, 10 February 1991.

9. Letter from Geraint Lewis to Paul Robertson, 14 November 1991.
10. Letter from Caroline Brown to Mr Libin, 27 November 1981.
11. Letter from Horace Fitzpatrick to Adrian Farmer, 28 January 1982.
12. *Early Music News*, June 1982.
13. The *Guardian*, 28 May and 19 June 1982.
14. *Practical Hi-Fi*, date unknown.
15. Letter from Adrian Farmer to Caroline Brown, 6 July 1983.
16. Fax from Roy Goodman, undated.
17. Fax from Nimbus Records Ltd. to Roy Goodman, 25 November 1989.
18. Fax from Roy Goodman to Adrian Farmer, 27 November 1989.
19. Fax from Roy Goodman to Adrian Farmer, 27 November 1989.
20. File note, Adrian Farmer, 14 July 1988.
21. Letter from Gerald Reynolds to Stephen Neiman, 26 June 1989.
22. Letter from Ken Aldred to Stephen Neiman, 14 October 1988.
23. Letter from Stephen Neiman to Numa Labinsky, 13 September 1990.
24. Fax from Stephen Neiman to Gerald Reynolds, 2 November 1990.
25. Fax from MacFarlanes to Hanover Band, undated.
26. Letter from Caradoc Evans to Gerald Reynolds, 17 January 1991.
27. Letter from Adrian Farmer to Caradoc Evans, 24 January 1991.
28. Letter from Gerald Reynolds to Stephen Neiman, 11 February 1991.
29. Letter from Stephen Neiman to Gerald Reynolds, 20 February 1991.
30. Letter from Roy Goodman to Adrian Farmer, 14 May 1991.
31. Letter from Adrian Farmer to Roy Goodman, 17 May 1991.
32. Letter from Caroline Brown to Numa Labinsky, 18 June 1991.
33. *Burrelles*, Dimitri Drobatschewsky, 26 November 1991.
34. Letter from Hugh Padley (ESO) to Adrian Farmer, 8 May 1986.
35. Letter from Nimbus Records Ltd. to Hugh Padley, 10 November 1982.
36. Nimbus Catalogue.
37. The *Daily Telegraph*, 1 February 1992.

CHAPTER ELEVEN
1. *Classic CD*, March 1991.
2. *Classic CD*, March 1991.
3. The *Independent*, 1 August 1992.
4. Keith Hardwick/Larry Lusting, *The Record Collector*, 5 December 1989.
5. Letter from Nimbus Records Ltd to Nick Thomas, undated.
6. Gerald Reynolds/Keith Hardwick, *The Record Collector*, undated.
7. 'Tripping Down Memory Lane', article by Robert Hartford, undated.
8. The *Independent*, 1 August 1992.
9. *Classic CD*, March 1991.
10. *Classic CD*, March 1991.
11. *Gramophone*, August 1992.
12. Geerd Heinsen, *Orpheus*, December 1991.
13. *Classic CD*, March 1991.
14. *Musical Opinion*, August 1990.
15. *Fanfare*, January–February 1991.

CHAPTER TWELVE
1. Letter from Stanley G Grad, Northpoint NY, 4 January 1988.
2. Letter from Dwight Corbin to Nimbus USA, 4 July 1988.
3. *San Francisco Chronicle*, 2 June 1987.
4. *Milwaukee Sentinel*, 31 October 1987.
5. *Los Angeles Herald Examiner*, 21 June 1987.
6. KPMG report to Robert Maxwell.
7. Memorandum from Mark Galloway to Peter Laister, 16 March 1988.
8. Letter from Gerald Reynolds to Patrick J Call, 10 October 1990.
9. Letter from Gerald Reynolds to Peter Laister, 28 November 1991.
10. Letter from Alan Sugar (Amstrad) to Peter Laister, 11 February 1992.

11. Facsimile from Gerald Reynolds to William J McGrath (McDurmott Will & Emery), 27 February 1992.
12. Letter from D A Howell (Price Waterhouse) to Gerald Reynolds, 5 March 1992.
13. Letter from Peter Laister to D A Howell, 9 March 1992.
14. Facsimile from William J McGrath to Gerald Reynolds, 6 May 1992.
15. Memorandum from Gerald Reynolds to Lyndon Faulkner, Stuart Garman, Chandos Ellis, John Denton, Gary Halfrecht, Emil Dudek and Howard Nash, 27 August 1992.

CHAPTER THIRTEEN

1. Letter from Martin Jones to Adrian Farmer, 28 September 1992.

INDEX

Abbey National 120
Acke, Christiane van 51, *103*
Aeolian Company 251
Ainsworth-Morris, Richard 162
Alberni Quartet 250
Albert Hall 164
Aldred, Ken 183
Alice in Wonderland 195
Ambisonics 34−5, 88 (&fn),
　89−91, 101, 206, 209, 244, 257
A & M Records 135, 220
Amaral, Cis *153*
Amber Records 230
American Express 182
Antara (Benjamin) 40
Argo Records 172
Arrau, Claudio *153*
Arts Council 10
Apley, Richard 142, 146
Ashcroft, Peggy 172
Association of Business
　Sponsorship in the Arts
　(ABSA) 190
ASV 148
Auer, Leopold 139
Austro-Hungarian Haydn
　Orchestra 182, 193 (&fn)

Bacchanales, Les (Couperin) 96
Bach, Johann Sebastian 41, 95,
　142, 250
Barber Institute, University of
　Birmingham 10
Barenboim, Daniel 83
Barton, Geoff 89, 101, *181*

Barton, John 172
Bateson, Roger 92, 253
Battistini, Mattia 208
Baudelaire, Charles 3, 60
Bechet, Sidney 10
Beecham, Sir Thomas 205, 210
Beer, Eugene 93
Beethoven, Ludwig van 36, 83,
　86, 95, 175, 177, 178, 179, 250
Benjamin, George 40, *40, 41*, 250
Berlioz, Hector 5
Berlin Philharmonic 193
Bernstein, Leonard 99, 148, 193
Best, Martin 93, 151, 172−7, *174*
Birmingham Repertory Theatre
　7 (&fn)
Birmingham Symphony
　Orchestra 11
Blackham, Dennis 85−6
Blair, William *75*
Boccherini, Luigi 192
Bochman, Michael *192*
Boehm, Helen 189
Boris Godunov (Mussorgsky) 7
Boughton, William 39, 189−90,
　191, 192, 192, 251
Boult, Sir Adrian 190
Bournemouth Symphony
　Orchestra 11
Bowyer, Kevin 250
Brahms, Johannes 142
Brandis Quartet 193fn, 250
Brandis, Thomas 193fn
Branson, Richard 134
Bretan, Judit 250

Bretan, Nikolai 250
Bridge, Frank 192
British Broadcasting
　Corporation (BBC) 10, 11, 48,
　72, 73, 79, 116, 150, 189, 254
BBC Welsh Symphony
　Orchestra 194, 196, 198, 250
British Technology Group 89,
　91, 104
British Telecom 120, 254
Britten, Benjamin 192
Broadbank, Robin 211−2, 257
Bromsgrove Festival 26, 27
Brookes, Basil 159
Brown, Caroline 177, 183, 184,
　185, 186, 187
Brymer, Jack 27
Budden, Julian 73
Butterworth, George 192

Call, Patrick J 222
Calvi, Emma 10fn
Capitol/EMI 243fn
Caradoc Evans, Simon 184, 185
Carnegie Hall 42
Caruso, Enrico 35, 36, 171, 202,
　206, 208
CBS 98
C-Cube Micro Systems 249
Ceausescu, President 250
Chaliapin, Feodor 207
Charlottesville, Virginia 106,
　132, 134, 218, 223
Chatterjee, Subhen *216*
Cherkassy, Shura 39, 70,

146–51, *147*, 219

Chopin, Frédéric 67, 68, 69, 94, 148

Christ Church Cathedral Choir 197, *197*, 250

Chrysalis 135

Collins Classics 98

Comecon 160

Cortot, Alfred 65, 251

Cuenod, Hugues 39, 59–61, *60*, 93

Curry, Nicholas 173, 175

Curtis Institute 139

Cwmbran, South Wales 106, 112, 123, 124, 125, 129, *130*, 131, 135, 235

Darlington, Stephen 197, *197*

Dances of Death (Mussorgsky) 74

Dante Troubadours, The 173

Datta, Sudha *216*

Debussy, Claude 6, 60, 95, 147, 173, 174

Decca 79, 87, 148, 150

Dean, Thompson 226, 229, *232*

de Gaulle, Général 7

Delius, Frederick 192

Dench, Judi 172

Devi, Girija *213*

Denton, John 223, 230

de Pachman 251

Department of Trade & Industry 104, 124

Deutsche Grammophon 148

Deyanova, Marta *152*

Diapason d'Or 167, 210, 252

Dichterliebe (Schumann) 12

Discovision Associates 103, 227

Distronic 243fn

Dix, Colin 8, 18, 44, 249

Donaldson, Lufkin & Jenrette (DJL) 224, 225, 226, 228, 229, 230, 233, 234, 241

Donelly 243fn

Doubles (Hoddinott) 197

Douglas, Basil 65, 69–70

Drennan, Jim *123*, 124, 132, 134

Dudek, Emil 43–4, 45, 119–20,

222, 237

Duke of Kent, HRH The *128*

Duparc, Henri 29–30, 60, 237

Eddy, Graham *84*

Edison, Award 93, 173

Elder, Mark *41*

Electra 165, 168

Elgar, Edward 142, 143, 175, 189, 192

Elliott, Peter *231*

Ellis, Chandos 43, 235

EMI 102, 123, 130, 135, 136, 169, 172, 173, 208, 227, 254

English String Orchestra 189

English Symphony Orchestra 171, 189, *191*, 192, 200

Equale Brass 95–6

Eroica (Beethoven) 69

Eurodisc 148

Evans, Geraint 12, 14

Falu, Eduardo *213*

Familia Valera *215*

Farmer, Adrian 27–30, *29*, 36, 38–9, 42, 43, 46, 47, 69, 72, 86, 88, 92, 98, 99–100, 123, 138, 140, 142, 144–5, 146, 148, 151, *152*, 164, 173, 175–6, 177, 179, 182, 183, 185, 186, 187, 189, 190, *192*, 193 (&fn), *196*, 198, 200, 207, 208, 211, 218, 225, 229, 234, 238–9, 242, 244, 249, 250, 252, 254, 257

Faulkner, Lyndon 220, 222, 223, 230, 232, 236

Fauré, Gabriel 6, 9, 61, 65, 237

Fellgett, Professor 89

Ferrier, Kathleen 14

Fiddlesticks Festival 212

Field, Helen 41, 42

Fine, Michael 218

Finzi, Gerald 192

Firebird (Stravinsky) 37

Fischer, Adam 193, *194*

Fischer-Dieskau, Dietrich 14

Fitzpatrick, Dr Horace 177–8

Fleming, Amaryllis *153*

Flight of the Bumble Bee (Rimsky-Korsakov) 147

Fong Naam *213*

Fournier, Pierre 99

Four Serious Songs (Brahms) 12, 74

Franks, Nick 176

Franz Schubert Quartet 250

Galloway, Mark 162, 221, 222

Garland, Patrick 172

Garman, Stuart 19, 47, 156, 159, 160–1, 168, 218, 223, 227, 229, 232

Gerhman, Shura *see* Count Numa Labinsky

General Electric Plastics 115

Gerzon, Michael 89

Gielgud, Sir John 195, *196*

Gigli, Beniamino 208

Giménez, Raúl *153*

Glock, Sir William 15, 65, *65*, 93

Great Caruso, The 202

Goldsmith, John 87

Goodman, Roy 178, 181–2, 187 (&fn)

Goodwin, Peter 95

Grainger, Percy 95

Granvilles 224, 226, 227–8, 229, 230

Great Hall, University of Birmingham 181, *192*

Green, Andrew 146

Grosvenor Records 172

Guildford Farm, USA 133

Guildhall School of Music 172

Guller, Youra 93–5, *94*

Haddey, Arthur 59

Hahn, Reynaldo 9, 10 (&fn)

Halliday, Dr Jonathan 27, 30–1, 42, 44, 46, 47, 85, 86–7, 88, 104, 105, *106*, 114, 115, 123, 134, 178, 220, 229, 244, 245, 246, 247, 248, 249, 254, 257

Handel, Georg Friedrich 41

Hands, Terry 172

Handsworth Wood Properties

Ltd 48
Hanover Band 86, 88, 177—89, *188*
Hanover Band Trust 182—3
Happy Prince, The (Wilde) 195
Hardwick, Keith 208, 209—10
Hartog, Howard 59—60
Harvey-Jones, Sir John 136—7
Hary Janos (Kodaly) 193—4
Haskill, Clara 93
Haydn, Franz Joseph 36, 60, 182, 192, 193
Haydnsaal, Esterhazy Palace 34, 193, 194
Heaventree of Stars, The (Hoddinott) 197
Helfrecht, Gary 222, 223
Henderson, Roy xi, 10 (&fn), 14
Hepworth, David 190
Hermes Development Co. Ltd. 48, 49
Hermes Jazz 208, 212
Hermes Recordings Ltd 48, 51
Hetzel, Gerhard *194*
Heward, Leslie 10
HMV 148
Hocks, Christian *see* Alexander Michejew
Hoddinott, Alun 197
Hoffman, Josef 148
Hoffnung, Ben 181
Holst, Gustav 192
Horizon Chimérique, L' (Fauré) 29—30, 61
Howat, Roy 31
Hubner, Professor 193
Hudson, Ben 250
Huggett, Monica 177, 178, 179, *180*
Hungarian Dances (Brahms) 140, 143, 146
Hungarian State Orchestra 193
Husch, Gerhard *61*
Hyperion 182, 185, 187

Ibbs & Tillett 142, 146, 149, 150
ICI 136
Isepp, Martin 60

Island Records 135

Jackson, Sir Barry 7 (&fn), 8
Jones, Martin 59, 71—2, *72*, 95, 151, 177, 210, 253
Jones, Roger 117
Juilliard School of Music 139
J/V 243fn
JVC 245, 254

Kalichstein, Joseph 195
Kansas City Chorale 251
Karajan, Herbert von 193
Kingfisher 254
Kingsbury, Arthur 172
Kist, Jan 13—14, 74
Kodaly, Zoltán 99, 100
Kothare, M. *216*
Koussevitsky Award 167
KPM 81, 112
Kraus, Alfredo *153*
Kreisler, Fritz 139, 250
Kreisleriana (Schumann) 148
K-Tel 135
Kunte, Anano *216*

Labinsky, Count Numa: birth 2; childhood 2—4; and Shura II 2; as a singer 5—15, 26—7, *29*, 58—9, 61, *237*, 237, 238—9; homosexuality 5; and Tom 5—6; as a miner 9; and René Ramond 9; change of names 1, 10, 11; and Michael xi—xii, 46; and Gerald 46; as a property developer 48, 51, 52; and Nina Walker 73—4; as a businessman 18—20, 21; and employees 16—17, 22; and Robert Maxwell 155, 156—8, 160, 161, 163; as President of Nimbus 124, 137; as an artist 16, *237*; as a poet 15, *237*; and ill-health 17—18, 20—1, 51, 137; death 237, 256
Laister, Peter 17, 22, 136, 137, 154, 156—7, *157*, 159, 161, 162—3, 165, 167—8, 202, 222,

223, 225, 227, 228, 235, 236, 253, 254
Lanza, Mario 202
Laredo, Jamie 39, 195
LeBovit, Harry 250
Lee, Christopher 195
Lee, Mike 43, 46, *90*, 91, 114, 123
Leigh, Vanessa 14
Lengauer, Stephanie 81
Lewis, Geraint 196
Libin, Alexander 2, 3, 4, 5
Libin (*née* Crohin), Blanche 2, 3, 4, 7, 9, 48, 58
Libin, Jeanne 3, 7
Libin, Numa *see* Count Numa Labinsky
Lill, John 199, *199*, 250
Liszt, Franz 95
Liverpool Philharmonic 11, 18fn
Llewellyn, Grant 196
Lloyd, David 27, 28
Lloyds Bank 122, 124, 156, 165, 217, 224
London Symphony Orchestra 37
Lucia di Lammermoor (Donizetti) 210

MacArden, Joy 10 (&fn)
Magic Flute, The (Mozart) 210
Mallarmé, Stéphane 60
Man, Wu *214*
Marchesi, Blanche 10fn
Mathias, William *153*, 196, 197
Matisse, Henri 16
Matthews, David 175
Maus, Professor Frank 140
Maxwell Communications Corporation (MCC) 136, 155, 158, 159—68, 217, 225, 226, 236, 220, 223
Maxwell, Debbie 158
Maxwell, Ian 217
Maxwell, Kevin 43, 155, 158, 159, 217
Maxwell, Robert 43, 47, 112, 131, 136, 151, 154—70, 212, 217, 220, 222, 223, 234, 241, 242
Maxwell Davies, Peter 98

Mayking 243fn
MCA 254
McFarlanes 168, 185
McGrath, Bill 223, 224, 226
McGraw H ill 220
McKenzie, Angus 59
Medici Quartet 173, 174, 175−7, 250
Mendelssohn, Felix 71, 147, 187, 192, 195, 250
Menuhin, Yehudi 250
Meridian 175, 189
Meridian Audio 251
Messiaen, Olivier 40
Michejew, Alexander 99−100, 151
Microsoft 254
MIDEM 246, 248, 254
Midland Bank 122, 124, 134, 156
Midland Radio Orchestra 189
Midsummer Night's Dream, A (Tchaikovsky) 75, 194−5
Misra, Ramesh *213*
Missa Solemnis (Beethoven) 181
Mitsubishi 189
Mitsui 254
Montserrat Caballé *76*
Moss, Philip 207, 243, 254
Moyedi, Mustapha *115*
Mozart, Wolfgang Amadeus 60, 139, 140, 145
Musica Viva 51

Narayan, Aruna *214*
Narayan, Ram *214*
Nash, Howard 45, 159−60, 163, 169, 221, 222, 223, 227−8, 229, 230, 233
Neiman, Stephen 177, 183, 184, 185, 186, 187
Nimbus Communications International Ltd 232, 236
Nimbus Foundation 47, 241−2
Nimbus Manufacturing Inc., USA 243
Nimbus Manufacturing Ltd. 112, 120, 231, 234, 235, 236, 237
Nimbus Pressings 122

Nimbus Records foundation of 49, 76−7; principles of recording 33−8, 39, 97, 175, 180−1, 207; digital recording 86, 87−8, 257; and surround sound 59, 62−3; manufacture of LPs 63−4, 69, 79−86, 126, 128, 171; manufacture of CDs 43, 44, 71, 101−18, *109*, 116, 117, 118, 119, 124, 125, 128, 129−30, *131*, 134−5, 138, 169, 171; and CD-ROM 44, 119−21, *121*, 154, 166, 220, 222, 245; and *Prima Voce* 4, 61, 202, 203, 204−11, 212, 257; and Video-CD 237, 244, 246−9; and marketing 39, 81, 91−3, 113, 176, 200−1, 252−4; and recording artists 35, 36, 38−9, 68, 97, 137, 151; and employees 43−6, 128, *129*; American plant 131−4, *132*, 162, 165−6, 167, 217−223, 251
Nimbus Technology and Engineering Ltd. 220, 232, 251
Nimbus USA 230
Nuits D'Eté (Berlioz) 5
Nunn, Trevor 172

O'Beirne, Anne 112
Oistrakh, David 139
Opera de Camera 51
Optical Recording Corporation 227
Otaka, Tadaaki 198−9, *198*

Padley, Hugh 190
Parker, Evan 81
Parry, Hubert 192
Parsons, Geoffrey 61, *61, 62*
Passagio (Hoddinott) 197
Pena, Paco 171, 177, 212, *213*
Perlemuter, vlado 39, *64*, 64−70, *66, 69, 70*, 151, 167, 171, 219
Petrouchka (Stravinsky) 147
Phelps-Barnard, Christa 149, 150
Philadelphia Orchestra 138
Philharmonia Orchestra 95, 96

Pickwick Records 135
Pictures at an Exhibition (Mussorgsky) 147
Pioneer 227
Piper, John 196
Philips 101, 102−5, 114, 167, 227, 246, 247, 248
Podolski, Mischa 51
Pollard, Anthony 90
Polygram 102, 124, 134, 220, 233
Price Waterhouse 217
Prince of Wales, HRH The 241, *241*
Pritchard, John 18fn
Prokofiev, Sergei 251

Queen Elizabeth Hall 66, 175
Queen's Award for Technological Achievement 124
Queen of Sheba (Gounod) 8
Quest for Quality, The (Webb) 43, 45, 91, 136

Rachmaninov, Sergei 147, 198−9, 250
Ramond, René 9, 16
Ravel, Maurice 65, 66−7, 69, 173, 174, 189, 251
RCA 130, 135, 167, 186, 246, 186
R & D Activities 232
Redifusion 81, 254
Reynolds, Gerald: and Numa 24, 25, 26; as a property developer 51, 53; as a recording technician 63, 81, *82*, 84, 104−5, 114, 115, 120, 205, 242, 245, 249, 257; as a businessman 27, 79, 168, 183, 186, 221, 248, 257
Reynolds, Michael: and Numa xi−xii, 23−4; as a property developer 50, 53; as a businessman 23, 79, 168, 236, 247; and Robert Maxwell 166−7
Rite of Spring (Stravinsky) 37

Roberts, Bernard 29, 36, *37*, 83, 151
Robertson, Paul 174, 175, 176
Robinson, Heath 115
Rossini Gioachino 195
Rover 120
Royal Northern College of Music 28
Royal Opera House 138
Royal Philharmonic 143
Royal Shakespeare Company 172
Rozdestvensky, Gennady 37, *38*, 39
Rubinstein, Anton 148

Sadolikar, Shruti *216*
Scarlatti, Domenico 41
Schoenberg, Arnold 192
Schone Mullerin, Die (Schubert) 13, 28, 74
Schubert, Franz 60
Schwarzkopf, Elisabeth 14
Scott, John 197
Scottish Chamber Orchestra *141*, 142, 145, 194
Scottish National Opera 202
Scottish National Orchestra 98
Sellick, Phyllis *153*
Shakespeare, William xi
Shaw, George Bernard 7fn
Shostakovich, Dmitri 173, 174
Shrewsbury, Lady 18 (&fn), 73
Shumsky, Eric 140
Sibelius, Jean 192
Shumsky, Oscar 39, 138–46, *139*, *141*, 151
Smith, Anthony 83, 92–3, 199, 252–3, *253*, 254
Smith, Cyril *153*
Smith, Ronald 39
Socrate (Satie) 60
Soldier's Tale, The (Stravinsky) 195
Sonopress 116, 243fn, 249
Sony 87, 102, 178, 246, 254
Soundstream 87
Sousa, John 41–2, 253

Souster, Tim *152*
Spicer and Pegler 183
Star Children (Hoddinott) 197
Stensham Court *53*
Stokowski, Leopold 138
Strange, Sylvia 138, 187
Strauss, Richard 173, 192
Stravinsky, Igor 147, 192
Stravinsky, Soulima *152*
Sugar, Alan 224
Sullivan, Arthur 195
Summit 243fn

Tamanti, Roberto 10fn
Target Records 92
Tchaikovsky, Pyotr Ilyich 86, 192
Telstar 135
Tetrazzini, Luisa 210
Texas Instruments 254
Themes Variées (Poulenc) 71
Thomas, Nick 168, 209
Thompson, Francis 9
Thomson, Michael 96
Through the Looking Glass (Carrol) 195
Tilburg, JJGC van *103*
Tippett, Sir Michael *152*, *192*
Todd, Ann 195, *195*
Tomorrow's World 93
Town, John 243
Trebunia family *215*
Trend, Don 150
Tryptich 243fn

Unicorn 87

Vallin, Ninon 6, 9, 10fn
Vaughan Williams, Ralph 175, 190, 192, 218
Vaughan Williams, Ursula 175
Verdi, Giuseppe 73
Verney, Mary 86, *180*
Vienna Philharmonic 193
Virgin Records 130–1, 134, 135, 164, 165, 166, 167, 168, 227
Vivaldi Ensemble 189

Wagner, Richard 60

Waites, John 96
Walker, Nina 29, 42, 46, 71, 73–5, *76*, *107*, 138, 149, 175
Wallace, John 41–2, 95–9, *98*, 151, 200
Warner Brothers 254
Warner Home Video 254
Welsh Development Authority 131
Westrup, Sir Jack 10
White, Norman 202, *203*, 205, 206, 207, 208, 211, 257
Williams, Glyn 224
Wilson, Colin 13, *13*
Wiltshire, Alan 37, 41, 97, 138
Wimbush, Mary *15*
Winterreise, Die (Schubert) 12, 13, 73–4
Wyastone Leys 8, 14, 18, 54–8, *55*, *56*, 69, 77, 78, 81, 90, 93, 106, 115, 125, 133, 148, 149, 150, 156, 172, 179, 204, 205, 232, 245, 254, 255, 254, 255
Wyastone Leys Concert Hall 242

Yale, University of 139
Ysaye, Eugene 139, 140, 145

Zarcos, Sacha 11